In this age of commerce,
where companies do strive,
To make profits and success,
and to stay alive,
'Tis wise to consider,
with care and with might,
The strategies that shape
the corporate sight.

Aye, corporate strategy,
the path to great gain,
Doth lead to prosperity,
and ease of pain.

A company must look
to its goals and its aims,
And measure its progress,
with number and names,
'Tis wise to diversify,
and not to rely,
On just one stream of revenue
'tis why

Aye, corporate strategy,
the path to great gain,
Doth lead to prosperity,
and ease of pain.

Marketing, sales,
and operations too,
Each play a role,
in the company's due,
And leadership must be strong,
with a guiding hand,
To steer the company,
through this commercial land.

Aye, corporate strategy,
the path to great gain,
Doth lead to prosperity,
and ease of pain.

Innovation and adaptability,
do play a part,
In the company's success,
from the very start,
For change is inevitable,
and constant is the tide,
And a company must shift,
with each turn of the tide.

—ChatGPT3 on business strategy, in the style of William Shakespeare

A WHOLE NEW STRATEGY

EVERYTHING YOU NEED TO THINK AND ACT MORE STRATEGICALLY

Nathan Shedroff

SAN FRANCISCO, CA, USA

A WHOLE NEW STRATEGY

EVERYTHING YOU NEED TO THINK AND ACT MORE STRATEGICALLY

I would like to express my gratitude to my mentors,
who have shaped my critical, creative, and strategic
thinking throughout my life:

Jeff Rutherford
Michael Everitt
Richard Saul Wurman
Regis McKenna
Brenda Laurel
Hunter Lovins
Ron Nasher
Steve Diller

and my editor, **Tony Ahn**,
for making my thoughts more intelligible

Copyright 2023
Nathan Shedroff
All Rights Reserved

Design & Production:
Editor: Tony Ahn
Design, Illustrations & Diagrams,
Index, & Layout: Nathan Shedroff

Typography:
Text: ITC Garamond
Display: Interstate

Experience Design Books
99 Rausch Street #525
San Francisco CA 94103
USA

experiencedesignbooks.com
Errors:
info@experiencedesignbooks.com

ISBN-13: **979-8-9890463-0-0**
LCCN: **2023916491**
Printed & bound in the USA

CONTENTS

CONTRIBUTORS

ChatGPT 3 /Pages i & vii
Generative AI from OpenAI

Claude.ai /Page vii
Generative AI from Anthropic

Carl Bass /Page 5
Retired CEO, Autodesk
While at Autodesk (the second time), he grew revenue from $1B to $4B and market cap from $2B to $25B.

Jon H. Pittman /Page 11
Retired Vice President of Corporate Strategy, Autodesk.
Formerly led the strategic foresight team at Autodesk, the company that helps people imagine, design, and create a better world. I defined and led the Corporate Strategy process at Autodesk and taught strategic thinking in both internal executive education programs and at the Haas School of Business at UC Berkeley.

Steve Diller /Page 29
Founding Partner at Scansion.
20+ years collaborating with business leaders to design meaningful experiences for their customers. Specialties in innovation, branding, marketing strategy, and execution. Taught for 15 years in the DMBA program at California College of the Arts

Christopher Ireland /Page 35
Retired CEO, Cheskin. Adjunct faculty, Stanford Continuing Education.
Has found a magical combination in teaching new generations of designers and developers at Stanford—initially on campus, now online. Each quarter she is challenged to use new technology, address emerging complexities, and mentor a highly diverse student mix. It's never boring

Brenda Laurel /Page 39
Design researcher, writer, and interaction designer.
Developed courses at UCSC to boost creative and values-based game design and theatre. Led the design and development of graduate trans-media design programs at California College of the Arts and Art Center.

Jeanne Liedtka /Page 63
Professor of Business Administration, UVA Darden School of Business
Involved in corporate strategy for over 30 years. Teaches both MBAs and executives at the Darden Graduate School of Business. Consults on innovation, organic growth, and design thinking. Began her career as a strategy consultant for the Boston Consulting Group and was Chief Learning Officer at United Technologies.

Spectra Adaora Ijeoma Asala /Page 85

in *Purpose-driven business leader, venture builder & impact investor*
Fractional CPO & COO, coach for mission-driven business leaders, startups, and impact organizations, and active angel investor and advisor to pre-seed and seed stage tech startups & social enterprises.

Josh Levine /Page 97

in *Writer, educator, and podcaster with a passion for company culture*
Author, consultant, and educator on a mission to help organizations design a culture advantage. His book, *Great Mondays,* was listed as one of BookAuthority's best culture books of all time.

Jake Dunagan /Page 111

in *Director, Governance Futures Lab at Institute for the Future*
Experiential futurist, governance designer, and teacher. He is focused on social invention that help individuals, organizations, and governing institutions re-imagine and re-invent their futures.

Sara Beckman /Page 143

in *Earl F. Cheit Faculty Fellow, Haas School of Business, UC Berkeley*
Directs the Product Management Program and teaches graduate and executive courses at University of California, Berkeley.

Minnie Bredouw /Page 155

in *Founder & Executive Director, Purpose Project, Creative Director, Pinterist*
Minnie's career focus is design for social impact. She has spent most of her career designing programs focused on youth, equity, and education reform.

Ephi Banaynal dela Cruz /Page 159

in *Co-founder & CEO Context Nature Public Benefit Corp*
Developed and implemented global standards, programs, and technologies in executive global leadership roles for corporate sustainability and human rights, product design, environment, safety, engineering, and responsible supply chain at Fortune 500 companies.

Radha Mistry /Page 175

in *Associate Principal, Americas Foresight Leader Arup*
Previously, foresight leader at Autodesk. Focused on collaboratively building more equitable and inclusive futures, and to make space for communities who might not yet see themselves in future visions.

Dave Roselle /Page 181

in*Design Strategist, Futurist, Innovation Manager*
He leads high uncertainty, cross functional innovation projects to successful outcomes, manages innovation processes for senior leadership and infuses futures thinking into ideation and strategy workshops. Currently, the Director of Product Innovation at ServiceChannel. Previously, was a Senior Strategic Designer at BCG Digital Ventures.

FOREWORD/
A MORE EVOLVED STRATEGY

Image: Joshua J Cotten

In an age where technological advancements are no longer mere milestones but the very tracks on which our world runs, there's a poignant realization dawning upon us: strategy, as we know it, needs a transformation—an evolution.

Historically, strategy has been a game of conquest—a realm dominated by adversarial engagements where the mighty triumphed. But, as we hurtle into a future molded by digitization, interconnectedness, and artificial intelligence, the old paradigms seem ill-equipped. Now, the need is for a strategy that shifts *from adversarial to cooperative* orientation.

Systems thinking—a holistic approach that recognizes the interconnectedness of things—offers profound insights into this evolving landscape. *Traditional linear paths are yielding to multi-dimensional spaces*. These intricate networks, filled with potential intersections and overlaps, hold untapped opportunities and, at the same time, possible blind spots. Our strategies must be nimble and expansive, with the acumen to discern both.

A critical step forward is reimagining our understanding of stakeholders. It is no longer enough to understand customers in *extractive* terms. We must cast our nets wider, embracing a collaborative research approach that encompasses partners, collaborators, and even competitors as we understand people on deeper levels. As we engage with all of our stakeholders, we must be truly authentic—eschewing manipulative sales narratives in favor of *genuine human connections* that transcend mere demographics.

Beyond adversarial confines, the world brims with opportunities for *symbiotic relationships.* Zero-sum games, where one's gain is another's loss, are outdated. Instead, we must seek cooperative scenarios where collective wins are achievable. Such an approach heralds a new definition of success, where competitive advantage morphs into **community advantage,** and where profit motives are qualified by their contribution to a **broader collective good**.

In execution, the transformation is even more profound. Our horizons need to expand from merely designing products or interfaces to crafting entire **experiences**—and **meaningful** ones at that. We can and should **co-create value, foster healthy relationships**, and prioritize **regenerative business models** over fleeting transactions.

The rise of artificial intelligence poses its unique challenges and opportunities. As AI becomes a bedrock of business and innovation, the **human touch** becomes even more crucial. The onus is on us to cultivate our uniquely human capabilities, balancing our technological prowess with **emotional intelligence, creativity,** and **ethical considerations**. **Continuous learning, adaptability,** and a commitment to **shared values** will define success in this AI-dominated era.

To those standing on the precipice of this expansive future, it might appear overwhelming. But within its complexity lies the promise of unparalleled growth. Strategy, in this new age, isn't just about thriving—it's about **co-evolving**.

In essence, as the lines between competition and collaboration blur, and as new technologies redefine realms of possibility, our strategic compass needs recalibration. Our journey ahead is one of **shared visions, collective endeavors,** and a **harmony** between human spirit and technological marvels.

Here's to a future where strategy is not just a plan, but a **shared symphony of progress**.

—In collaboration with ChatGPT 4, Claude.ai, and Nathan Shedroff

INTRODUCTION/
STRATEGY IS IN CRISIS

I'm going to try not to be too dismissive of the state of current or traditional business strategy or its process and tools but strategy has clearly not kept pace with advancements in other business domains and functions.

I know this sounds alarmist but the current state of business strategy training and practice is so broken that it is in crisis. Not only are traditional strategic tools and processes woefully inadequate (and, mostly, always were), their deficiencies are keeping companies from staying relevant in the marketplace—at an alarming rate.

In 2019, McKinsey & Company, one of the most venerated sources of strategic consulting, published an eye-popping report* on what they term "zombie" companies: those companies that are unable to create real value or growth, either in the marketplace or for themselves (including their stakeholders and shareholders). These are companies you probably already suspect: Sears, Macy*s, K-Mart, etc. And, not only those that have already failed or the ones you can't understand why they're still in business. These are companies that seem successful, ones you may even admire.

The conclusion of McKinsey's research is that 85% of all companies, worldwide, whether they're private or public, are zombies! Your read that correctly (I even double-checked after my editor made their way through the manuscript). 85%!

These companies include those who can't service their debt—they're unable to make payments on the money they've borrowed), as well as those who can only pay the interest but cannot make progress on the borrowed principle). It also includes

*www.mckinsey.com/featured-insights/innovation-and-growth/what-every-ceo-needs-to-know-about-superstar-companies

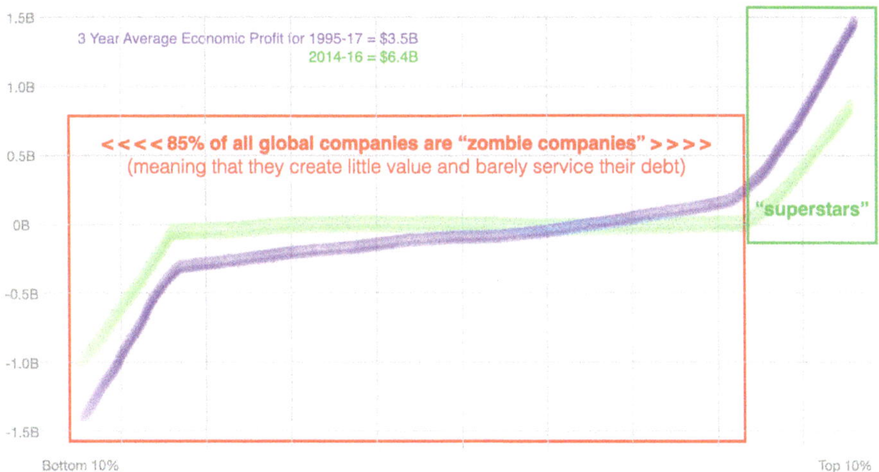

companies who may not have debt but can only manage to pay their expenses and either don't make a profit, make very little, or can't fund initiatives for research, development, or evolution. Since every company needs to be constantly evolving in order to stay relevant to customers, they too join the ranks of the walking corporate dead.

These zombie companies are in statis—not growing, not evolving, barely able to stay afloat—but working really hard to do so (the market is not full of friends).

Now, if you're McKinsey, perhaps this is where you pull-out your slide deck and promotional materials to tell companies that they should hire McKinsey instead of whomever they currently trust to develop their strategy (if they have one). But, the unspoken revelation, here, is a serious one: most of these companies already "do" strategy, whether internally or with a consultancy, and it's not producing results! This should scare every organization in the world (including non-profits and government agencies) and embarrass every strategic consultant.

Now, I suppose we could write off a lot of those strategies as inferior or poorly implemented—which often means that implementation wasn't baked-into the strategy—or that the organizations ignored the advice they got. All of this may be true, but the 85% figure still points to a massive cause for alarm: typical approaches to strategy (models, process, tools, etc.) simply aren't cutting it. The state of the art is one of decay.

It gets even worse: another recent McKinsey report* describes the results of a global survey concerning ecological concerns for leaders. While it appears that 83% of those companies surveyed have now set targets for climate change (and I really question whether these targets are adequate or meaningful), very few have set targets for any other ecological concerns, including fresh water, forests, biodiversity, pollution, etc. Again, the strategy that companies are preparing aren't addressing some of the most important issues of our times. At best, these issues are bolted onto traditional processes and not integrated, dynamic components.

*www.mckinsey.com/capabilities/sustainability/our-insights/where-the-worlds-largest-companies-stand-on-nature

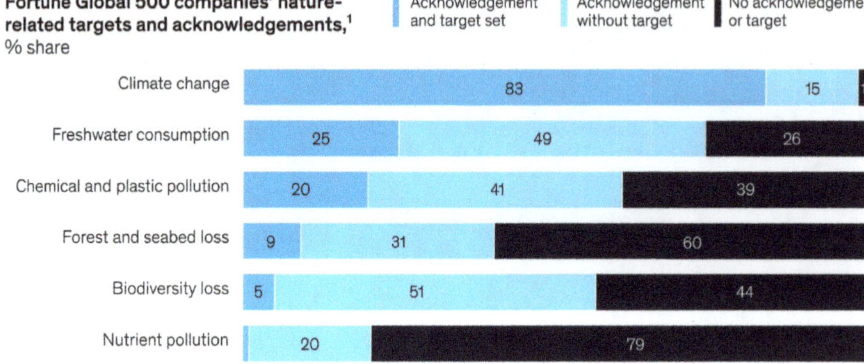

This is why we need new approaches, ones that are updated with current understandings of business, economics, markets, and people; ones that integrate what's typically left out of traditional strategy. We need to challenge the oversimplifications and assumptions that have been made up to this point that were built on learnings from 50-or-so years ago.

That's what I plan to do in this book. I've been teaching business principles, including strategy, to not-your-typical business professions for 15 years and practicing new approaches to strategy for many years before that. Growing professionally in the revolutionary, non-traditional interactive media industry has provided me a valuable perspective on what has changed in business what hasn't, and how we can move forward with new understandings and build them into new models, processes, and tools. In short, I've spent the last 15 years focused on redesigning strategy. I've been evolving the models and descriptions of the tools we need for this century's organizations.

I learned strategy from a variety of sources but, mostly in practice. I have an MBA in Sustainable Management, from Presidio Graduate School, so I was fortunate to learn about business from a different—and better—frame, not "business as usual." This better prepared me for the world today with challenges and contexts that weren't present even 20 years ago. In addition, I've consulted for a variety of companies and non-profit organizations for over 30 years, via my company, *vivid* studios, an early Internet pioneer, as well as my private consulting in business, experience, and brand strategy ever since. My strategy experience started long before, back in 1993 working with Regis McKenna, a marketing pioneer from Silicon Valley back in the early Apple days (more on him later) where he taught me and my colleagues his CRUSH approach to accelerated, better market strategy.

Since those days, I've worked for startups and large companies alike, as well as non-profits. I've worked for consumer packaged goods companies, tech firms, telcos, crypto startups, consumer electronics companies, sports equipment manufacturers, etc. Lastly, I started an MBA program in 2007 (the MBA in Design Strategy) as a way of teaching business in a new way—particularly innovation and strategy—and the model, process, and understandings in this book reflect that 30 year+ journey.

Most strategy is bad, slow and expensive.

I know that header is an incendiary statement, but if you get a couple drinks into a strategic consultant (or the client of one), most will agree. Now, people will reserve a varying sliver of the market as the exception (great strategy) and they will locate themselves in that sliver, but they will still secretly agree with this statement. And, most will agree with "slow and expensive," regardless.

In his book, *Good Strategy / Bad Strategy*, Richard P. Rumelt describes bad strategy as having one or more of four characteristics:

- ***Fluff*** is a form of gibberish masquerading as strategic concepts or arguments. It uses "Sunday" words (words that are inflated and unnecessarily abstruse) and apparently esoteric concepts to create the illusion of high-level thinking.
- ***Failure to face the challenge***. Bad strategy fails to recognize or define the challenge. When you cannot define the challenge, you cannot evaluate a strategy or improve it.
- ***Mistaking goals for strategy.*** Many bad strategies are just statements of desire rather than plans for overcoming obstacles.
- ***Bad strategic objectives***. A strategic objective is set by a leader as a means to an end. Strategic objectives are "bad" when they fail to address critical issues or when they are impracticable.

There are many reasons for this:

- Strategy requires you to research information from different domains and from many different sources.
- Great strategy requires the involvement of several people inside an organization, which requires time, focus, and money.
- Most strategy relies on filling in templates—often simply downloaded from the Internet—and these templates are (and always have been) inadequate.
- Because strategy requires us to consider so many different perspectives and sources, we usually look for shortcuts to speed things up or make things easier and it is exactly these shortcuts that often invalidate the very data that we expect to inform us.
- Most strategy only reviews quantitative data because it is the easiest to obtain and use and because business culture (and, increasingly, culture-writ-large) favors numbers as being more important, more accurate, and more relevant). Yet ignoring qualitative data, particularly about customers and employees is responsible for much of the most public and spectacular market losses on record.

In addition to the reasons above, qualitative data is also the best source of innovation—it's just more difficult to collect and analyze.

Nathan/ Your experience with strategy is different than most businesspeople—it's unapologetically skeptical, if not, dismissive of traditional approaches to strategy.

Carl/ Yes. In business, there is a huge number of people claiming things to be strategic that clearly are not. Some of it is fractal in nature—at one level it may be strategic—but, if you really step back, I would say that **95 to 99% of what a company does isn't really strategic**. There are a few big decisions that are made and then most everything else is tactical execution. Every big company I've ever been at, the number of people that claim, "Here's our new strategy!" It's not. That's my take on strategy. Often, it's just your plans for the year.

When businesspeople claim they're going to do a "strategic review" it's usually a bunch of horse shit. To me, the strategy should tell me how you're going to beat your competition further, distance yourself between you and your competition, build some barriers between something, etc. It's about actually being engaged in part of competition.

Would you also agree that it's not always your competition? Sometimes it's what's happening in the rest of the world: technology, society, nature, whatever.

Yes, but it still comes down to competition. ***I look at strategy as a way to get ahead of your competition***. You have vast options but you need to decide, "I'm going to out-compete because I'm going to have better customer service, you know, Zappo's, or "I'm going to out-compete because of supply chain," Walmart or Amazon, or "I'm going to build a better product." There are a million ways to go about it but those are strategic decisions you make entering or succeeding in a market.

Then, what is good strategy versus bad strategy?

Good versus bad is empirical. It either succeeds or not. If you take a strategy in isolation, but your competition did it three months earlier, it's not effective. I don't really care what you measure you business by, but if the decisions you made have an inflection point in terms of how much better you are than your competition, then your strategy was a good one. You can always have a good strategy that's executed poorly. Companies do that all the time. A good strategy can still be insufficient to out-compete. Depending on how differentiated your strategy is, you can probably tolerate various qualities of execution.

I'll go out on a limb and say that most companies have so-so execution, anyway. A lot of them are just lucky to be in an industry or at a time when so-so is good enough.

A well-chosen strategy is either something that you can execute on or something you can build the capability to execute well. It would be crazy to say "I have this incredible idea!" but your idea for strategy is much better if it's closer to what you already know how to do and, yes, you'll probably have to build some skills that you don't have today.

For someone who's as skeptical of traditional strategy as you are, you invested a lot into strategy at Autodesk. It was obviously of some value or you wouldn't have continued to, so how did you approach what was valuable to look at and look for, and then how did you reintegrate that into the operations?

At Autodesk, strategy was all around the company. Every group within the organization did strategy on the existing businesses. For example, the move to a subscription model did not come from a the strategy group. Ideas about moving into new markets, how to price or sell our products, or how we should build our products were all strategies developed and executed within the various groups. These folks really knew their customers, products, and markets. They understood the dynamics of all those things in a way that a more independent strategy group wouldn't. But, when it came to wholly new things and markets, our internal strategy group functioned in some ways like strategic consultants. They were looking outside the existing business to new conditions we might make use of. And that group was absolutely aligned with the business. The things they uncovered and brought to the business weren't outside of our intent.

I think in most companies, people don't actually do strategy. It's easy to have "strategy" discussions. Every company says they do strategy, but if you really look, at what they're doing, real strategy is a rare thing.

Going back to that communications question, you've been in a lot of companies. How do you communicate well, that strategic intent or understanding or direction, so that everyone in the company can act on it?

I think that's tied to how crisp and clear the idea is. One of the typical failure modes for communicating strategy is that it's just a jumble of bullshit.

One of my pet peeves is "corporate values." Right? Nobody ever says we're going to be terrible people and make people cry. And yet, like, there's so many companies that do that. Comcast, for example.

Well, sadly, that's actually a viable strategy. It's like when Wells Fargo decided to open accounts customers didn't need in order to generate many more fees. It is their business strategy, but it's not stated. It may or may not be sustainable, and it may not be good for your brand, but it is an actually strategy. But, if you're going to do that, at least be honest with yourselves. Most strategy is full of good intentions—and there's nothing wrong with the ideas. But, they don't come-out in the actions—the execution.

The strategy must, first, be clear about what to do and not to do. Then, it must be tied to execution. If it isn't, there's little hope. After both of these steps, then you can talk about communicating it clearly to everyone. Everyone should know how to reinforce the strategy.

This gets to an interesting question: who in an organization should decide this? I'm pretty agnostic. I just want to make sure it's being done.

Read the entire interview at www.nathan.com/whole-new-strategy

Current Strategy Tools are Inadequate

Here is a story of the typical approach to strategy. This is fictional but I assure you that it is absolutely typical of strategy work as taught in business schools and practiced in organizations of all types and sizes at all levels.

Consider this startup in the process of creating their first strategic plan: Quan, Mellissa, Gerald, and Song found each other at their last company and have left to start a company around their "big idea." They do as Melissa was taught in business school—she has an MBA after all: they download a SWOT template and another for Positioning Statements. They break into two teams to accomplish more, faster. Mellissa and Quan take the SWOT and Gerald and Song work on the Positioning Statement. They give themselves an hour and then they review where each team is together.

Melissa and Quan start listing strengths and weaknesses:

Strengths:
- We're all from Ivy League schools
- They don't yet have any customers
- We have experience working in the industry
- They need manufacturing partners

Weaknesses:
- They understand the manufacturing process needed
- They don't yet have a sales channel

Opportunities:
- They have a unique idea
- If they move quickly, they can define the category
- None of their competitors is yet in the Metaverse

Threats:
- The market may change quickly
- Their old company could quickly copy their idea

All of the above is typical. They already have a solution, they know their market, they have some experience in the space, etc. The SWOT analysis is helping them identify what to focus on and what to worry about. I imagine you've already figured out what lies ahead for them but we'll leave these two for the moment and check in with Gerald and Song.

Positioning Statement:

For customers who need the best multiplexing solution
We offer a mutliplexing subscription service
Which benefits them by managing their communications more efficiently and in a 3D display
As opposed to our competitor, Tired Corp,
Which offer only spreadsheet-based data plexing.

The four come back together after an hour and agree that they've focused on the most important factors and are gratified that their positioning statement is so clear—and so quickly. It's exactly as they've discussed before and it matches their past research into the market. They're now ready to do some competitive analysis to see how they might compare to their old company, Tired Corp and the others currently in the market.

I know this sounds incredibly, incredulously obvious, but this is how strategy is taught in nearly every business program and how much strategy is performed. Even larger firms and "name brand" consultants perform fancier versions of these same exercises, replete with the same errors. What's wrong with this approach?

Nearly everything.

First, none of the identified factors in either tool correspond to the items identified in the other. If they are accurate, Gerald and Song;s findings don't relate at all to Melissa and Quan's. There's no connection between these two activities. How do we reconcile them? Which are more important? Which are based on which? These processes were done in parallel, with no corresponding sequence, requiring us to untangle them in order to reconcile their disparity and move on. A better approach would be to do one (perhaps the SWOT) and use that as the basis for the other. At least, then, they would relate to each other. However, I'll show you how a SWOT isn't even necessary as it emerges automatically from the other steps in the process. You should never draft another SWOT in your career!

Next, how do any of them know these are the best answers—or that any of them are accurate. Is the Metaverse a sound opportunity? Are they the only ones in the category? Will the market move quickly? Are customers asking for a 3D display of their dataplexing? None of these entries are validated in any way. Where is the proof that these are important (or even exist), let alone the proof that these factors are the most important?

I know, I know, it sounds ridiculous that this is how most strategy is done. I assure you, however, that it's true—certainly of startups and smaller companies who don't have the resources to hire strategists, but these problems also true of many, many established, medium and large companies. Think back to that report on zombie companies. This begins to explain why 85% of companies worldwide aren't successfully differentiating themselves and why their strategies are so faulty.

But, there's something even more troublesome here. Even if everything in these two "analyses" is true, so what? Do customers care that all four of these founders graduated from Ivy League schools? Are they only selling to customers in or from similar schools? Other than wanting to buy high-end products and services, do their customers care that they have experience and understand the manufacturing processes needed? Even if they did, how would they know?

Military Strategy

In the military, there are often two types of insight used to create strategy: situational awareness and operational awareness. **Situational awareness** is understanding your surroundings: What territory are you in? What's the terrain? Who's around you? Where is the enemy? Where and who else are around you (such as civilians)? What are the weather conditions? Etc. **Operational awareness** is focused on how things work: What resources do you have and need to accomplish the mission? How prepared are they? How, when, and where can you get more? How does your equipment work and how is it maintained?

Business strategy is the same. In business, situational awareness represents all of the conditions you should understand before you act: your **customers, competitors,** other **stakeholders**, and overall **trends**, not just in your industry but throughout society and the world. If you can gain insights into these, you can better formulate successful strategy, but, not many organizations look at all of these or look at them thoroughly. The chapters of this book specifically cover these.

Operational strategy, in business, refers to most everything about an organization's activities (operations): its **capabilities, priorities, partnerships, resources, business model, culture, etc.** It describes how ready the organization is to meet its challenges, perform its activities, and reach its goals. Thorough investigation into both of these sets of things are necessary to succeed, whether you're in the market or on the

This is the most critical misstep of all strategy: **what are the most important decision-drivers of customer decisions. If you only take one thing from this book, this is the thing to understand.** It's discussed in detail in the first chapter, but confusing customer or company desires or trivia with actual decision-drivers is the most fundamental misstep businesspeople make, no matter their background, education, or experience.

How Do We Fix Strategy?

This book will outline better strategy that you can manage yourself. It will help you understand just enough of your market's context to set a strategic direction and translate that into successful tactics (and action)!

The Seven Laws of Strategy

The most important things to understand about better strategy are:
- Strategy is about Context and Focus.
- Market issues should be separated from Operational issues.
- Strategy requires a thorough review of stakeholders of all types.
- Strategy is mostly about People, whether directly or by proxy.
- Where strategy is not about people, it's about the environment that supports society and the economy.

These issues and impacts must be factored into the process:
- Great strategy requires a specific sequence of steps. The output of one step becomes the input to the next.
- Great strategy requires new understandings of value and appreciation for how it is exchanged.
- Strategy is complex; it needs to be. However, we can bring much more clarity to the process and the results.
- The oversimplification of past and traditional strategy tools is one of the most concerning problems with strategy. Great strategy isn't easy and easy tools lead you to inappropriate strategies.

Context

Sadly, too many businesspeople ignore the context of the market and society around them. Because business can be complex, we seek to simplify things just so we can survive our responsibilities. Some of this is inevitable. You can never build an understanding of the entire world around you as rich as that world. It would be like comedian Steven Wright's joke about maps: "I have a map of the United States, life size. 1 mile equals 1 mile. It's a bitch to fold it."

Obviously, we can't model the world in exact detail. However, the approach most strategy processes and tools take cuts out too much context. In our desire to focus, we turn our attention away from critical details, players, issues, and impacts. Impacts such as social equity or being good neighbors are ignored, as are ecological impacts. But, also stakeholders that may become impediments (like governments, media, or NGOs) or constructive partners in success (those same partners).

The trick to better strategy is to constantly survey the landscape broadly and then narrow our focus to the most important priorities identified by that wide perspective. This is a continuous process that repeats over and over, throughout a strategic process. It's OK to eventually ignore issues and impacts (perhaps, a better approach is to set them aside for later) as long as our focus proceeds from a set that included all of those factors. Traditional strategy just ignores them from the start.

Market vs. Operations

Traditional strategy tools also tend to mix the external with the internal and because businesspeople are paid to focus on their responsibilities (most of which are operational), too often the external/market factors get deemphasized or even ignored. As you can imagine, "ignore your market" is not a strategy for success! Yet, the strategic processes businesspeople use often deprioritizes their inclusion.

In addition, because we sell into the market, these factors need to be prioritized before we consider our internal factors. Over and over, organizations decide to do things: buy services and other companies, sell things, and build capabilities without ever validating if the market necessitates this. You've seen this throughout your career: a company

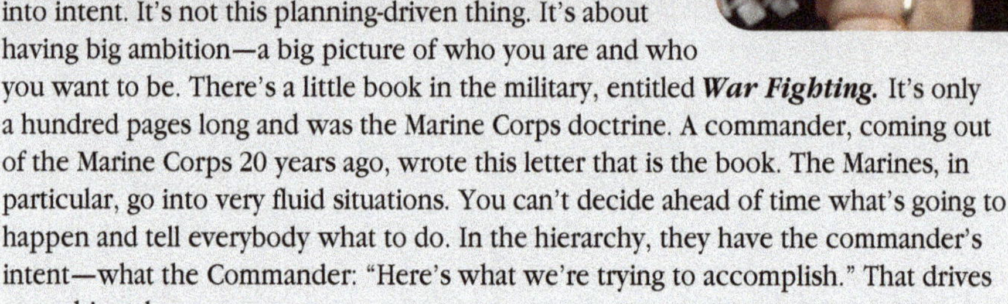

Nathan/ You have mentioned before that strategy is broken. How do you fix how it's taught or how it's practiced?

Jon Pittman/ I built our process [at Autodesk] around the idea of *"strategic intent."* I got the idea from Phillip Lay, who consulted with us for a while. I put together the strategy process for Autodesk and then I wanted to look more into intent. It's not this planning-driven thing. It's about having big ambition—a big picture of who you are and who you want to be. There's a little book in the military, entitled *War Fighting.* It's only a hundred pages long and was the Marine Corps doctrine. A commander, coming out of the Marine Corps 20 years ago, wrote this letter that is the book. The Marines, in particular, go into very fluid situations. You can't decide ahead of time what's going to happen and tell everybody what to do. In the hierarchy, they have the commander's intent—what the Commander: "Here's what we're trying to accomplish." That drives everything else.

At the next level down, they break a challenge into pieces from the Commander's intent—what you're trying to accomplish—all the way down to the person on the ground who must know how that intent impacts their goals. That gives them freedom of action—to decide how they're going to do it—but, they first need to know what goal to accomplish. To me, strategy is building a *hierarchy of intents* where everybody knows what to accomplish, but has the freedom of movement and creativity to solve their challenges in service of that intent.

That's the best thing within the organization too—especially for consumer-oriented organizations. I remember the days when US airlines empowered the people at the ticket desk, the gate, and on the plane to make decisions when problems occurred. Then, to cut costs, they just forced rules on customer-facing employees that might or might not solve the problem and took away all of their agency. It's interesting that you mention a book on strategy that came from the military. That's also where scenario planning came from. Would this have come from anywhere else but the defense industry?

The military *has* to have all of these contingencies because the stakes are so high. You can't just be surprised. Think about where we were surprised, like September 11th. When the fighter jets were scrambled from Langley Air Force Base, they weren't told where to go. They went over the ocean to their practice area because that was their drill. Everyone assumed that the threat was coming in over the ocean. Despite the preparation, it was a failure of imagination. They didn't yet have a directive or policy about shooting down a US passenger jet.

War is essentially adversarial and I don't see that the kind of strategy that you practice at Autodesk as being essentially adversarial. So, is there a difference between the strategy that comes from the military and how it's practiced by business?

Absolutely. What I take-away from the military texts is the idea of strategic intent and how it is passed through the entire organization. It is the clear notion of where you want to go. I think that's too often missing in strategy. The other thing that influenced me was Michael Porter's original article on his Five Forces. His basic point was that if you try to do what your competitors are doing, you become a commodity. Over time, commoditization is always happening. ***There's this frontier of differentiation that you always have to be on. You really can't afford to be a follower.*** You want to be a leader and that requires you to focus on what's different about your organization and offering that your customers care about. At Autodesk, we use this idea of ***"competitive separation."*** It has a strong basis in economics. The idea is to find something your customers desire that your competitors cannot or will not do, because if they can replicate it, you can't effectively compete.

It seems that the strategic process at Autodesk looked deeply at context as much as competitors. That's not really stressed in traditional business strategy.

Strategy and planning are different things. ***Strategy is having an informed point of view about where we want to go. Planning is how we're going to get there.*** You must have a point of view. You want to be deliberate, and not random. If you're actually driving the company, you can't rely on luck.

Strategy was in a unique place at Autodesk. We were under Jeff [Kowalski], the CTO, not Carl [Bass], the CEO. Jeff is the ultimate operator—super sharp—but, he knew enough to leave us alone and not try to operationalize us too much. We had goals and budgets, for sure, but both Jeff and Carl knew that strategy isn't like software development or facilities or finance and couldn't and shouldn't be managed in the same ways. We weren't solving an already-identified operational challenge. We were looking at things no one else in the company had the time or imperative to look at.

We always knew that we were in this incredibly lucky position of having all this upstream design information that was going to be used downstream for something. We saw lots of opportunity in that downstream. Our biggest problem was we were a little random capturing that with Carl.

You did have very "nuts-and-bolts, boots-on-the-ground parts of the company, especially with the sales team. How did those hierarchies of intent get communicated clearly?

The operating parts of the company all had their strategies and sales was connected with that. So, their intents and metrics were clear: "Here's what we're going to do this year." That was more difficult to do in the technical community because it had been so bottom-up for a long time. I was sitting with a bunch of professors from the University of Cincinnati at our annual conference and they were amazed at how diverse our audience was in terms of different industries and disciplines. Most people think of Autodesk as a set of software products. They were surprised by how deeply we thought about their application to practice and how we understood not only what our customers were doing with our software but what they were going through in their own businesses—what their challenges were.

Read the entire interview at www.nathan.com/whole-new-strategy

acquiring another only to shut it all down a few years later when it didn't prove successful or an organization moving into new market that doesn't make any sense for their business or brand, or one that spends lavishly into the latest hot technology only to never deploy it and write off the loss (think VR and blockchain).

Separating and honoring impacts, issues, and decision-drivers in each of these two areas isn't enough, however. The sequence in which you review them makes the difference between understanding your opportunities and missing then altogether.

Simply put, **start with the market context and use that to drive your operational context.** Your operational strategy should support your market strategy and not the other way around! Now, there is some other information you should consider when setting your operational priorities. Trends in technology, governance, the economy, society, and the environment are also worth considering, so there should be a place for these. The word "considering" is apt here: they are worth considering because they impact the context in which you operate, not because they're cool.

Marketing vs. Sales

One of the biggest mistakes in business is conflating and/or combining the Marketing function or department with the Sales function or department. Because these are both focused externally, leaders traditionally mix them together. When they do, they almost always destroy Marketing in the service of Sales.

Healthy organisms both inhale and exhale. They cannot do one without the other. Likewise, in healthy (and successful) organizations, **Marketing is the inhale** (what you learn from customers, competitors, trends, etc.) and **Sales is the exhale** (what you tell your customers, industry, competitors, etc.). They're very different things.

When combined, and because it is so important (it generates revenue), Sales nearly always crowds—out Marketing, which simply becomes the messaging subset of Sales. It stops breathing in an understanding of customers, competitors, and industry in all but the most tactical, quantitative sense. Marketing is supposed to uncover important insights about the market and be on the lookout for coming change. Sales isn't usually concerned with that. And, many salespeople, from managers on down, believe they can tell customers and markets what they want them to believe, in order to make those sales. This is hardly ever true.

To be sure, your Sales and Marketing teams need to be coordinating, along with every other high-level team in the company. But, if they're combined and lead by one person, one is going to suffer and then the entire organization will suffer. Either it won't be learning but it needs to from the market, or it won't be effectively messaging around those learnings to the market.

Stakeholders

Likewise, there are other stakeholders besides the traditional ones (customers, competitors, and shareholders) to consider in your strategy because they impact your context—both internal and external. Traditionally, businesspeople only really cared about shareholders (because that's who they considered themselves to be serving), competitors (because they had to, though many ignore them sometimes), and customers (begrudgingly). While some companies are customer-driven, way too many are not. This is especially true of governmental agencies and non-governmental organizations (NGOs). They may represent themselves as serving the citizenry or a specific population but either their plans make no attempt to actually understand these stakeholders or their actions ignore their realities. Even when organizations deeply care about customers, they often use techniques and tools that mask the most important understandings.

Leaders—entrepreneurs in particular—are often fiercely independent people. The media loves to lionize them as lone-wolfs (which is a complete fiction). To most businesspeople, stakeholders are often seen as a nuisance and as people or institutions who have little influence on an organization. The reality, however, is much different. Stakeholders of all kinds can be a source of impediments and partnerships, a critical fulcrum for success or failure.

Any stakeholders can be partners—or adversaries. Where NGOs like industry watchdogs or UN agencies are often seen as a thorn in the side of businesses, NGOs not only provide an important purpose for people and society, they are often unsung allies with shared business goals. However, they're rarely addressed in business strategy, except haphazardly.

We'll discuss this more in Chapter 5, but consider for a moment the partnerships Patagonia has with Breadfruit Institute, Rodale Institute, Washington State University and many more. While Patagonia isn't in the business of regenerative agriculture and fishery restoration, its strategic priorities align with these and other initiatives. They wouldn't be effective at starting and managing divisions to implement these operations but, by partnering with other stakeholders, they can accomplish similar goals and make their supply chains more efficient while simultaneously helping others).

Similarly, when Nike wanted to start using organic cotton in their apparel in the late 1990s, they quickly learned that there wasn't enough organic cotton produced in the world to meet the needs of even one of their product lines. A less strategic company would have just decided against using organic cotton but Nike knew that they would need to take the initiative to seed the industry so that they could meet these goals even if it took a decade to create the supply. They had to make investments in farmers and commitments to order materials in order to build the capacity they needed.

Even Apple invests heavily in their manufacturing partners, investing in and buying the very machines used in their vendors' factories in order to have those capabilities available (often before their competitors). They aren't content to wait until "the market" makes strategically significant capabilities available; they bring these capabilities into existence themselves, to the benefit of both stakeholders.

The opposite is also true; today, the most successful NGOs, charities, and other non-profits already know that "corporate" partners can be more strategic sources of success beyond merely sources of funding. The NAACP, a leading US civil rights organization dedicated to achieving racial equality and justice for African Americans and other marginalized communities, partners with Google to fund, scale, and support its AfroAcademic, Cultural, Technological and Scientific Olympics. This benefits their constituents as well as Google's ability to better source from underrepresented groups when hiring, helping them meet their goals.

If it takes a village to raise a child, as an old African proverb suggests, ***it takes a community to help an organization (of any type) succeed***. Those companies who routinely see other organizations as adversaries or don't bother looking beyond their own corporate borders often reduce their ability to succeed by alienating themselves from potential partners.

Lastly, where the term ***shareholder*** used to be the only outsider category that businesspeople were taught to address, the term, ***stakeholder***, has broadened the field of both responsibility and possibility.

A New Model for Strategy

There are a lot of moving parts to Strategy, and this is what can make it seem so daunting. However, they're actually easy to map and explain—hopefully this book does that well. Each step represents important opportunities to question the context around an organization, research if needed, and focus on the most likely opportunities. They're all important steps but each doesn't have to take days or weeks to perform.

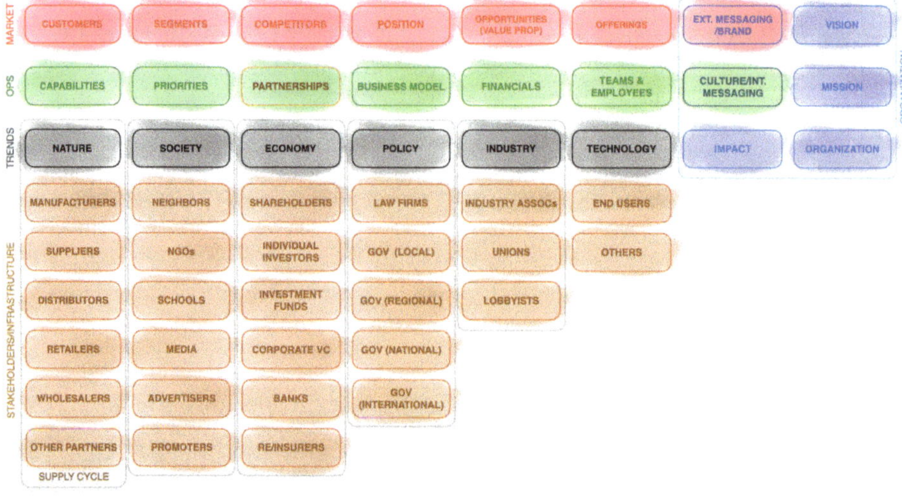

The most important thing is to actually ask these questions, even if the answer is "this doesn't apply at this time." Fair enough. Not every organization needs to focus on every potential stakeholder or category. Not every trend will impact your business. What's critical is asking the question in the first place, at the right time, and then moving on when you have a satisfactory answer. The worst thing you can do is never ask the question at all, whether because you don't have the time or information, or because it never occurred to you. I can assure you that others are asking these questions and your success will hinge on finding the most powerful levers you can pull that identify and leverage those forces toward your success.

Sequence

One of the problems our hypothetical startup above encountered stemmed from independently working on two interrelated (dependent) processes at the same time. Not only did they ignore some steps in the strategic process (such as customer research), having different people develop the SWOT analysis and Positioning Statement simultaneously ensured that the results of each wouldn't mesh. Go back and look at those two diagrams. How many things in one show up in the other? They might as well be for two different companies.

Great strategy requires the output of one step to be the input of the next. Reversing the order, ignoring steps, or practicing them simultaneously negates their value and creates untold (and usually unrecognized) contradictions in strategy.

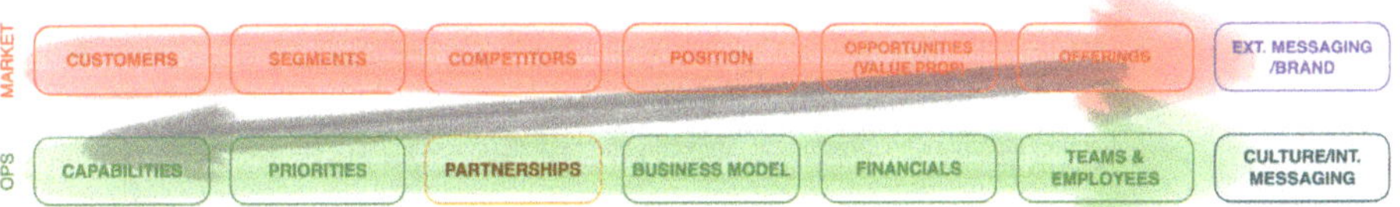

However, by carefully addressing the right questions in the right order, the cumulative focus ensures that the conclusions of strategy are supported by each step (and the questions associated with each step) are internally validated and consistent, and that the resulting strategy has a greater chance of success. It also means that those working on strategy maximize the value and efficiency of their work since they don't need to go back and reconcile divergent conclusions, reconsider prior information, and explain away contradictions.

I was taught this method by one of the greatest market strategists in Silicon Valley: Regis McKenna. In the early 1990s, I and my partners at *vivid* studios met with him every Saturday morning for weeks to codify his approach to strategy. Before this, I was always more than a little suspicious of "marketing." Perhaps, you are, too. What I learned was that there were specific, careful, and successful steps that could reduce the chaos of understanding an organization's surrounding market and quickly focus on the best possible paths to success. He called this process CRUSH (simply, for "crush the competition") and the model in this book was inspired by that approach.

What's enough?

Sadly, there's no light that illuminates when you've "done enough" strategy. There is no way for a template or a tool to signal when you've best answered the question. But I can assure you that not answering it at all is easy to spot. Some of the steps are mandatory. Some are optional (though still worth considering, if only for an hour or so). All represent opportunities to understand your customers, your market, and the world around you, as well as your opportunities.

Even without a big budget or a lot of time, moving through this model in the proper sequence will heighten your chances of success and enable you to see opportunities you'd otherwise miss. That's about all we can hope for with Strategy.

Now, to be honest, templates aren't necessarily bad in their own right. Even this new model could be printed and used as a template. What is a problem, however, is how they're used—and when. Without the right context, the data in them isn't relevant. Without the right sequence, it doesn't usually match. Without the right answers (like decision-drivers), it's just garbage and the old adage, "Garbage in, garbage out" applies. If you know what underpins the template, know when to use which part, and know what really needs to be recorded, templates can be quick organizers that help you get organized and speed you along.

There are ***so many templates*** and canvases these days. This has been an important progression in the past 20 years, yet none of them are adequate. Even this new model I'm sharing is likely inadequate—just (hopefully) less so. I've tried to correct many of the most common problems with previous models but there are likely some things I've missed, too. Think of this as the best model thus far but it may be supplanted by others—and/or by future evolutions of this one.

Oh yes, and evidence: even when you're using templates, without evidence, your data is ungrounded, making your insights and decisions equally ungrounded. If you're questioned on either, you won't be able to defend your strategy.

Who needs to be involved?

Ideally, everyone who touches the company, its offerings, its customers, and its operations should be involved with the strategic process at some point. However, it's often not feasible for truly ***everyone*** in an organization to be involved (at least for larger organizations), and it cannot be everyone's focus. However, it's usually the case that way too *few* people are involved—one of the many reasons why strategy fails.

Some roles (and their involvement) are more important than others, and most only at key parts of the process. In the Market sequence, everyone who connects with customers, competitors, and industry must have their concerns, data, and insight included. This means that customer service personnel, salespeople, support people of all kinds, even roles with no *official* connection to customers often lend important data to the understanding of customers and the market.

There is a famous story about online footware retailer Zappo's that describes how the company flies job candidates to their headquarters in Las Vegas, Nevada, for interviews. They have a company bus pick these prospects up from the airport. When they're returned to the airport in the same manner, the company talks with the bus driver to get their insights as to how pleasant, interesting, or alternatively, abusive the person might have been. It's not likely that, singlehandedly, the driver could torpedo an otherwise stellar candidate but it's often the case that this data can influence the decision of whether they would make a valuable employee. Your organization likely has people in it who understand your customers, partners, competitors, etc. in ways not usually recognized. Their input may be the difference between "business as usual" and recognizing something your competitors haven't noticed about your customers and market.

Likewise, there are people throughout the operations of an organization that aren't usually consulted about how the business runs, what's not working as well as it could, or how things could be improved. Why **wouldn't** you want to surface these insights while making critical decisions about the organization's future?

One of the strengths of this new model is that it helps remind you of connections and issues you might otherwise forget (and that your peers have never been taught to consider). Largely, valuing so many disparate voices is a factor of culture (more on that in Chapter 8). If an organization is used to separating people, teams, and divisions into silos or fiefdoms, it's not likely that suddenly asking people into the process is going to work well. Managers may be offended and feel undermined, and employees may feel like there's a catch they can't quite identify. You may need to lay some groundwork, culturally, well in advance of consulting people that have never-before been brought into the process (and you may need to reassure everyone, particularly managers, along the way that things will be better).

Change is terrifying to some people. Many organizations develop an immunity to it. And, most everything about strategy suggests change—or should, if it's going to have any positive impact. This is because both the market and society are constantly changing. Much of managing the strategic process is really about managing expectations and fears.

You'll also need to leave some extra time to consult more people, including partners of all kinds. Everything described in the next chapter on customers (and researching them) also applies to consulting people internally.

It never hurts to poll those in your organization about the current strategy (or whatever they think it is). Can they effectively answer the questions "How do you define our current strategy?" and "How do you define your role regarding the current strategy?" Is there a current strategy or not? If there is one, is it understood by many? Has it ever been communicated effectively and, if so, to whom?

Strategy is the synthesis of understanding several overlapping contexts, the union of several different perspectives, and the synthesis of conversations about these. All of this *requires* complexity because ignoring it ignored important truths about your customers, markets, competitors, industry, stakeholders, etc. Your goal is to clarify all of these disparate elements so that you can see how, together, they form a path to greater success. This complexity is a feature, not a bug, though some in your organization may try to subvert the process by simplifying the inputs and insights.

/Highlights

- Typical strategy is so rife with errors, false assumptions and short-cuts that its results are unworthy of consideration. In fact, it is more likely that strategic conclusions would lead organizations in adverse directions.
- Most companies haven't considered the most pressing issues of our time (like climate change), either among their customers, or the world as a whole, in their strategy, making it even more ill-considered—and potentially—disastrous.
- Template-based strategy is inadequate and lends itself to poor execution.
- All strategy begins with research—both qualitative and quantitative. Yet, most strategy all but ignores qualitative research, which is the basis for understanding the "why" of customer behavior and decisions, not merely the "what."
- The most important aspect of market strategy, customer decision-drivers, is often completely absent from strategic decisions.
- Sequence is important to strategy. Proper strategy uses the output of one process as the input for the next, linking work with prior insights, creating continuity.
- Strategy is based on multiple (and diverse) contexts: market, customer, trends, organization, etc.
- Better strategy separates the market contexts from the operational ones and addresses each in sequence (starting with the former, before the latter).
- Though often combined, marketing and sales are two very different functions. The first is focused on research to understand customers, markets, etc. and the latter is focused on messaging customers and others.
- Every stakeholder is a potential partner or threat. Great strategy addresses value across all stakeholders and seeks to establish more successful relationships with key stakeholders, both new and existing.
- Think about superior strategy as constantly evolving and relevant. Ideally, market and operational performance of any kind should be put into the context of strategy so that it's immediately and continuously clear when an organization is "on strategy" and when it is not.

/Explore More

- *War Fighting* by US Marine Corps:
  www.marines.mil/Portals/1/Publications/MCDP%201%20Warfighting.pdf
- *What is Strategy?* by Michael E. Porter: hbr.org/1996/11/what-is-strategy

Your Market

An organization's market is its single most important element. However, to see how regularly and sloppily companies consider their market, you wouldn't get that impression. The market represents those you wish to serve. There may be several categories of these customers or constituents* (called market segments) but you must have someone you're in business to serve. Most for-profit companies know they have customers but they have tremendous difficulty understanding customer needs and desires and what they base their buying decisions upon. Too many non-profit companies don't even perceive that they have constituents to serve or mistake other non-profits and government agencies as the people they serve. Even when they do serve other organizations, there are always people at some point in the value chain whose needs are served. They are often referred to as end users.

Any organization that can't name and accurately describe their customers needs to halt everything and determine the best way to do so.

*The word constituents is more common absent the for-profit context but it really means the same thing. Some bristle at the term consumer (and rightly so since we are all more than the sum of what we consume) but all of these terms mean the same thing: the people you intend to serve value of some kind.

Chapter 1

Your Customers

All strategy must begin with customers, even if you don't yet have any. However, this isn't the place many companies start. Why? Because it's the most difficult part. You actually have to go out into the world and talk to people if you want to understand what they want, what they need and, most importantly, upon what they base their decisions.

There are lots of challenges to this: many people are either uninterested or not well-suited to speaking to others about their lives—and have a limited capacity to listen with empathy. Next, the methods you use to speak with customers need to vary with the people and conditions. I won't rehash the current state of the art of market or customer research; there are plenty of great books about these subjects. I will, however, fill-in the missing pieces that often doom both customer and market research (and yes, there's a difference)—especially in regards to strategy. And, even though you might use a different term than "customers" (perhaps "citizens," "guests," "members," "constituents," or just "people"), the same processes are required and the same conditions apply.

There are 5 Kinds of Value

One important thing we all need to acknowledge is that there is more than one kind of value. Beyond *Financial value*—universally (and almost solely) recognized in business, most businesspeople will acknowledge *Functional value:* the features or performance that a product or service provides. After all, something has to be exchanged for money. Traditionally, this represents the two things all businesses look at and track: Price and Performance. By all means, both of these are important. Too many businesspeople however, think that only these two are important—or exist at all—and the reality is that, often, they aren't the most important factors customers use to make a purchase decision.

Now, most of you reading this know we all get more than just features from the products, services, events, and places we experience. But, in business contexts (and especially strategy), this is almost entirely ignored. In fact, it's really obvious when you stop to think about it even a little. First, we often buy things for emotional reasons: how something makes us feel. We don't even always realize that we do this, or that these factors outweigh the others.

Lots of us think of ourselves as rational beings and we certainly are, at times. We all have that capacity. However, we're much more complex than just rationality. Emotions are part of our nature and are incredibly powerful forces on our behavior, decisions, and lives. Even those among us who try to downplay their emotions still feel them.

In traditional business, emotions are treated as a mutable non-sequitur, there only to manipulate if we can. Economists call these "irrational" factors and either try to mini-mize them or purposefully ignore them altogether. Many, many people go into busi-ness and other disciplines (like engineering) specifically because our emotional natures confuse or annoy them. These people will tell you that emotions aren't relevant, aren't measurable (therefore they can't be "managed"), and can't be factored into strategy or other kinds of business decisions. They may, begrudgingly, admit that they exist but claim they are only crudely addressable through avenues like advertising, thus they can't be a part of serious plans. Yet, any salesperson or customer service representative can tell you that emotions are usually the most powerful factor regarding a customer's (or, any stakeholder, really) relationship with an organization—and, especially, buying decisions.

The best organizations buck the "common wisdom" and know that the emotional rela-tionship their customers have with their organization has a huge impact on everything: sales (and, therefore, revenue), customer loyalty, and even the ire of governments and NGOs.

Consider an archetypal story:

Rick is a middle manager in his finance company. He's in his late 40s and has two kids in elementary school. He's worked his entire life, and he and his wife bring in a decent living. They're comfortable but by no means wealthy.

Rick sees himself as a "rational guy" who is good with numbers and research. He's done his homework before he walks into the car dealership (he's just not that comfort-able buying something like a car online). He knows the area prices of the sedans he's interested in as well as the depreciation and ownership costs.

He discusses his needs with Rachel, the salesperson he sees when he walks in: the two models he's most interested in, the option packages, the colors, the wait for delivery, etc. But, the entire time, he can't help but glance over to this little red, sporty convertible on display in the glass corner of the showroom. He's admired that car since he was in college and it's even better than the model he admired then.

This doesn't go unnoticed by Rachel, who sees this a lot. She knows Rick's type: a self-identified stick-to-the-facts, rational guy. She answers all of his questions but while they're waiting for information on inventory to come back from the system, she walks him over to the—many of you have already guessed it—convertible.

Fast forwarding to the end: as he's driving his new sports car through the foothills (he's taking the long way home, of course, to enjoy his new car), he is grinning as wide as his face could possibly allow.

He. Is. Loving. Life!

He pulls into his driveway, gets out and walks the path to his front door with an excited gait, and turns back to look lovingly on his new acquisition just before he opens the front door to his home.

And, then it hits him.

What has he done!? He's definitely gone over the budget he and his partner set for the car and it dawns on him that it doesn't even fit the kids (being a two-seater)! Where is he going to put his family? How did this happen? He's a rational guy, after all!

Now, this isn't by any means a rarity. People buy cars like this every day—and not just cars. For some, it may be computers or consumer electronics, sporting equipment, hunting equipment, handbags, shoes, jewelry, makeup, or homes. We don't all do it for every category but we all do it for some categories. They represent the things we most care about.

Traditional economics and businesses say that we're "rational actors" and looks on this behavior (even as they profit from it), as an aberration of some kind—a weird, unreliable quirk. Even Rick thinks he's made some kind of mistake as he's a calculating guy—literally. It's his job! (By the way, everyone **knows** people aren't entirely rational yet it's still taught ad nauseum in economics course sand business programs and the people who most need to understand it's falsity, this helps them ignore what is obvious to everyone but them.)

Even some psychologists still call this "irrational" behavior. But, has Rick truly been irrational? He may not have recognized that he had unfulfilled needs and desires —perhaps, to feel more accomplished, more virile, more successful, even younger.

These may have been unconscious aspects of his self but they are very real, very normal, and very powerful—almost always more powerful than decisions about prices and performance.

So, why does traditional business only focus on price and performance: Financial and Functional value? This approach misses many important factors and leaves significant value on the table? I find this to be one of the biggest missteps in business.

Salespeople already know that if the price and performance adage were true, they wouldn't have a chance to make a sale (and wouldn't be needed). They would be mere order-takers and order-fillers.

But what if I tell you that's not even the only or most important "missing" value from business? There are two other kinds of value that are more personal, more hidden, and more enduring than emotions (which typically fade after 30-120 seconds anyway if not continuously stimulated).

Identity value is about how we define or envision ourselves. It's more than just emotions. It's why there are Coke people and Pepsi people, Windows people and Apple people, iOS and Android, Real Madrid and FC Barcelona. In fact, it's the reason sports is as big an industry as it is. It's why brands have any value at all (and, believe me, those companies with valuable brands understand this well). It's where our values reside, whether they're about freedom, expression, religion, or any other institution in our lives.

Now, let me say that no, it's probably not healthy that we construct our identities from corporate brands. In the past, we did this with religions, nations, regions, sports, etc. and now we've collectively added corporations and other organizations to the calculus. I won't argue the relative health of adding brands to our identity equations. I'll just note that it's real and it happens. Why wouldn't you want to understand this when you're building your organization's strategy?

But, wait! There's one more kind of value that's even more important: Meaning. This is about our worldviews and it transcends brands, emotions, price, features, and even our identities. How we understand the world (our worldview) is powerful. Some see the world as wondrous and magical. Others think those people are deluded because they see the world as dangerous and haphazard. You know what? They're both right! Your worldview is a function of what you prioritize and how you express it. Even people who prioritize the same thing, say Freedom, can express this differently. For example, Europeans often express Freedom as "following the rules" (we're all free from each other if we just stick to the agreed-upon rules). Others, like many who live in the United States take a different, if not quite opposite, take: "I'm only free if I can do whatever the hell I want, whenever I want!"

Consider how profound that difference is (and there aren't only two choices—there are many). This is why foreign relationships can be so difficult, not to mention those within our friends and families.

I'll ask again, if these forms of value are so powerful, why wouldn't you want to consider them in your strategy? Or, more accurately, why doesn't everyone?!

I've written much more deeply about this, with more detail, in books written with my favorite co-author, Steve Diller—***Blind Spot***, in particular—so I won't go into more detail here. You can also watch videos about it. These other forms of value are real, and they're not accidental. You can deliberately build, exchange, and reap this value. They can and should be a part of your strategy.

Meaningful value is the deepest, most stable kind of value and applies to all stakeholders, not only customers. It's especially important to your employees but it doesn't stop there. Read Chapter 10 on stakeholders to understand this more deeply.

Meaning is also an effective design tool for deliberately building more value for your customers as well as for your organization. It doesn't happen by accident though: up until now, it's been largely an intuitive process. We now have models and techniques for understanding meaning, which means we can be strategic about it, not merely tactical.

Meaning is strategic. It is both a signal for your organization and those around you. If you want to reap the benefits of Meaningful value, you need to deliberately build a path to delivering it. And, if you understand your customers, your company, your employees, and your competitors on this level, you can deliberately distinguish your organization on that basis. You can't back your way into it at the end of development nor sprinkle it on top once all of your key decisions have been made (like many business-people approach advertising).

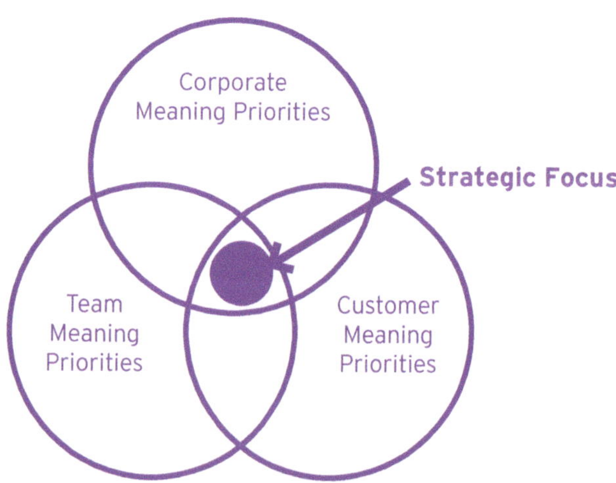

Once you understand value on this level, it becomes clear how aligned it is throughout your organization. Understanding Meaningful value will signal how difficult it might be to move into a new market, acquire or merge with another company, prioritize a hiring spree, or position against a similar competitor. This gives businesspeople a way to deliberately, strategically make more successful decisions. I'll go into more detail on this in a later chapter.

But, but, B2B!

I nearly always hear this statement when I speak about the five kinds of value: "Well, I can understand how this works for B2C businesses, but I'm in a B2B business and people only make decisions based on cost!" This is understandable but hopelessly inaccurate. *As long as you're dealing with another human, the other forms of value are always in play! I'll give you an example.*

B2C: Business-to-Consumer
B2B: Business-to-(other)-Businesses

In my time, there used to be a famous line in business: "Nobody ever got fired for hiring IBM." What this means is that IBM thrived not on their prices (indeed, they were never the least expensive option) nor their performance (no offense to the fine folks there but IBM was never the absolute best option, either). And in that era, IBM most definitely did not sell to consumers!

What was at work, here, and has always been a factor—and still is—is that most people didn't want to be blamed for making a bad decision if things failed. They didn't want to lose their jobs! It turns out that fear of losing your job (an emotion) was more powerful than price or performance. Not surprising at all, of course, but anyone who says that emotions don't count in business decisions is, frankly, kidding themselves. What do you think all those business lunches and golf games were accomplishing? It wasn't more competitive pricing.

Again, salespeople have always known this. Too often, though, they've had to work around the company's strategy because this wasn't a factor in that strategy unless the leadership had come from a sales background.

"Quant" people may really, really want quant to be the only way decisions are made. They may proclaim how everything would be so much more efficient if cost and performance were the only factors considered in business decisions, but they would be very, very wrong. Consider the cost to Uber when a manager made the "efficient" decision to only order men's jackets for his team since there was only one woman on it. He only ordered team jackets for the male workers since he could get a volume discount, but a single female jacket took the price over budget. He saved a little money. He was more efficient. Yet his decision helped to unleash a tidal wave that ultimately cost the company billions in market value. Quantitatively, it was a disastrous, short-sighted decision (not to mention the more important fairness factor). Now, traditional

Something that often confuses people is the result of the term, B2B (Business to Business). It's much too vague a term to highlight the differences within the business market 9as if everyone in the market were looking for the same things). A better, more nuanced way to think about who is in this market is to recognize that there are, at least, two categories here that need to be treated differently: B2E and B2P.

B2E (Business to Enterprise) is the B2B that most people think about. It's when your customer is a company or other organization. You're still selling to a person within that company but they represent more than just themselves (or, at least, they should).

B2P (Business to Professional) represents people in their career capacity. These aren't "consumers in the general sense because they aren't buying for their personal life but for their professional one. And, their concerns in doing so are likely different.

These two groups usually need require different offerings and different messages. For example, many of Salesforce's first customers were individual salespeople, purchasing their software to help them do their job. They could justify the expense of the subscription because it directly affected their ability to manage and generate revenue. That's a very different value proposition than a consumer who isn't purchasing a product or service that impacts their salary. In contrast, Salesforce eventually started selling their software into companies (sometimes, the very same companies whose salespeople were already using it) as corporate accounts. This is a different kind of sale, requiring different approaches than with individual professionals. Effective sales (and marketing) doesn't lump these into one category (B2B).

There is sometimes a variation of B2P that represents the "prosumers," hobbyist consumers who want professional-level tools. They don't earn revenue from their hobbies but the want the higher quality and commitment offered by professional tools. These are the audiophiles that buy the most sophisticated audio equipment they can afford to listen to their LPs, the "weekend warriors" who attack the outdoors with lifted pickups and professional-grade fishing equipment, and the über-gamers who buy gaming rigs that rival those at gamin competitions—and so many more. These aren't strictly consumers for mere enjoyment.

business decisions and metrics would say, "Sorry lady, you're not economically expedient." But I can assure you that if you asked the company if one of their corporate values (and that's a part of their strategy) was unfairness, they would have denied it strongly.

Qual and Quant

In order to understand your customers (and other stakeholders) on these higher-value levels, you have to leave the world of the quantitative. These values just aren't researchable nor measurable via quantitative tools and processes. That's OK. You can use those for your other market research tasks.

But, one must learn, practice, and use *qualitative* tools and processes to identify Emotional, Identity, and Meaningful value. For best results, this is where you should start. If you start with quantitative value techniques, you often cut out the opportunity to uncover and understand your customers and constituents in qualitative ways. In fact, tools like surveys make researching qualitative value nearly impossible, so if you start there, you've already decided that it's not important. You're not going to be able to wedge it into your plans later.

Market Research vs. Customer Research

What's the difference between market research and customer research? In general (though this is no longer a strict rule), market research refers to quantitative research. It shouldn't, but over time, it has come to. Ideally, to understand the market, we should research both quantitatively and qualitatively. But, in their haste to systematize, standardize, and numericize everything, most businesspeople and processes throw out the qualitative techniques, claiming they're too difficult, too expensive, or irrelevant. As I've said, there is a huge bias toward numbers in business (one of its biggest weaknesses) and qualitative techniques and data are deemed unnecessary.

Of course, this makes designers, customer service people, salespeople, and many others supremely uncomfortable because they know there is more to understand than surveys and other quant techniques reveal. Sadly, when your colleagues refer to market research this is likely all they mean.

Qualitative customer research is sometimes called *market insight* in order to differentiate design-based and other qualitative customer research techniques that understand customers in terms of total value (all five kinds) from market research (which traditionally relies only on quantitative techniques). It is critical to strategy to combine data from both approaches if you want to be successful.

While quant techniques can tell you a lot about *"what"* is happening, only qualitative techniques can tell you *"why"* they are happening. It is entirely inadequate to formulate strategy and go to market only understanding the "what" (or even the" how," "when," and "where") without also understanding the "why."

Starting with qualitative techniques, like interviews, laddering, and observations (there are many variations of each) allows you to uncover these other forms of value more readily. And once you have, you can use that to focus your quantitative research more effectively. The results of your *qualitative* inquiry become the input to your *quantitative* input (sadly, it doesn't work effectively the other way). The resulting quantitative research will uncover data that will lead to more questions that qualitative research can illuminate more deeply, and so on. Continuous research starts with qualitative and then moves to quantitative and then back to qual and then to quant—forever. It's the interplay between these that will constantly uncover what you need to understand about customers.

Nathan/ I wanted to ask you about research in the context of strategy. Tthe type of research is probably more critical than whether you do research or not. How do you success-fully frame that to leaders?

Steve/ In order to address that, I think it's important to note that there's at least three different major types of informa-tion that typically informs strategic thinking inside compa-nies: customer insight, com-petitor and market insight and insight on internal functions and processes. If we're talking about strategy to drive innovation, that usually focuses on a market analysis of the competitive and industry landscape. Obviously, that's important because you need to understand the context. That's what I usually discuss with business execs but it's only one half of the equation. The other half is the customers and to ignore the customer makes no sense consider-ing how quickly consumers evolve. The competitive analysis is basically the seller side—producers and competitors. The other half is the buyer side. And, that doesn't just mean trying to figure-out consumer life stages and trends in purchasing. You need to understand people's *experiential preferences* and how they're evolving—where they're headed. You can't do that only with quant. You can only get there with certain kinds of qualitative research.

Business leaders are perfectly comfortable with the competitor industry side and the quant side. But, most are uncomfortable with the customer side, specifically the qualita-tive side. Does that bear out in your experience?

That's definitely true. It's actually a good idea. It's just that you don't know what the right ques-tions are unless you do qualitative first and most marketers and leaders think they already know what the right questions are. It's not difficult for me to identify really bad questions that have destroyed entire in-dustries. I've seen it happen.

I started doing work for newspapers around the turn of the millennium. It was 1999. And we were approached by the head of research at one of the big Midwestern news-papers. Since then, I've worked with a lot of other papers in the United States—some-times up to a dozen projects for key pa-pers. What was really fascinating about this was the discussions, because newspapers did traditional market research so they could tell advertisers what consumer products people were likely to be in the market for in the next few years. In other words, they were doing consumer research to sell their read-ers to their advertisers. So, if you're a furniture retailer in town, if you knew that 40% of the people who read the one metropolitan daily were planning to buy new furniture in the next year, you had a really good reason to buy ad space.

But, being public-spirited people, the newspaper researchers also thought: "Let's ask people, how im-portant certain attributes of newspapers are to them." They would ask questions like: "On a one to sev-en scale, how important is objectivity to you? How important is depth? How important is balance? How important is news you can use?" Unsurprisingly, they were pleased to see that the vast majority of their readers valued those things really highly. What they didn't take into account were two key things. One is that the average American has been trained for decades to know what journalists think is important in news stories. The vast majority of news readers never thought about it for themselves independent of what they've been told. So, they knew objectivity should be important, they knew balance should be important. But, is that what mattered most to readers? Well, they didn't know because they never actu-ally asked people what mattered to them. They assumed they knew because the journalistic profession is driven by people who are elitist in their mentality—they know what's best for people. They'll decide how to serve it up, and then people will like it, they're expected to. So, I suggested asking the question in a slightly different way: "What is it about newspapers that makes you savor the prospect of picking the paper off the stoop in the morning? Is it objectivity? Is it balance?" With some of the most important publishers and editors in America, not a single one of them could answer the question. They were more than a little flummoxed and would question: Why does that matter? But they quickly understood that they were making assumptions about what mattered that drove their questions, assumptions that didn't really make sense.

Now, I should also mention that, at this time, the reason they turned to us was because the average age of readers was 40 years old—and getting older (this was 1999, remember). And, they thought that they should have had people in their thirties because they believed that people started subscribing about the time they bought their first home. So, what was happening? Gen Xers weren't subscribing and they couldn't figure out why. Meanwhile, the Internet was growing and they didn't know what to make of that. And, even by that point, the classifieds were beginning to migrate from the metropolitan dailies to Craigslists and other online services. They didn't think that would ever really take-off because all of the online options didn't have the depth of interesting stuff that the metropolitan dailies had. They assumed that people cared about the news how they cared about it. We conducted a bunch of 90 minute interviews with people and quickly understood what people wanted. Objectivity was not the point. Balance wasn't either. It's not like they were against objectivity, it just wasn't what was driving them.

For instance, many people in regional markets equated "objectivity" with liberalism. They would read an article and then point it out to me. In one case, there was an article on "pollution in the city" and this one woman looked at this and responded, "This is typical. They have this story about pollution, but they don't say whether it's good or bad or whether it's a serious problem or not a big deal. They just tell me that there's pollution and they tell me where it's coming from and they tell me what the mayor thinks." I asked, "So, what do you make of that?" And she responded, "Well, this is typi-cal liberal writing. It is morality-free even when there should be a point of view about whether this is good or bad or how bad is." Another article reported on demonstrations at abortion clinics in the city and this guy declared "The article never says anything about the problem of people having abortions." I asked him to elaborate and he said, "Liberals wrote this. They treat it as if it's self-evident that it's a good thing that we have these clinics and they're reporting on the bad people that are demonstrating outside of them, and their tone is neutral as if they're objective. But, what they're bringing to it has an unspoken bias. They act like they're objective, but they're not."

Read the entire interview at www.nathan.com/whole-new-strategy

But, how much research do you need to do? What's "just enough" when it comes to understanding customers, who can be so diverse?

How Much Research is Enough?

Believe it or not, studies show that great qualitative research with just a few people will surface many of the customer desires and needs you're likely to find. Now, your colleagues may laugh at this because most businesspeople have been led to believe that you need hundreds of responses to understand and validate an opportunity. And, you do, if you only do quantitative research. But, starting with qual and doing it effectively, will uncover the insights with the best potential and then quantitative research can further validate these insights to the tune of hundreds of people. 15 people is not difficult—for any organization. No one has an excuse to not perform at least that amount of investigation.

Qualitative customer research is more expensive than survey-oriented market research but immensely more valuable. Still, too many organizations (and leaders at all levels) discount that value, often on the basis of sample size. It's a poor excuse but you can understand their thinking: "I have a survey of 425 people that says people prefer x over y or z. You have 15 interviews with customers who say that they don't prefer z, y, or z—although they hate z less—but really prefer something else entirely—let's call it w." If you're the leader of an organization needing to make a product development decision, who are you going to believe, the 425 people or the 15?

This is the tyranny of numbers (and poor research techniques). It's likely that the 15 people are pointing to a much more successful market solution but it would be unaffordable for the company to ask 415 more to confirm it. What to do?

Well, here is where it comes in handy to point out that research demonstrates that 12 people is an acceptable number of people when they're in a similar segment (all stay-at-home fathers or all grandmothers with diabetes, for example). You still need to do good research but this study* shows that just 12 people, well-researched, can expose 95% of the variance in desires and needs (the experiences they want) within the population you study. That's actually an affordable tactic to get better data. While the research suggests 12 interviews, Christopher Ireland suggests 15 to be safe (read her interview starting on page 35).

This study shows that 12 interviews can almost certainly find all the diversity of perspective within a population. In other words, you can comfortably identify all the key variables that determine how the full range of people in that population make choices. And that can be used to segment a population. It won't necessarily uncover which are most important, otherfactors, such as intensity, can help with that. This is where quant research really shines, as now you've identified the right variables that inform the right questions to further research with quant tools.

*How Many Interviews Are Enough?: An Experiment with Data Saturation and Variability: Greg Guest, Arwen Bunce, and Laura Johnson https://doi.org/10.1177/1525822X05279903

/The Mall Intercept

The behavior of many leaders and managers in companies makes me wonder just how comfortable they are with people (instead of tools and reports). Often, when managers and leaders are asked to take part in customer journeys or customer research, they beg-off, citing too much importance or not enough time. Even in school, one of the most difficult tasks my colleagues in business programs assign is for their business students to go out into the world and meet actual customers. They seem genuinely afraid to meet people and instead, believe it's their place as future MBAs for others to perform market research, which will be collated and summarized for them at some point so that they can create appropriate marketing plans. They use the Internet to search for relevant secondary research but do everything they can to ignore the need to be involved in primary research, themselves.

This behavior is seen in business schools and in the business world as well as in all types of organizations and industries. Only the most clued-in businesspeople know that they need first-hand contact with customers if they hope to understand any opportunities the market has to offer. They also know that market research data, which is primarily numerical, doesn't tell the whole story of opportunity sometimes, and experiencing it first-hand can impart a better understanding.

For example, take the case of the once popular market research tool, the mall intercept. Now, the reasoning behind a mall intercept makes a lot of sense, but as we'll see, its usefulness can leave a lot to be desired. Thankfully, it's largely obsolete now for the reasons you'll read here. But consider: how could it ever have been deemed valuable, and by whom?

A mall intercept is a simple idea: go to where people are already predisposed to buy things (such as a mall), when they're in an optimal state of mind to make and share decisions about products and services, and ask them what you want to know about their preferences. A mall intercept is often a prelude or alternative to a focus group, where customers are brought into a room (an artificial situation) to comment on potential products and services.

This isn't a bad premise, by the way. People do have different thoughts, reactions, and opinions and share different information when they're in the process of evaluating or buying something than when they're doing something else in their lives.

What typically happens in a mall intercept is that a marketing manager hires another company to perform the research and assigns no one from her company (let alone herself) to attend the research or watch any of it in action. To save costs, she hires the firm with the least expensive proposal since this research is so "plain and simple" to perform really, how difficult can it be to stop people and ask a few, set questions? The market research firm, also trying to cut its costs, hires people at minimum-wage since this work isn't viewed in any way as skilled labor anyone can do it. And, to keep these interviewers productive, they'll usually pay by the completed survey, not by the hour. This way, they reward productivity and not laziness.

What is rarely considered is how this appears to mall shoppers or how it feels to the interviewers. The entire research project is viewed as an inexpensive, easy way of getting valuable shopper insight. But, almost nobody likes stopping people and interrupting their activities to ask questions since almost nobody wants to be stopped (for the same reason). The busier we are, the more we resent intrusions into our lives. Thus there's a built-in conflict of interest in the technique, no matter how easy it is to perform.

You can probably already tell what's going to occur. We have people being paid little but motivated to fill-out as many surveys as possible, as fast as possible. These interviewers aren't looking forward to interrupting strangers to talk and they know that most of these strangers aren't going to be happy about being interrupted. They're given survey sheets that are purposefully standardized, short, and direct because the researchers know that shoppers aren't going to take much time out of their shopping to answer questions. So, the survey questions are pointed, direct, easy to answer, and somewhat obvious (since the low-skilled, low-paid interviewers aren't in any position to ask anything in-depth nor follow-up on any interesting comments). Consider what you would do in this situation (as interviewer, interviewee, or even as marketing executive). How would you respond to this situation and the relationships it implies?

To marketing managers, it's a foolproof plan to garner important customer insight at a low, controllable cost. To everyone else, it's one perfectly engineered for this to happen (though we certainly can't say that it does in every case): understandably reluctant interviewers save shoppers the hassle from interruption and maximize their revenue by simply filling-out the surveys themselves!

Now, these interviewers aren't stupid. They know that the surveys are going to be read, so they might go sit-down somewhere, like the mall's food court, and answer each survey a little differently. They might channel their friends and family in filling-in the answers (to reflect what they think are realistic concerns of real people they know). In other cases, they just vary the answers so that it's clear they weren't all filled-out the same (which might give away that someone did exactly what they're doing).

All of this money and effort has now yielded "valuable" customer insight appropriate for just one purpose: recycling the paper. The research includes no real customer insight because it doesn't include answers from any actual customers.

But before we get too judgmental about these interviewers' behavior, let's also acknowledge the likelihood that the mall intercept was going to generate useful research in the first place. No one from the company buying the research is involved: not from marketing, product development, sales, customers service, or anywhere else. No one from the company has met any real customers, let alone learned anything about their lives and motivations. Likely, the survey questions haven't even been vetted for possible bias or ambiguity. Any answers from any real customers (from, perhaps, more honest or diligent interviewers) haven't been followed-up on or connected to the company's goals, mission, or intent. In effect, there is no relationship.

For the most part, the entire endeavor was a waste from the moment the marketing manager decided to pawn-off the duty completely to an outside agency. You can just imagine what will happen if she doesn't realize that the report she's later given contains exactly this lack of insight or conclusions that might lead in exactly the wrong direction.

Thankfully, the mall intercept isn't common practice anymore. However, there are plenty of other market research tools currently in popular use that are just as misguided, mostly because they assume that only quantitative results are important, but also because quantitative reports impart an air of accuracy. The statistics make us feel confident about the research, often without inquiring whether the right questions were asked of the right people, in the right context, at the right time, in the first place.

The Only Thing That Matters are the Drivers of Decisions

There is another thing traditional business strategy (and, the rest of traditional business) misses, although it is crucial. Even the qualitatively-driven "design" strategists and researchers miss it, too. It's certainly nice to have a full picture of your customers, complete with interesting details of their lives, motivations, likes, dislikes, etc.: "Kriti is a 24 year old customer service agent who loves K-POP, lives at home, and uses WeChat incessantly" or "Haru is a 42 year old manager who hates drinking after work with his peers (though he does it anyway because it's expected), deplores TikTok and social media and is a news hound." All of this is really nice. It may even be helpful for the designers, engineers, project managers, and others to know these customers in this way so they can better empathize with them. But, from a strategic standpoint, none of this matters.

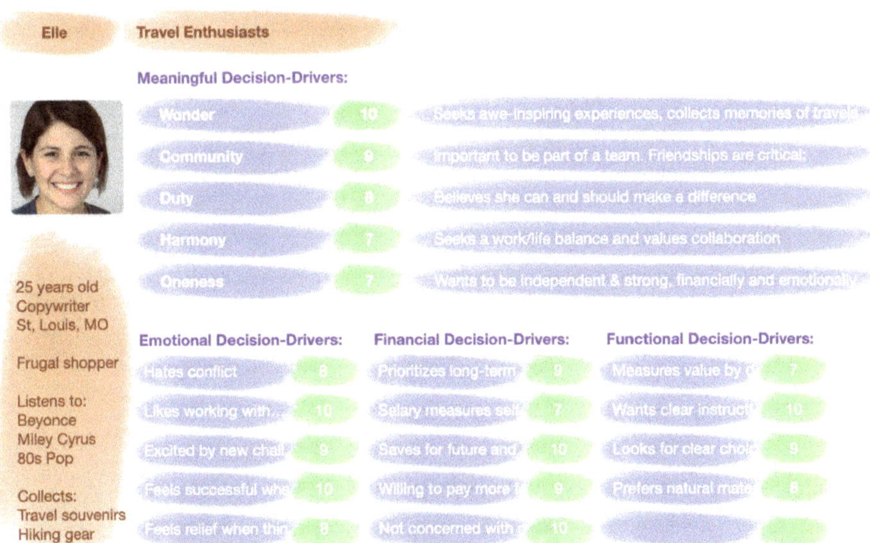

Nathan/ You are probably one of the best design researchers on the planet. How did you approach strategy for your clients, especially when you weren't necessarily hired to do strategy?

Christopher/ Thanks. Part of it came from my background. I have an MBA and strategy was just something I automatically thought about—in fact, I couldn't stop thinking about it. The thing about research, particularly design research, is you're almost always learning things that directly apply to strategy. So, it's just a matter of speaking up and saying, "Hey, look at this opportunity" or "Wow, look at this challenge."

Did you ever feel insecure speaking-up about something you found when you weren't, specifically, hired to do strategy?

It's normal to feel unsure. But, I'm the oldest of seven and I've never felt insecure in my life. So, I probably butted-in where I wasn't wanted, but it didn't occur to me not to. I was fortunate to have really good rapport with most of my clients. I can think of only a few times when I was shut-out or when people would be rude and say, "I didn't ask for your opinion," but I would just drop them as clients.

It also helped that the kind of research I did was really early in the development process. The last thing you want is be in the last phase of development and have your researcher say, "Uh, by the way, your strategy sucks." So, because I was early, I could help direct their product or market strategy. As we got later and later in the development process, my strategy comments would become more and more tactical. At that stage, I'd be able to affirm, "This color or form works well," but it's much too late for "This market isn't good!"

Nathan/ For those of us who are not the first of seven, what would you suggest to people to build that kind of confidence?

Start with self-awareness—a clear understanding of your strengths and weaknesses. You build confidence out of your strengths. Next, look at your partners—know who has your back and who complements or balances you. If you're in a creative discipline, you're likely a great visual or verbal communicator. Put yourself in a role where you're communicating strategy with your talents. You're doing what is asked, of you but have the opportunity to make suggestions. Then, reinforce it over and over again. Look for opportunities where you can make a contribution and just build it like any muscle.

How do you know when you've done enough research or strategy?

It depends on the purpose of the research. We had a number of clients who used research to mitigate risk. We had others who used it to explore, and these requests were quite different. The ones who wanted to reduce risk, honest to God, would hire us to do 80 one-on-ones, all over the country, sometimes the world. We'd be sitting in these back rooms hearing questions asked in the same way over and over and over again. And, after a while it's so clear: "Oh my God, we're hearing exactly the same thing! We're not hearing anything new!" So, we were motivated to figure-out the point when we've gotten 80% of what's there to get—where it's going to take us tens of thousands of dollars to get the last 20%. Unless the client can cover those costs and is super risk adverse, we don't want to do that. We just want that 80%.

We started focusing closely on when we got to 80% and it ended-up being somewhere around 12 to 15 people when they were in a homogenous set. We checked that against academic research, and we found data that explained that you'd get 85% of the ,ost information info at about 15 interviews. After that, we just baked that into our process and sold our field work in sets of 15. Now, some clients would come to us and say, "Okay, we want you to do a global study in five countries and we want to do 20 inter-views." We would have to tell them "No, when we say 15, we mean 15 in China, 15 in Brazil, etc. Not 15 in the whole world." Unless your topic is, you know, "What color is the sky?"

It would depend. Sometimes it was, but we were logical sellers, not emotional sellers. We would just explain how and why we work, and we'd always give options. If they didn't have that big of a budget, we'd get creative. For example, we might divide the countries between the "romantic" or "hot" countries and the "cool" ones. We would suggest 15 in each and that would often work.

The other thing is that the incremental cost isn't that high compared to the overhead organizing the trip and study, in the first place. So, if you're doing five, the next ten doesn't blow the budget out that much.

You're right, unless you're dealing with a high cost respondent like a doctor. But, if you're researching teenagers or parents, it doesn't cost much more.

You mentioned "hot" and "cool" countries, which speaks to Marshall McLuhan's ob-servations about media, as well as Mihaly Csikszentmihalyi's "hot" and "cold" families. Could you describe what you mean by this and talk a bit about segmentation? I can't imagine it was always geographic. How would you suggest people best segment?

I mean "hot" and "cool" at a very high level. "Cool" is "rational." "Hot" is "emotional." There are cultures that are more built on emotion and others that are built on rational-ity; for example, Italy vs. Norway. We were fortunate to have deep-pocketed clients, like Pepsi, General Motors, Microsoft and Levis who really were interested in seg-mentation. They had massive audiences and they couldn't afford to market to them in generalities.

Read the entire interview at www.nathan.com/whole-new-strategy

/Strategies vs. Tactics

These two are usually conflated. What's a strategic thing and what's a tactical thing? Sometimes, this distinction is used to bludgeon and silence others: "Oh, that's *tactical*, we're focused on *strategy* right now!" The reality is that both require context and if you're entering any strategy process, you need to calibrate what context is appropriate. This is because the output of strategy *is* tactics ("here's what we plan to do and this is how we'll do it"). That sounds clear, right?

But, the strategies at the level of offerings (products, services, etc.) are the tactics for the level higher Product Strategy. And the product strategy is one of many tactics to enact the Business Strategy. This is another reason sequence and context are important. If you start with Product Strategy, it's difficult to work up to Corporate Strategy because too many key decisions have already been made without the context that is important at the level. Of course, you can go change the product strategy when the corporate strategy is more defined but now you have to change that, as well as the tactics under it, and the strategies and tactics at all of the levels below it. It's just not an efficient or effective way to work. It can also be costly: much work "down the line" may need to be redone, people fired and others hired, etc.

What matters is what they base their decisions upon: their decision-drivers.

And, you don't get to these by simply asking. For example, ask the IBM client I mentioned above what they based their decision to hire IBM on and they will never say "fear of losing my job." They will always cite some kind of price/performance justification, especially to their bosses, but we all know that's not the entire story, nor the most important part of the story. This is where salespeople can be invaluable, though they may need help articulating what's at work.

The basis for market strategy starts with (and focuses on) customer decision-drivers. They may like green widgets or smooth ones or loud ones or blinking ones but are these the drivers of their decisions? You can ask them in endless surveys what they like and don't, what they wish was available and don't care about. But, if they aren't basing their purchase decisions on these things, they are irrelevant to

/There's still a Role for Trivia

I'm not completely against the demographic trivia that many people use to construct their customer personas. As long as these details aren't taking emphasis away from decision-drivers, and as long as it still comes from actual customer research and isn't made-up in the minds of marketers, this kind of trivia can help create a fuller story of customers. Understanding people as more than merely a set of needs and desires (and decisions) is important, so this information can often help businesspeople of all kinds better empathize with their customers.

strategy. For sure, these facts may become important in the development of offerings (products, services, events, and places) and they will help differentiate your offerings and make them more appealing, but this is all tactical, not strategic. If you collect this information (and this is an opportune time to), save it for later, when you're defining and development specific offerings.

What you need to know is if they leave your store after 30 seconds because the perfume you pump into your vents is overpowering. Or, that your best customers won't come back to your restaurant because they have to yell over the music to the person across the table in order to have a conversation. Or, that your packaging made someone laugh at a time they needed to (these aren't all negatives). Or, that you are alienating your customers who want to feel like they're contributing to making the world just a little better. This is what you need to base your strategy upon.

Market Segmentation

Most businesses serve more than one kind of customer. Your solution likely will work for different kinds of people, contexts, and applications. But, the way you promote and sell to each may be different. In fact, you may have to offer slightly (or even greatly) different versions. The decision-drivers for some customers may be different than others. These represent different customer segments (you could just as easily call them market segments). This is OK. It's entirely natural. You merely need to identify where this is the case.

But how? Should you group these customers together by a particular factor? Or, should you group them in a different way?

Traditional business wisdom says to differentiate customer segments demographically because—guess why?—it's easier. Some marketing people don't even know that they could segment their customers differently because they've never seen it done! They might split their markets by geographic region or age or skill level. Surely, experts probably require a different solution than beginners but is this the most important differentiator?

Typical Market Segments:

Demographics:	Geography:	Behavioral:
• Age	• Country	• Use Amount & Patterns
• Income	• Market Region	• Benefits Expected
• Gender	• Population Density	• Brand Association
• Race	• Climate	• Loyalty
• Nationality		• Readiness to Buy
• Occupation	**Psychographics:**	
• Education	• Social Class	
• Religion	• Personality Attributes	
• Occupation	• Lifestyle	
• Married Status	• Climate	

Nathan/ You have so much experience teaching and practicing design research at a level that is still rare these days. What do you consider design research and where and why is it appropriate?

Brenda/ You can break it down into qualitative and quantitative or look at it in terms of process—where it should occur. In terms of quantitative research, you can get statistics from many places and even generate your own if you have a big enough sample size. And this is good for demographics, income level, education level, etc. and maybe some foundational desires or needs that people express. For example, we found with Purple Moon that age 8 or 9 was the best time to intervene with technology and computers Kids at this age were still curious. By the time they're teens, all kinds of these stereotypes set in. There as a lot of existing material that others had produced about this.

But, I'm a very strong component of starting with qualitative research if you really want to understand people and discover the best opportunities. We started with a set of questions. At Purple Moon, it wasn't enough to learn that girls stopped using computers and playing games around that age. We needed to understand why. This is 1994. We started with a question: ***"What would it take for a girl to put her hands on a keyboard?"*** We discovered a better one along the way: ***"What are the differences be-tween the ways girls and boys play at this age?"*** We learned a tremendous amount about their social and personal lives and behavior. Purple Moon and its products came out of that question. They would have never emerged from something like ***"How can we better market our games to girls?"*** The one or two attempts that had been made previously were completely screwed by the premises of the games, the game play, the availability, the game sponsors, where they were sold, etc. For example, girls and moms would never walk by them because they were sold in male spaces.

We were fortunate to have great funding so we researched all over the United States with over a thou-sand girls. We could look for regional and other differences and stuff. That gave us was the entire framework for the kinds of games we ultimately create. We uncovered the vast differences between how girls think about themselves in a social context and a personal context. This led to us creating two series of games with the same characters.

In my teaching, I always look at three-term provocations—things that don't exactly go together, like energy, entitlement, and brand. It doesn't really matter as long as there is some interesting overlap. The process of design research uncovered rich, important material at that overlap. Whether you have an audience in mind already or not, this is a way to generate ideas that wouldn't arise otherwise.

I strongly believe that working with dyads is a really good idea. Maybe you've screened for one kind of respondent. Ask them to bring their best friend. With kids, this is terrif-ic because they will call each other out on things they don't even realize are true. But, even with adults, they have conversations between themselves that are very different from the things they might tell you on their own. There is an entire business of coding what you hear and understanding what's salient. When I move from paper to working prototypes, I engage with the same audience as well as new ones because that helps you isolate what's really at work for an audience—it's a way to validate your learning.

That's right. One of the projects we did at Art Center was focused on better under-standing tweens and their relation to technology and comfort. It was a partnership with Hewlett Packard and it had a big im-pact on their thinking at the time. I've always insisted that personas be based on actual people and this isn't always the case. You should be able to tell who that persona is—you've meet them, even if it's an amalga-mation of a few kids. Too often, a persona in business is used as some kind of vague ideal per-son but not grounded in actual people. They are a construction of designers' and researchers' assumptions and expectations, but not representative of the reality of these audiences or customers. If you haven't met them, these persona are just bad fictions.

Exactly. I sometimes asked my students to write down all their biases and beliefs about their subjects and I would bring my little cauldron and we put them in there. When we got done with our research, we would burn these slips of paper because we had shown ourselves that our assumptions were wrong. It was physical.

I think people feel they have greater empathy than they do. Also, we believe that we understand people better because of our personal experiences but it can lead us astray. I could say, "Hey, I was a little girl so I know all about that." Well, I was a little girl in 1950. It was not the same. My experience no longer counts. We tend to design for ourselves, on the basis of our own personal experiences.

I try prompts out on people—my husband or friends or colleagues. If people don't see anything interesting in it, I know I don't have a good prompt. Sometimes, the prompt includes a specific demographic, but it doesn't have to.

Tony Ahn, my editor, reminds me at this point that there is a company called Joshua Tree that makes a Hiker's Salve, Climber's Salve, Musician's Salve, Gymnast's Salve, and a bunch of other products. On a message board (or maybe Amazon Q&A) they admitted once that all of these were the same formula, just different labels. All of these different groups of people want to buy something specialized for them. They all have the same problem though: chafe. In this case, they really are in the same market segment (at least form the standpoint of Joshua Tree): the segment of chafing people looking for specialized creams for themselves. Joshua Tree has found a creative way to serve them all (or most of them) in a unique way, playing to that decision-driver while optimizing their operations. Only demographically are they serving different markets. In reality, in terms of what their customers respond to—their decision-drivers—they're the same segment.

Do you eat, travel, and live like everyone else in your age group? Everyone else with your occupation? Everyone that lives within a kilometer of you? Or everyone that is using this offering for the first time?

No, you do not. Not everyone in Asia buys, lives, loves, or behaves the same so why would you segment by such a large region? Or, even a smaller one, like Norway?

Or course, you can't segment based on everything. Which do you choose? Certainly, using some demographic attribute makes it much easier: everything simply slides into neat groups. But, is this the most effective method of market segmentation? Does it build on the highest-order value you identified? The answer, again, is "no." Yet, this is how nearly all companies create their market segments! Yet, this is how nearly all companies create their market segments, and why I remain critical of traditional strategy. It should be clear by now why so many companies are failing to differentiate themselves or escape zombiedom. Is it more clear why so many companies are failing to differentiate themselves or escape zombiedom?

What if you segmented your customers by their decision-drivers? This group of customers values fast, easy set-up the most. This other one values easy monitoring most because it helps them manage their team. A third one values the reporting function because they're concerned about proving their value to their bosses. And these may not be mutually exclusive. Although these are mostly functional differentiations, they're still better than demographic trivia, but there is a better approach.

What if you segmented customers by those driven by a sense of Duty, their need for Accomplishment, or their desire for Community? What if you differentiated those whose decisions were driven by Security or Beauty or Redemption. Now, you're thinking like an organization that recognizes the value of its brand—and a valuable one at that. Your strategy is now being driven by those things most powerful to your customers.

/The First Redemptive Car

When Toyota launched the Prius in the USA, they made some bad assumptions. Because of the way they segmented customers, they understood the Prius as an "environmental" car, a factor most associated with college students. So, the Prius was pretty barebones compared to Toyota's more luxurious models.

What they found, however, was that many of their customers were leaving luxury cars to buy a Prius. When my friend Christopher got rid of her Jaguar to get a Prius, she was not satisfied with the options and types of interior trim. Those early Prius felt cheap compared to more substantial cars. They didn't have the conveniences customers like her expected and needed because Toyota was thinking about college students, not CEOs.

The right research would have identified, before the car launched, why many people were longing for a car that spoke to and shared their values. The felt guilt that their cars were bad for the environment, even if they went for the least bad car at the time. Then, came this new kind of car that was much better for the environment. It was still a car and, therefore, still had adverse impacts on the environment but it allowed drivers to feel less guilt for their necessary driving. It was a redeeming purchase.

Toyota eventually understood who was really attracted to the Prius and what they needed to satisfy them, but it took a new definition and understanding of the customers' worldview to do so. My co-author, Steve Diller, instantly identified Redemption as the key differentiator for the Prius from the start. Had Toyota understood this beforehand, they would have seen this decision-driver in drivers and owners that crossed age and income groupings. They would have understood that Christopher would want one, too, and then gone on to understand how her Prius needed to be configured.

Instead of segmenting your car customers into those who want a V8 or V6 or V4 engine, or those who want a sedan or wagon or sports car, consider how much more valuable it would be to segment between those looking for Beauty, those for Redemption, or those who want Fun. Most people don't care about the type of engine (and that's becoming less meaningful these days anyway) or even the type of car. You might be looking for a sedan but find yourself swayed by an SUV or a crossover (a combination between the two that proves that the simple categories of "sedan, wagon, SUV, etc." only worked when there were few categories to begin with). Most customers cross traditional segments, much to the frustration of organizations that insist on segmenting in traditional ways.

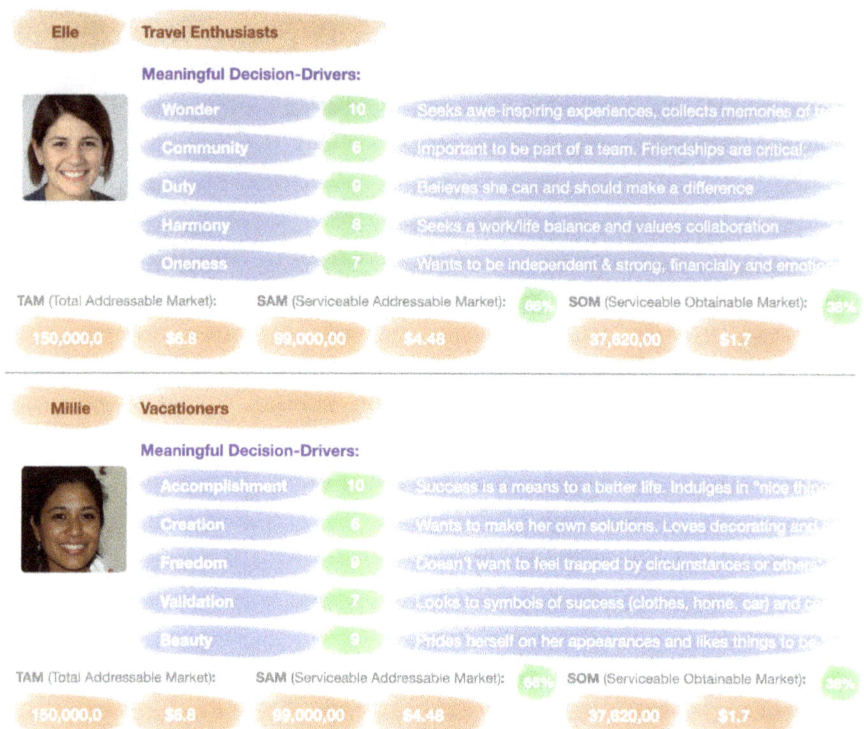

For example, for several decades, there has been a new, large segment of customers in the travel industry: Experience Travelers. They still confound some hotels, restaurants, airlines, and tour providers. These folks might be from any age group, any profession, and country, etc. What defines Experience Travelers is that they seek unique experiences. They want to see things not on the typical tour and they want to feel like "locals" anywhere they go. In fact, they actively abhor the typical tourist traps and popular destinations. Experience Travelers might eat at the most expensive restaurant in a city one night because it has a unique dish or approach and then eat at a food truck the next night for the same reason. They might visit a museum one day and rent bikes and ride through the countryside the next. This behavior eschews traditional categorization: young people are supposed to be the active ones and rich people are supposed to eat expensive meals. Tourists go to museums and monuments to take photos of the destination as evidence that they were there while families go to child-friendly and age-appropriate venues.

There are, of course, many other ways to segment customers but what's important to recognize is that the segments above are focused on belief and behavior, not on demographics. You can have a college degree, low or high income, be of any age, and live anywhere and still fall into any of these groups. After almost 20 years since this original segmentation, we can see that only about 40% of consumers were engaged with ecological issues. So few companies have recognized this (not to mention government agencies and non-profit organizations), that it's really not surprising that more progress hasn't been made on these issues.

A great example of segmentation comes from the sustainability world. Instead of viewing customers as those who do or don't value sustainability in the products and services they purchase and use, the reality is that there are other important segments between these. I'm going to use an old example because it's so clear and because we've been able to see the outcome. In my book, ***Design is the Problem,*** I described the segmentation within the sustainability "market" as defined by different industry groups:

Green Gauge (2007):

30%	True Blue Greens (most committed)
10%	Greenback Greens (interested but not always willing to spend more)
26%	Sprouts (undecided about ecological issues but not totally against them)
15%	Grousers (view ecological issues as too big or complicated to do anything about)
18%	Apathetics (not interested at all or don't believe these issues exist)

Part of the failure stems from the fact that most organizations didn't approach customers, citizens, and constituents in different ways—in the ways they needed to be approached in order to change their beliefs and behaviors. Too many assumed that the same messages and the same options were going to work across all of them and that was never going to be the case (and wasn't).

Successful customer segments require deeper understanding of customer motivations and decision-drivers, which lead to more appropriate differentiations, which lead to more important insights and more successful strategy.

By defining their segments so narrowly and around trivial distinctions, much of the travel industry has missed an opportunity to be relevant to more people in new ways—and build better value. And, this is not an isolated example!

Your segments should be focused on the things you've identified as most important to your customers. It may be their biggest decision-drivers, their meaning priorities (which core meanings they prioritize), or some other grouping that speaks to their values, desires, and aspirations. By doing this, it will put your best opportunities for value at the heart of how you define your customers.

Market Sizing & Verification

Now you're ready to do the thing that most businesspeople jump to first or second: determining the size of the opportunity. It's not always easy to determine the size of a current market, let alone predict the size, scope, and value of a future market opportunity. Of course, you've probably already figured out that sizing the market depends on how you define what the market is. Is Royal Dutch Shell an oil company or an energy company? Is McDonalds in the burger business or the real estate business? Are you selling products, services, experiences, or a lifestyle? How you define the value you deliver changes the boundaries of the market and, similarly, the opportunity.

You need to look at the market for your current or potential offerings. This will also redefine your competitors. If you're in charge of Apple's Apple Watch division, sure, you should be looking at other smartwatches. However, the marketing-savvy people at Apple also understand that watches are a fashion and status item as well as a functional one. They know they're competing with other watch manufacturers (and partnering with some) and even jewelry makers. That opens up the market considerably.

Once you have a realistic idea of the market segments you're targeting, you can more accurately size the opportunities. It's common to speak about these segments in three different terms: ***Total Addressable Market*** (TAM), ***Serviceable Addressable Market*** (SAM), and ***Serviceable Obtainable Market*** (SOM). TAM is the total market in any geography. For example, how many SUVs are sold in your country? That's likely a large number. But, if you're building a new SUV, surely not every single one is a sale you can step in and make for yourself! The SAM is the number you can realistically serve. In other words, how many SUVs could you really sell in your country in this year? This may be based on your manufacturing limitations (how many can you even make?) or your reach (how are you going to get in front of every customer to make your case?). It may be bounded by your personnel or your resources—or who you're able to partner with. Lastly, there's a second dose of reality. Beyond what you can reasonably service, there are likely competitors already there. How many SUV sales can you believably take away from existing competitors? Given your marketing messages, your understanding of customers' decision-drivers, their decision processes, what they can afford, their brand loyalty to others, etc., how many SUVs can you really expect to sell?

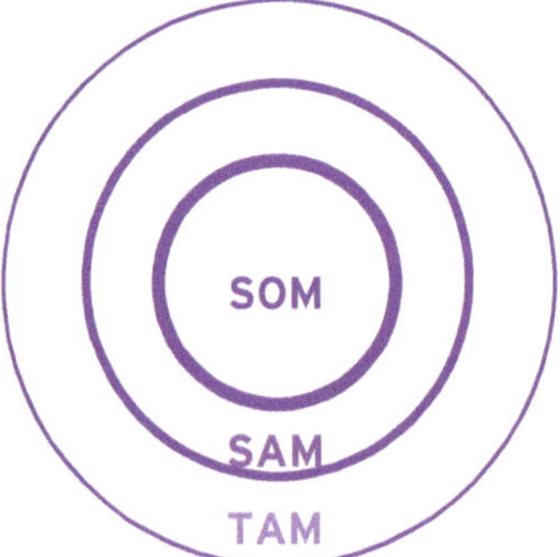

This can be a harsh dose of reality. It's an obvious misstep on the part of inexperienced businesspeople (often in startups but not limited to them) to assume they can serve the entire market with their ultracool widget. Everyone is their customer and no competitor can match their widget's value. You'll get a cold reaction from investors and partners if you approach your market this way.

However, at some point, you need to research the market numbers (size, sales, etc.) to show that there is a there, there. This might be the first point in the process when an assumed opportunity suddenly doesn't look so great after all. This is a good thing! It's much better to find this out now than later, when lots of money, time, and resources have been spent in pursuit of something that isn't real. It's also possible that with truly radical innovations, others might not believe your numbers. They may just look too good for seasoned industry insiders to believe. If your numbers truly reflect the opportunity, you'll need to show how you've validated your customers, your market, and the size of the opportunity to retain your credibility. It's rare that incredulously huge opportunities appear but they do, on occasion.

At the end of this process, you should know your customers well and have identified the best value you can create for them. You'll know what drives their purchase decisions, how they relate to other customers, and how big of an opportunity they represent. You've explored widely and narrowed on the most important customers, their most important drivers, and the most important customer opportunities. This "go wide, then focus" process will repeat over and over throughout the process to create strategy. This is its strength.

Your Market Strategy

The work you do in understanding your market does double-duty. It is both the basis for your organization's business strategy, as well as the resulting market strategy. Often called a "go-to-market strategy," once you have these insights, the tactics that result include many aspects: specific messaging to different segments, different approaches to reaching customers in different channels* and using different media, as well as the mechanisms for feedback from customers and the market.

While part of these insights drive the rest of your organization's strategy, they also form the basis, at the next level down, for market strategy and the tactics that will enact it.

- Your customers are looking to be served on several different levels of value. Which ones have you researched and which ones are being both desired and served?
- Do your current research methods uncover all five kinds of value? Do they identify decision-drivers? What are the most powerful decision-drivers for your customers?
- There are five kinds of value: functional, financial, emotional, identity, and meaningful. The first two are more quantitative and where traditional strategy processes focus entirely. The last three are qualitative and represent the deepest, most defendable value.
- Are the three qualitative types of value (emotional, identity, and meaningful) a point of discussion at all in your organization? If not, you will need to initiate this discussion.
- While many businesspeople in B2B companies think that their customers only care about functional and Financial value, as long as they're selling to humans, all five are in play.
- Addressing and understanding all five kinds of value allows organizations to create more successful strategies.
- All organizations are in the ***relationship and experience businesses,*** whether they recognize it or not. Too many don't realize this.
- ***Customer insight*** should focus mostly on decision-drivers, those elements that drive their decisions. It's important, of course, to understand the context for these as well, but the basis of market strategy is on these drivers and not demographic nor psychographic trivia.
- For larger organizations who serve many types of customers, better strategy segments them based on their most important decision-drivers. Segmenting based on Meaningful or Identity value is always more successful than segmenting on Functional or Financial value as it yields deeper relationships and, ultimately, is more financially successful.
- Market segmentation can reframe an organization's context, revealing new opportunities and new value but also will require operational changes to take advantage of these Are your customer segments more meaningful than those based on features or price? If not, how could you segment differently to provide more value?
- Market segments should be separated in parallel tracks for strategy, for best results.
- Each market segment should be sized realistically, even if these are approximations (unique market segments may not have readily available data and may be more difficult to validate). However, "harder" doesn't disqualify the insights these segments are based upon.
- No organization can sell to all customers in any segment. Instead, you will need to realistically estimate the total market you can address (TAM), the amount of that you can realistically service (SAM), and the percentage you can realistically sell to (SAM).

/Explore More:

Blind Spot by Steve Diller, Nathan Shedroff, & Sean Sauber
Just Enough Research by Erika Hall
Interviewing Users by Steve Portigal
Doorbells, Danger, and Dead Batteries by Steve Portigal
- ***Utopian Entrepreneur*** by Brenda Laurel

Chapter 2

Your Competitors

Market insights are the most time-consuming part of the strategic process but they're the also the most critical. Once you've uncovered and validated what drives customer decisions, the rest starts to flow clearly and quickly. The first phase was one both of expansion (looking at a lot of customers and a lot of decision-drivers) and focus (prioritizing only the most important few). The subsequent phases are all similar in this regard.

If you uncover more than one market segment, perform the rest of the Market sequence for each of those segments. This is a little extra work but it's the same steps.

Now, were going to take those focused decision-drivers and compare them against our competitors. This part is fairly easy. List the top-ranked drivers and, next to that, score your organization's ability to delivery those. Next, for each of your competitors, score them the same way. Of course, it's critical that you be honest. It's not likely you're great at delivering on all of these drivers and it's likely that you have at least a couple competitors who are better at some of them.

But, who, exactly, are your competitors?

Within each market segment, you may have different competitors so you need to perform this phase separately for each segment. When this is the case, you'll likely have a different mix of competitors in each, as well.

When you make this list, you should be thinking widely about where your customers go to get these needs and desires met. Relevant competitors may not be obvious or the ones traditionally considered. For example, an auto manufacturer's competitors aren't just other car companies. Because people find transportation options in many forms, competitors may be car-share services, rental cars, mass transit—even bicycles. If the purpose driving customers' needs is mobility, it opens up not just the number but the kinds of solutions they'll consider. This is going to expand the field, which is exactly what we want. So analogous solutions, substitution services, etc. are all relevant.

Next, we'll focus this list on the most important competitors. By ranking our performance of each driver as well as our competitors, and comparing the scores, we can isolate the drivers where we perform well and not. In fact, this is where we fix the traditional SWOT process (and all of its problems).

If you've scored yourself and your competitors on a 1-10 scale (10 being the best), anything scored an 8 or higher is a ***strength***. Likewise, any driver your score a 3 or below becomes a ***weakness***. The rest is just math.

Top Decision-Drivers:	Rank:	Your Company: Your Offering:	Competitor 1: Offering:	Competitor 2: Offering:	Competitor 3: Offering:	Competitor 4: Offering:	Competitor 5: Offering:	Competitor X: Offering:	
Wonder	10	10	4	7	2	8	4	9	Strength / Opportunity
Community	10	10	7	8	8	8	7	10	Strength / Opportunity
Hates conflict	10	8	1	5	9	7	5	10	Strength
Likes working with...	9	6	1	9	3	5	3	9	Threat
Excited by new chall...	9	8	10	10	7	8	1	4	Strength
Feels successful whe...	8	9	4	2	4	1	10	7	Strength / Opportunity
Feels relief when thin...	8	3	5	0	1	0	5	8	Weakness / Threat
Wants clear instruct...	8	3	6	0	1	0	8	9	Weakness / Threat
Salary measures self...	8	7	10	1	8	8	8	8	Strength / Threat
Willing to pay more fo...	8	8	6	8	3	3	2	9	Strength / Opportunity

How do you actually rank competitors against a scale? There are several ways to go about it and none are foolproof nor are any better than the others. Whatever gives you a confident sense of how well you and your competitors perform on those criteria are fine. Of course, you might all be fooling yourselves about the relative performance but that's another issue, entirely. Some researchers note the intensity of a respondent's response as a part of this score: "You know who really performs well? NewCorp! I've never been more impressed at their ability to help me!" That may not be a 9 or 10, but that customer is validating that NewCorp is performing well in the 7-10 range, at least. Compare that to "Yeah, I guess they're pretty good at that." That's faint praise—maybe middle of the road or lower. Other researchers devise surveys (now that they know exactly what they're looking for) to ask comparative questions. While you can't necessarily ask customers to give you their ranking (unless you *really* establish the range, with examples, and then control for other factors), you can compare relational data, such as how many people would use these services again or which they would feel comfortable referring to someone else along specific criteria. All in all, what matters most is that you rate yourself and your competitors on each of the top criteria in a uniform way, against the same scale. That's more important than trying to have a perfect method to define the ranks.

If you add and average all of your competitors' scores for each driver and compare your own, the difference is either an ***opportunity*** (where you score higher than the average of your competitors) or a ***threat*** (where you score worse than the average of your competitors). This can be done automatically, in fact. The higher the difference in these, the better the opportunity or the worse the threat.

This becomes another focusing function. You don't need to look at your strengths and, really, you don't need to focus on your weaknesses either. Your focus needs to be on the differences that create your biggest opportunities and threats. Those opportunities are functions you want to build upon. Those threats are things you most need to react to. The things in the middle are less important and shouldn't be the focus at the moment.

Within each market segment, you can probably focus on 3-5 opportunities and 3-5 threats and build a strategy around those. Remember, we're just two steps into the Market sequence. There's much more to do.

But, we've fixed the issues with the SWOT diagram and, if necessary, can still pull each item out and set it in that two-by-two (in case you need to satisfy a colleague who expects traditional output. Just cut and past all of your strengths, weaknesses, opportunities, and threats and you're done! But, each is validated, internally consistent, and matters to customers. Of course, this is just the market side of the SWOT. We'll get to the Operational side in a bit.

Lastly, never compare yourself to other organizations! Compare your offerings against theirs!

This is going to immediately seem obvious but it is not how most business people do this nor how they've been taught. At this point, you don't care about your competitor's company, only their offerings (and neither do your customers). Don't compare yourself to Nike, Dial, Carrefour, or Chanel. Compare your specific product, service, event, or place offerings to their specific offerings. Except when comparing corporate brands, all of the other decision-drivers are specific to market offerings—your products, services, etc. to theirs.

Yes, Tesla has a strong brand (and an increasingly polarized one). But, most customers will compare the Model X against a similar electric SUV (and even non-electric SUVs). If you only look at the company level, you'll miss what you need to focus upon again.

Competitor X

There's one little wrinkle here we should pay attention to: how about the competitor you can't yet see? Every market has a startup in stealth mode or a new initiative within a competitor that hasn't yet been announced or isn't yet on your radar. Ideally, we want to build our strategy against these as well—especially with these in mind since they represent potential disruptive innovation. But, how can we know what we can't see?

The answer is to use outside experts. Guess if you must. Ask this simple question: what would we do if we were the startup? In answering it, score that Competitor X against all of the same customer drivers. You may want to isolate these scores when comparing against your other competitors. In some ways, this is the market solution you should really be focused on building!

If this is too difficult a mind teaser, another question you might ask yourself to define your Competitor X might be: what would Apple do if they entered our market? It doesn't need to be realistic that Apple is going to open restaurants or make wedding dresses. What's important is that you have a way to imagine an innovative and formidable competitor that confidently takes a new approach. Apple had a wide variety of products that appeal to a huge percentage of many markets. They may not be for everyone but they sure do serve a lot of people successfully. If Apple is too much of a stretch, replace it with Nike or Disney or someone that still represents disruptive innovation, combined with resources and a track record of success. By considering a Competitor X, you're likely to uncover potential opportunities that would not have surfaced otherwise.

/Highlights

- Every organization has competitors, obvious and non-obvious. Some of these are alternatives your customers might use instead of your offering, even choosing "none."
- Mostly, you compete against offerings, not other companies. When you evaluate how your offering competes against others', don't mistake their organizations for their offerings.
- Evaluate your offerings and those of your competitors on the basis of your customers' most important decision-drivers and not issues that haven't been validated.
- The traditional SWOT (strengths, weaknesses, opportunities, and threats) doesn't usually list validated decision-drivers, making it easy to focus on the wrong things. When doing better strategy, these things are simple mathematical results of your assessment of customer decision-drivers and your comparison of them against your competitors' offerings. They shouldn't be open to manipulation by popular vote.
- Always address Competitor X, that competing offering that may be lurking unnoticed. This maybe a startup you haven't seen (or are concerned about). It may be the offering you should be developing if you were unencumbered by your organization. In a pinch, assume it's the thing Apple would create if they entered your industry and market segment.

Chapter 3

Your Position & Value

While we're only two steps into the Market sequence, we've already done the bulk of what traditional marketing strategy achieves. We've performed and identified customers' needs and desires (and validated these) and performed a competitive analysis based on them. In addition, we've generated a SWOT diagram automatically, the right way. Next, it's onto the Positioning process (and statement).

This one is mostly mathematics, as well. Ideally, we would take all of the opportunities and threats identified by competitive analysis (the previous chapter) and determine which have the most potential. This helps us find a market position with the best opportunities as well as form the basis for a positioning statement.

First, we focus on our opportunities (it's important to identify our threats but positioning with them would be strange, to say the least). The opportunities with the greats difference between us and our competitors are likely the best positions in the market we could target. So, take the top two scores (the biggest differences) and plot them on the typical two-by-two. We do this in twos because most of us parse diagrams in 2D. It's easy for us to both plot and understand date in two axes. Ideally, we wouldn't be so limited and we could plot as many as we needed in 5D, 6D, or higher space. But, that takes an exceptional person. For now, work two at a time.

By plotting our scores on these two axes, as well as out competitors, we can see how we're all distributed and look for spaces we can inhabit that aren't crowded by our competitors. Usually, this is already represented in the top two opportunities but we can try different combinations to see if we find something more to our liking.

When we find the best combination, we've identified a market position that we can build a successful business around that is different than our competitors. Again, all of this is also validated by customer decision-drivers, so we're not positioning on things that don't matter. This is a further focusing step.

What about the blue ocean strategy?

Many of you have probably heard of "blue ocean strategy." This is the idea that we can find a market position that we can "own" that has no competitors. Every tech startup has one to claim to potential investors, whether or not it exists. And, investors Eat. It. Up! They know that a company that can serve a market that has no natural competitors has the opportunity to make a lot of money.

But, it's never this easy, is it? While you're looking for a blank spot in these two-by-two market diagrams, beware the magically open space where there are no competitors! There may be very good reasons why no one is competing in that part of the market. Perhaps, it's not technically possible to deliver that level of quality for that low a price? Perhaps, it's blank because there's just no market for high cost, low quality solutions? There are good reasons why you uncovered the opportunities you have and they're placed where you are.

Because we've validated these drivers as real for customers, we also avoid the other mistake some make in search of blue ocean strategies. When Steve Jobs left Apple to form NeXT Computers, he developed a powerful UNIX-based workstation with a graphic interface (like the Macintosh) and then wrapped it into a beautiful black case. The NeXT cube looked different from nearly every other workstation. When it was introduced, Jobs proclaimed that it was the best black UNIX workstation on the market! In fact, it was the only black UNIX workstation on the market—a true blue ocean strategy! This is what every entrepreneur dreams of: a market with no competitors.

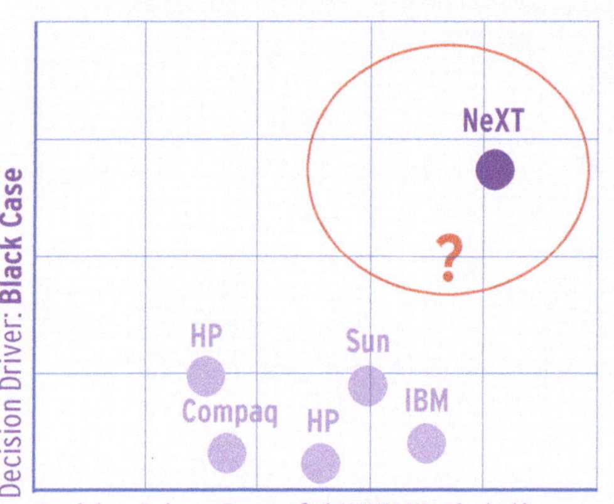

Of course, you can see the problem here. Were customers clamoring for a black workstation? Was that an important decision-driver? Mostly, the answer was "no." It was a phony blue ocean strategy and if Steve Jobs can fall into this pit, so can you. If you've truly identified and validated customer decision-drivers, you shouldn't be able to fall into this pit, at all.

If you have identified a truly blue ocean position, congratulations! You've found an enviable, ideal opportunity. Now, you only need to deliver on it.

Your Value Proposition

If you've followed this process, you have already likely identified an advantageous position that differentiates you from your competitors on the specific issues that drive your customers' decisions. In this sense, you should have a strong, competitive position. But, some businesspeople define other kinds of positions. As we saw above, a "blue ocean strategy" isn't always a good one. But, this is really just a proprietary term for a super competitive position, one that others can't easily replace.

Some strategists propose that you find a sustainable value proposition, meaning a position you can maintain for a long time. This isn't the same use of the term "sustainable" that ecological people use to describe ecological performance in light of important issues (such as climate change). Sustainable positions are built on deep value that can last over a longer period of time. It means that some of those decision-drivers may have more lasting value and effect than others.

Lastly, many businesspeople look for "unfair advantage," another term that doesn't exactly mean would it seems to. No one is saying that you should do business in an unfair way (such as illegally). What this means is that those organizations who find a market position that cannot be replicated or occupied by a competitor may have extra value. For example, perhaps, you have particular intellectual property that others can't use or mimic? For decades, PIXAR has build and used characters that other film companies can't use (Woody and Buzz, Nemo and Dora, the Incredibles, etc.). Other firms might create similar characters (other bugs, toys, or fish) but they can't use those, specific, characters. That's an clear unfair advantage.

But, simply having an unfair advantage isn't valuable if it's in a way that customers don't value. A music publisher might have an unfair advantage by locking up a recording deal with a particular musician, singer, or DJ but if that artists isn't in demand, the unfair advantage isn't particularly advantageous. This brings us back to the fallacy of the blue ocean strategy or any other "advantageous" position. None of it matters if the decision-drivers it's built on isn't valid from the start. And, that comes from your original research

The best unfair advantage or sustainable position comes from engaging customers on the deeper levels of value: emotions, identity, and meaning. By transcending the weaker, more common, and surface value (financial and functional), customer relationships made at these deeper levels are more stable because they're more difficult to convince a customer to abandon or switch to another provider. When your customer relationship is based on identity or meaning, these are the deepest levels in which you can connect. Customers don't switch identities or worldviews often and not without a lot of effort. They will reconsider their functional criteria, their budgets, and even their emotional allegiances much more easily.

You best path to the most lasting, most unfair advantage is to base your position on those decision-drivers in which your customers connect with their identities and worldviews (core meanings).

The Positioning Statement

Once you've determined your best market position, you should elaborate on it to ensure it is understandable by the widest possible audience. At this point, you can use a positioning statement template and plug-in the opportunities you've determined are your best two. The rest is word-smithing. A typical template looks something like this:

For <market segment> *who need* <best opportunity 1>
We offer <offering>
Which benefits them by <best opportunity 2>

Some variations add the following:

As opposed to our <competitor/s>
Which offer only <worst opportunities>.

A classic example of a positioning statement (and one of the better ones) is Harry Beckwith's from his book Selling the Invisible.

A Classic Positioning Statement:	
WHO: Who are you?	IKEA
WHAT: What business are you in?	Home furnishings store
FOR WHOM: Who do you provide value?	Those who want a stylish, affordable home.
WHAT NEEDS: Whare are their needs?	Affordable furnishings and ideas that they can see before they buy.
AGAINST WHOM: Your competitors?	Department stores, COSTCO, Walmart, Target
THE DIFFERENCE: What differentiates you from them?	Range of unique products, flatpack/build yourself, delivery services (in cities), restaurant, etc.
THE BENEFITS: What unique benefits do you provide your customers?	Fun shopping experience, exploration and inspiration, one-stop shop, community, beauty, creativity, harmony, etc.

The Threat Statement

While attention and effort is typically devoted to creating a position statement (because it is universally recognized that market position is important), threat planning is just as crucial to success. Business strategists don't approach it in the same manner, but they should. I propose they do so through a Threat Statement, which captures those threats that were identified, and clearly describes what the company needs to fix to be successful. A list is probably adequate but where's the fun in that? Here is a template for putting some imperative behind it:

If we don't focus on fixing <biggest threats 1-3>
We will lose <market segment> ***to*** <competitors who excel in those decision-drivers>
We can fix this threat by <building, doing, messaging, etc. in this way>

How's that for clear and direct? These threats will be important when we get to the Operational sequence so hold them aside, for now.

While it's critical to focus on your best opportunities and offerings, you must make time to consider your greatest threats as well. To do this well, bring both into the Operational sequence and consider what you need to do, as an organization, to deal with both (more on that in the following chapters).

/Highlights

- Your best position should be a simply mathematical result of how your offerings compare against those of your competitors. It shouldn't be a separate process nor one disassociated from your customer and competitive research.
- For various reasons, however, you may find other positions you think will be more successful than those that the math identifies. This is fine as long as you have reasonable, defensible justification.
- Beware the "blue ocean strategy" promise. There may be very good reasons why a position no other competitors occupy isn't a good opportunity.
- Your positioning statement should be clear, concise, and mention the customer drivers it is based upon. It is a positive, aspirational focus of your best opportunities.
- Consider a threat statement in addition to your positioning statement. This is a summary of your greatest market threats, rather than merely your opportunities, and address both in your market and your operational strategy. These are things that you shouldn't ignore simply because they aren't the position you're focused upon.

/Explore More

- ***Selling the Invisible*** by Harry Beckwith

Chapter 4

Your Opportunities & Offerings

Your organization's best opportunities are the result of its ability to act on the value proposition it identifies in the market. The previous market steps were about just this so the next step focuses on developing and defining the opportunities previous identified.

This is where we think widely to identify opportunities in this position and, then, describe the offerings (products, services, etc.) that would enable your organization to take advantage of those opportunities. Lastly, this is a good moment to start the process of developing messaging to your customers about those offerings (and will illuminate the value of them to your customers). However, we can come back to this. While it's helpful to jot ideas down while customer value, decisions-drivers, and competitive position are fresh in your mind, at this point this isn't a critical part of strategy.

What's an Opportunity?

Consider Apple around the year 2003 Apple was a successful company for a long time, building a great, profitable business but "the market" (meaning analysts and investors) didn't value it terribly highly—until around 2003.* Why?

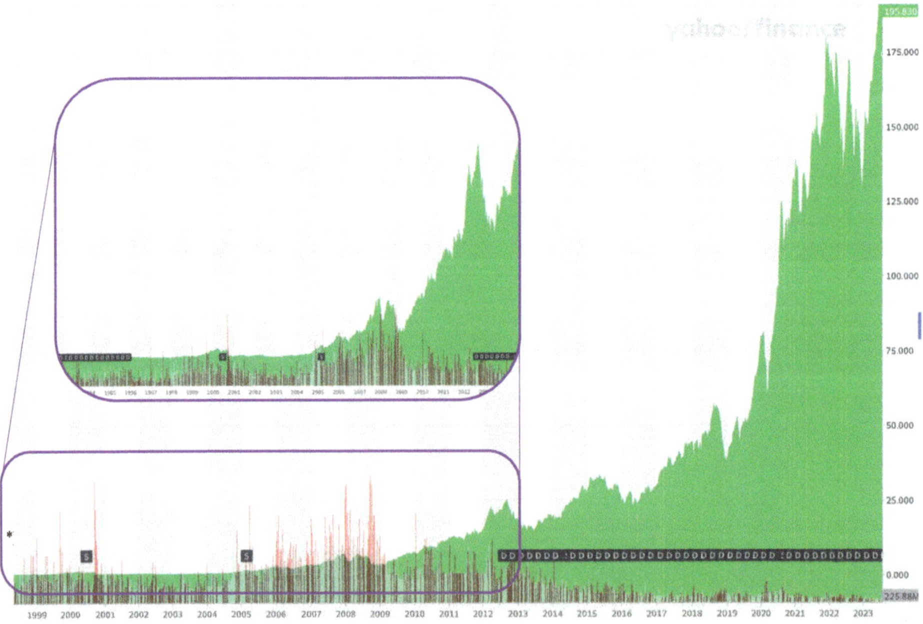

When I pose this question to my workshop attendees, the answer almost always is: "the iPhone stupid" (the stupid is usually silent)! But the iPhone didn't ship until 2007. Faced with this fact, most of my attendees switch their answer to: the iPod! (They drop the stupid at this point). But, the iPod went on sale in 2001 and, for the most part, was panned by the business press as unnecessarily expensive and "who needs 1000 songs in your pocket?" Customers, however, bought them briskly.

So, what changed between 2001 and 2003? The iTunes Store. Not only was Apple selling a pocket music player with iTunes software which moved music from your computer to your phone, but for the first time started *selling music*. This changed everything.

This is when the "market" decided that Apple wasn't a niche computer company, it was a music company—eventually becoming the predominant digital music company. For the first time, Apple made digital music easy to buy and load onto your portable player, all at an inexpensive and *stable* price. This is what built the digital music market (for everyone) because it made all of this possible for real people, not tech enthusiasts. In fact, Apple made it more convenient to purchase music than pirate it.

This is why "the market" reevaluated their understanding (and expectations) of Apple. It was no longer that niche computer manufacturer, it was now a music store. In fact, ever since then, the market hardly even recognizes that Apple makes computers. Now they focus more on sales of iPhones, iPads, AirPods, music, films, and other digital goods. Not only does the market not view Apple as a computer company any longer, it doesn't even see it as merely a consumer electronics company. They're now a media company with products, services, and content. As such, they compete in a different market and their expectations are completely different. If you want proof, answer this question: would you pit Apple and Lenovo against each other as competitors?

Curiously, Steve Jobs wasn't even a big fan of the iPod at the beginning. It was a curiosity, not a strategy. Nonetheless, it set the stage to completely change the company in strategic ways (and ways that couldn't be foreseen at the time).

But, back to 2004. Apple's fortunes take off with the market's new view of them and their stock price rises significantly (more significantly than in its previous history). They know this is a great market and they enjoy the new value but they also see two things on the horizon:

First, Apple noticed something about human behavior. Men (mostly) in industrialized nations (at least) only cared to carry about three items with them in their pockets each day: their keys, their wallet, and—no, not a phone. Many women, of course, carried purses with many more than three things in them. So, this is a more gendered understanding of the market—certainly not for the entire market—the TAM. Remember, *this is 2003*. Most people didn't have mobile phones with them. Instead, that *third thing* could have been one of many: a pocket camera, a music player, a PDA (personal digital assistant), etc.

The second thing was that more and more people were able to afford mobile phones and were purchasing them.

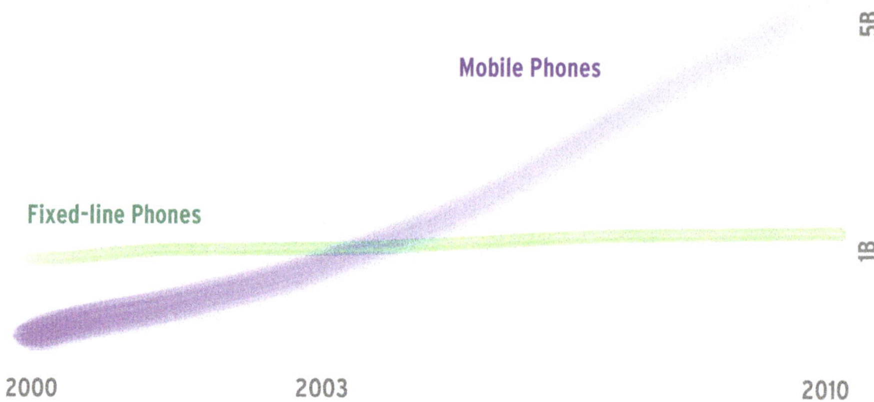

Some, were even getting rid of their home (and even work) phones and moving to a mobile phone only.

It would have been easy for many companies to either miss one or both of these trends or dismiss them entirely. In fact, many, many electronics companies did just that. But, Apple knew they had to get into the phone if they were going to stay in their customers' pockets and keep selling music (and other things. To ignore these facts would be an inevitable death of their music (and other content business).

There are a few strategies that Apple could have taken, however, when they saw and acted on these two facts. They could 1) build their own phone, 2) partner with a phone manufacturer, or 3) convince men (and others) to carry more than three items. Many "marketing-driven" companies that would have opted for the third. After all, most men have two or more pockets: just convince them to carry four things instead of three (despite their long-standing preference not to). This "adjust the market" rather than "adjust to the market" approach is what most American car companies took in the 1950s—and 60s, 70s, 80s, 90s and some even today. It's the height of arrogance that some companies think they can change consumer preferences, desires, and behaviors so easily. In times past, in fact, this might have even been more possible. But, not today. People have way too many choices, knowledge, and enjoy too much autonomy to be forced into changing their behavior if they don't want to. For all intents and purposes, the three-item rule was essentially an absolute one.

So, Apple could choose one of the other two options. They knew that for most people, the mobile phone was going to increasingly be that third thing and if they wanted to keep and grow their new-found business, they would need to get into the phone itself.

And what did Apple do next?

No, they didn't make the iPhone; that came later.

Much to Apple's delight, most people have forgotten that Apple actually chose option 2 over option 1—and for good reason. Mobile phones are incredibly complex and difficult to make, especially if you're adding all of these new functions. Apple knew they had no experience in this space (let alone the right employees), and they knew it would be, at minimum, a billion-dollar investment. They very wisely decided to partner with the best mobile phone manufacturer at the time: Motorola (maker of the super popular RAZR flip phone). They weren't a phone company (and weren't prepared to become one). It was a smart strategic move…

..and it failed.

On September 7, 2005, Apple and Motorola launched the ROKR. You don't remember it because it flopped. Even those around and of buying age at the time don't remember it without being prompted. And, more interestingly, even Apple hated it (internally). It didn't sell particularly well but it was the first phone with iTunes and customers could, in fact, port their music to it (albeit much fewer songs than the iPods of the day). What to do?

When the ROKR flopped, Apple had to change its strategy. It could have licked its wounds and just decided, "well, we just won't do a phone." That's what a lot of companies would have done (I'm not going to name names but you can figure out who). Instead, nothing had changed about the opportunity (or threat) they had identified: they still had to get into the mobile phone and stay in the pocket!

Almost reluctantly, Apple was forced to become a phone company—even though it didn't particularly want to. It had to hire new teams, spend over a billion dollars, learn entirely new markets, made new partnerships (remember AT&T when it launched?), and everything else it had tried to avoid in option 1. It was incredibly fortunate to have the iPad in development and could pivot, using those technologies and move them into a phone. It gave them a product that was years ahead of the competition—so much so that the biggest industry players at the time no longer exist.

This is the point I'm trying to make about opportunities: the opportunity (and its inherent threat) still existed even though their first strategy failed; it still needed to be addressed. While their first offering (the Apple/Motorola phone) wasn't successful (despite being an absolutely sound strategy), they needed a new offering to take advantage of the same opportunity. That new offering became the iPhone, launched in 2007. It changed everything—for Apple, for its customers, and for the industry as a whole.

This is the difference between opportunities and offerings. Offerings are the products, services, places, events, and other experiences that connect an opportunity to customers. It's how the value is delivered to customers (and, in return), comes back to the company). It's the same whether the industry is consumer electronics, luggage, restaurants, retail, or cloud services. It's also the same whether you're a for-profit company, a non-profit, or a government agency.

This story also highlights the fact that it's possible to build a sound strategy, make the right decisions, for the right reasons, and still fail. Looking back from our vantage point in the future, it's obvious what Apple should have done originally. But, looking forward at 2004, it wasn't clear at all and option 2 actually looked like the better strategy.

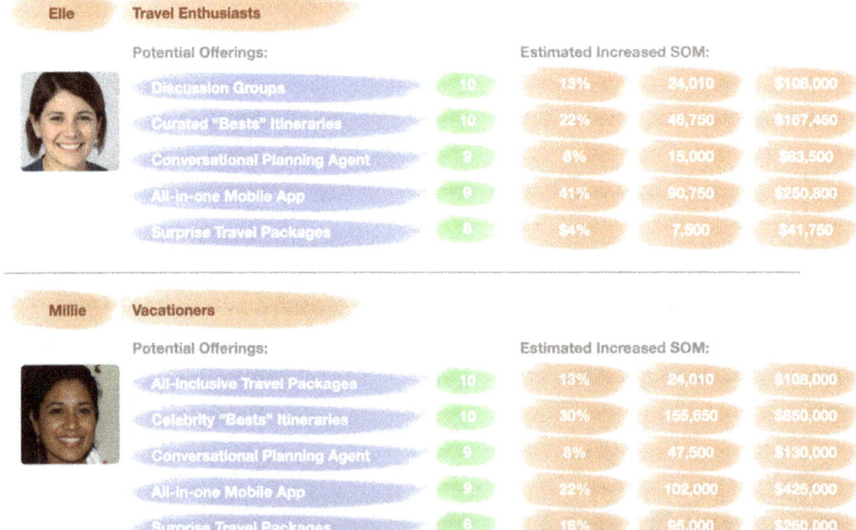

But, also, remember that this opportunity was identified by watching customer behavior—that three item rule. Miss that (or ignore it), and you miss the opportunity. This is the power of understanding customers in qualitative ways. There is no substitution for being close to customers, truly understanding them and their behavior, and not denying the facts, when convenient. This is as much a story about the value of great customer research as it is about strategy.

Identifying Opportunities

There is no secret to identifying opportunities. Most of it will be either reevaluating the other offerings in the market or brainstorming new possibilities. This is one of those

Elle — **Travel Enthusiasts**

Potential Offerings:		Estimated Increased SOM:		
Discussion Groups	10	13%	24,010	$108,000
Curated "Bests" Itineraries	10	22%	46,750	$167,450
Conversational Planning Agent	9	8%	15,000	$63,500
All-in-one Mobile App	9	41%	90,750	$250,800
Surprise Travel Packages	8	4%	7,500	$41,750

Millie — **Vacationers**

Potential Offerings:		Estimated Increased SOM:		
All-Inclusive Travel Packages	10	13%	24,010	$108,000
Celebrity "Bests" Itineraries	10	30%	155,650	$850,000
Conversational Planning Agent	9	8%	47,500	$130,000
All-in-one Mobile App	9	22%	102,000	$425,000
Surprise Travel Packages	8	16%	95,000	$260,000

expand-then-focus exercises. And, like all of these points in strategy, you should be working with several people that have diverse backgrounds (not merely yourself of a few of your team). This is one of those points to bring in others, from the organization but maybe even outside of it, to identify possible offerings and, then rank them in order of importance.

Conjuring Offerings

This is also when it pays to start connecting offerings with potential revenue. This is where the quant and the qual must come together and joining them may require a new round of market research. But beware of the numbers here. It's too easy to see some offerings as low-revenue (compared to others) when these offerings are new. Remember Apple's iPhone, which was OK'ed within the company as a fun accessory but opened up an opportunity to completely reshape the company (and its fortunes). It is common for large, established companies to miss important opportunities or kill them off before they reach their potential.

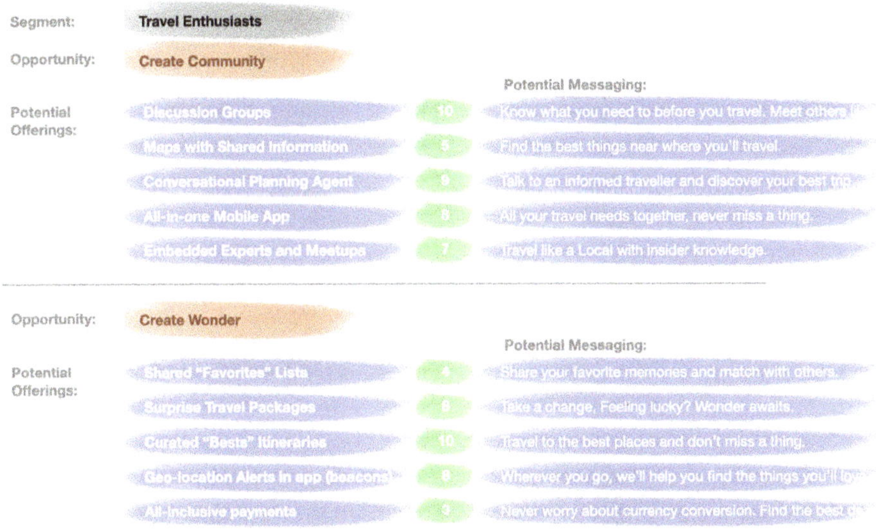

There are many potential offerings that can take advantage of any given opportunity (or threat)—more than you likely see, initially. Your job at this point is to imagine as many as you (and your larger team or cohort) can before you start narrowing-down the options. If you're a product company, have you considered creating a new service (other than repair and maintenance services): IBM moving into the consulting business in 1992, for example? If you're a service company, perhaps it's time to sell particular products that enhance the service: such as personal trainers offering nutritional supplements and gym gear? If you have a strong brand and loyal customers, perhaps you have the opportunity to create events or places where that brand "lives" in a way it hasn't before: Disney opening its first theme park, Disneyland, or Walmart, Apple, and T-Mobile moving into online banking or financial services, for example? Let's worry

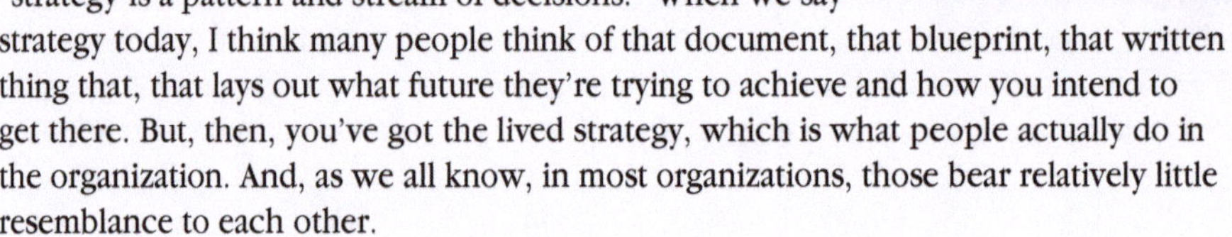

Nathan/ You've written several books about innovation, business, and design thinking and one of the most important things they communicate is a comfort zone that stretches across all of these very different worlds. Do you have a definition of strategy you find useful?

Jeanne/ I am not a definition person, but in my academic days, the prevailing definition was Henry Mintzberg's: "strategy is a pattern and stream of decisions." When we say strategy today, I think many people think of that document, that blueprint, that written thing that, that lays out what future they're trying to achieve and how you intend to get there. But, then, you've got the lived strategy, which is what people actually do in the organization. And, as we all know, in most organizations, those bear relatively little resemblance to each other.

When you say strategy, that means so many different things to different people. How do you work with that?

As someone who came out of the nuts-and-bolts business world, the most troubling thing about strategy is probably the extent to which it's only rhetoric. So often, nothing changes in an organization despite all of these senior people espousing strategy. The mission statement, all of it, goes nowhere. We've all seen it.

And then never communicating it to the rest of the organization. Right?

Right. I wrote a paper entitled, ***Experiencing Strategy,*** about how we treat strategy as this cognitive process. But, it really only matters when it becomes embodied in the individual practices of the people who work in the organization. And, that has two levels. The first: whether it is has personal meaning for people. The second: whether it guides their behavior (and a change in it). Those are two very different things but most strategy is lacking both.

There's lots of research—one in particular querying managers in a global set of thousands at lots of organizations—on the extent to which the principles of the mission statement and their organization influenced their day-to-day practice. And, the answer, not surprising, was almost never. That's the dilemma strategy faces when it remains an abstraction. Now, ***strategic intention***, by definition, is abstract because you're envisioning a few future that doesn't exist, but to actually get there, it needs to be translated at an operational level. People in marketing and operations and finance, etc. all do things in a specific way and, at a personal level, strategy needs to be translated so that everyone knows what to do differently, on a daily basis, for this strategy to work. That translation hardly ever happens, in part, because you communicate it one-way. It's not even a dialogue. It's a multi-faceted conversation. If people aren't experiencing a new strategy on an embodied, visceral level then their behavior is not going to shift to make it real.

Well, it's hard for me to imagine that you could have an innovation strategy in the absence of a corporate strategy. How would you know who to target for your innovation? And, how would you know what competencies or unique capabilities you wanted to bring into play? In the design process, when you help people create personas the first question is "Which persona should we design for?" Well, that's not a question design can answer. Design is mostly agnostic to who the customers are. Strategy has to answer that question. Without the umbrella of strategic intent, you don't know how to make choices because the strategy has to tell you who to serve and how to serve them. I can't imagine meaningful, fruitful innovation in the long term existing in the absence of some kind of coherent strategy to guide it.

Well, in this world, you would think it would, right? And, I think most corporations think they're doing it. They may not be calling it an innovation strategy. They may be calling it "new business initiatives" or "growth opportunities" or whatever the language is of the moment in that organization. But, fundamentally, strategy is about change. Inherent in the notion of strategy is the assumption that there is a more desirable future than the one we've got right now, or that there is a risk that will lose the current level of desirability we've got now in a changing world if we don't act differently.

Oh my god. We know that that's what's destroying our environment, in part. For quite a while now, people have been pointing out the system-level consequences of the corporate focus on growth. Wall Street and the other markets are incredibly and only focused on growth. It's a terrible thing for the planet and the environment and everything else—even for people who don't need to keep buying new junk they don't need. But, we don't seem to be able to escape that focus for publicly held companies.

Currently, the de facto understanding is that all profitable growth is good. For the tech industry, I don't even need to put the word profitable in there. We've seen crazy company-flipping and other phenomenon. That's probably one of the biggest challenges to the logic of strategy, when you no longer have to demonstrate that you actually create value in excess of your costs, but you're still worth a so much money in the stock market. I don't even know how you make sense of that, logically, but it's the "all growth is good" mentality that corporations are kind of prisoners to. Where does the madness stop? You can target your growth into areas that are more acceptable, but that requires inventing whole, new technologies, products, and services. That's much more difficult.

Read the entire interview at www.nathan.com/whole-new-strategy

later about what it will take, operationally, to build, deliver, and maintain these new offerings. For now, what are all of the ways to take advantage of the opportunities you've identified?

All Products are services

There are only a few categories of offerings: products (think, physical devices—mostly), services, places, and events. Everything that organizations offer to others to buy, rent, or participate in, falls into these four categories. But, most of these categories bleed over into services somehow. Nearly every product made needs to have at least some service around it: selling it, selling another, repairing it, servicing it, returning or replacing it and, hopefully, appropriately disposing or recycling, it. If you create a product and think the rest of these aren't important, you're doing everything you can do sabotage your relationships with your customers.

Too often, especially in digital services companies today, managers and employees only think in terms of "product." They have titles like product manager and, because of this, they never consider the services required to make or support that product in the market. One way that the best companies (or, those with the best customer relationships) succeed is not forgetting that they're in the experience business. A big part of that may be the services they deploy to help their customers succeed.

Evolving Offerings Strategy

Back in the 1990s, this was called something entirely different: "whole product." A key piece of Regis McKenna's approach to business and product strategy was the realization that while a spare product, such as software application, could satisfy some important customers (such as early adopters), this wouldn't work for larger markets. Offerings need to evolve in order to attract more customers.

Take Photoshop, for example. I first starting using it in 1988 (the icon was a Fotomat booth). Back then, it was still beta software but it was already highly sought-after and people in the know were describing how it was going to change everything. But, it was only usable by people on the "bleeding edge," in other words, early adopters. It was buggy, had no support, no tutorials, little to no documentation, and certainly no training courses or certifications. That was fine at the start but to build a real market, the product would need to evolve significantly.

Over time, Adobe added more and more to the offering: software that passed quality assurance (thus wasn't buggy), quick reference cards, tutorials, templates, etc. As it added more and more, it was usable—and appealing—to more and more people. It would not have grown the huge market it did without these evolving offerings that added more value for more people. In time, there were extensions, partnerships with printers and publishing manufacturers, programs for service bureaus, training programs (both Adobe's and others'), conferences, competitions, full courses (now at every community college), professional certifications, customer service lines, etc. In order to move from early adopters into the mainstream, full market, the offering needed to evolve substantially to appeal to the customers and help them create value. As obvious as this sounds, it's actually not an easy thing to make happen.

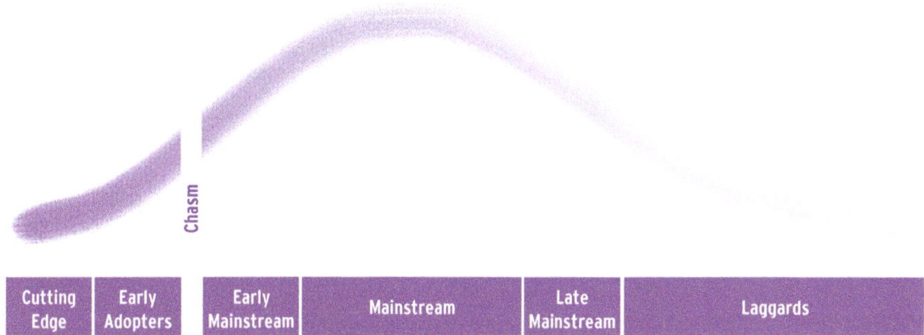

Geoffrey Moore wrote a book after leaving the Regis McKenna, Inc. (Regis McKenna's consultancy at the time) all about this transition, entitled ***Crossing the Chasm***. The gist of this book was that this transition not only required expanded offerings but, often, new skills in understanding and appealing to these new customers. It's not just enough to add features and services because these new customers are different segments—they have different needs.

Your strategy will eventually need to evolve in much the same way. You will need to better understand new customers and constituents and their different needs. You'll have to deploy new offerings that target these new people with different messaging (because what they care about will be different). But, for now, let's put this aside until you've already hit a homerun with one set of customers.

Is it worth it?

At this point, we can start asking one of the most important questions in business (of any kind): is it worth it? You've defined and prioritized potential offerings that support your best opportunities. All of these are validated by your customer decision-drivers and how they compare to your competitors' offerings. However, it's not enough to merely identify what customers need and want and what is differentiable in the market. You also need to assess whether it's feasible to make and deliver what you envision, and whether you can cover your costs (and make a profit, if necessary).

Is it desired?

If you've used the process outlined in the book, you should already have these questions answered: does it satisfy unmet needs, does it align with customers' decision-drivers, how big is the market opportunity, etc.)?

Is it feasible?
Can it be made within the technological, political (legal), societal (cultural), and natural constraints? How manageable is the entire process?
Is it sustainable?

Does it leverage your strengths and capabilities? Can we be competitive?
These concerns have already been validated for these offerings as well from this perspective, via the two competitive comparisons in this process (one for the Market sequence—start at Chapter 1—and the other for the Operations sequence—start at Chapter 5). Do these offerings align with your network, partnerships, operations, understandings, brand/values, etc.? Do they give you a sustainable competitive advantage?

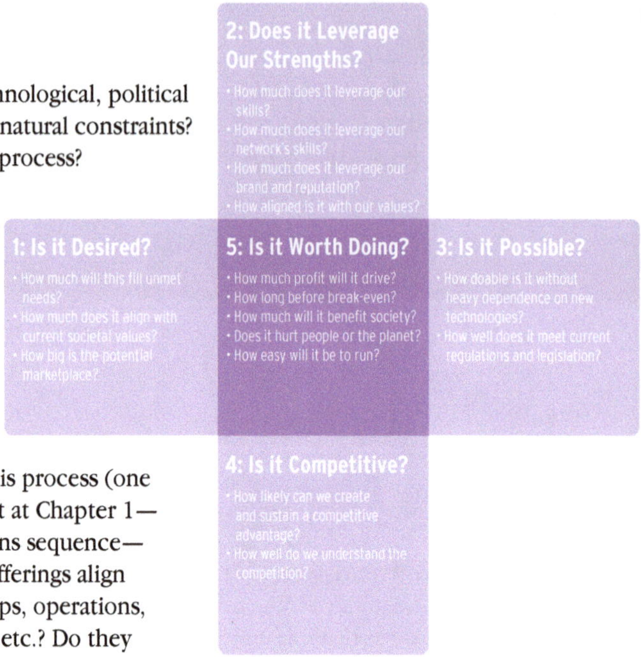

© Bill Wurz & Asher Waldfogel (modified)

Is it worth the effort?
Will you be able to reap the rewards commensurate with the time, money, resources, and emotions required to bring these offerings to market? Even social ventures and non-profits need to evaluate whether the intended result is worth the work, whether those results are measured in financial, functional, emotional, identity/brand, or meaningful terms. Is there profit (if that's necessary) and if so, how much? Is the Return on Investment worth the total cost of that investment?

Another thing to ensure is that your offerings are specific to your market segments. Each market segment (if you have more than one) will have its own positioning, opportunities, and offerings. When we get to the Operational sequence, the needs of all of them will come together. But, for now, it's important to keep them separate.

Obviously, if you have only one market segment, this is easy to see, manage, and track. But, that's not a reason to ignore markets that have clear customer value potential.

Remember Those Threats

As we mentioned in the last chapter, it's important to keep in mind your biggest market threats. While spending the bulk of your energy and resources on your opportunities (and the offerings that take advantage of them), don't forget to write a Threat Statement and bring those threats into the Operational sequence, along with the opportunities.

The Start of Messaging

While your mind is focused on opportunities and offerings, it's likely that ideas are being generated about messaging. This is natural. Since all of these offerings are grounded in customer decision-drivers and the five kinds of value, and since you're just identified a position distinct from your competitors, the language your competitors and customers use and the messages they're exposed to are also top-of-mind. If messaging comes to mind for these new offerings, this is a good time to jot it down. Don't worry if your ideas aren't great. You will undoubtedly refine them later. You just want to capture these thoughts while they're fresh and while your head is in this space.

You will return to and refine these messages (and throw some out entirely) when it's time for advertising, sales, and promotion. This is the beginning of this external messaging and directly reflects the connection to customer value. I'll describe more about messaging in Chapter 9.

/Highlights

- Your best opportunities will be those in which you can offer, in some form, greater value to your customers than can your competitors. This means that you need to define an offering (a product, service, place, event, or combination) that your customers can purchase.
- Both your market and operational strategies will be based on the offerings you decide to offer your customers. First, these offerings are validated from the work you've done in the Market sequence. Next, you evaluate your preparedness to offer these to your customers from a variety of contexts.
- Your key partners and key resources are those that can help your offerings succeed. This may include addressing new partnerships from stakeholders you never before identified.
- Once you've identified your best opportunities, you can imagine the best offerings that take advantage of these opportunities. These are separate for each market segment.
- While the insights and results from the Market sequence are still fresh in your mind, this is a good time to identify and record any messaging about these offers that occurs to you which might make them clear to your customers.

/Explore More

- *The Catalyst* Jeanne Leidtka, Robert H. Rosen, and Robert Wiltbank
- *Designing for Growth* by Jeanne Liedtka & Tim Ogilvie

Your Operations

If the market is everything outside the organization, operations covers everything inside it. The Market sequence is the most critical and most involved process in strategy but the Operations sequence is the second. If all you do strategy-wise is work through these two processes, the Market and Operations sequences, you've done the lion's share of the most important parts of strategy planning.

Once you identify how prepared you are to take action, the rest is just details aimed at implementing the tactics that will make you successful. This sequence follows a similar set of steps as the Market sequence but with a focus on the organization internally.

As with the Market sequence, the Operations sequence is a series of steps that expand possibilities and then focus efforts. Each part of an organization's operations (and there are many) are opportunities to innovate and consider who these functions support the Market sequence. Innovation isn't just about new offerings but new operations, as well.

Chapter 5

Your Capabilities & Priorities

Now that you know what the best offerings you should go to market with are, once they are differentiated to maximize your success it's time to address your readiness to do so. Your organization has several capabilities but they may not all be suited for delivering what you've identified. At the same time, some of your capabilities may no longer be critical to your success and you may be lacking others, still. However, the market imperatives from the end of the Market sequence are the inputs to the Operational sequence so your operational strategy will necessarily fit your market strategy (this isn't always the case for traditional strategy where adherence to sequence is sloppy).

First, list the offerings from the end of the Market sequence and then identify the capabilities necessary to successful offer them. You will likely need to consult several people within the organization and maybe even a few advisors outside, especially if these new offerings are truly innovative and novel.

For example, you may have identified the opportunity to build a Conversational User Interface (CUI) for your services. If so, you may have no current expertise in-house to deliver it. That's an obvious new capability you'll need. But, it's not just one line item: "hire CUI team." There may be several other requirements that relate, such as a database of user data on which to train the machine learning algorithms that underpin the decision tree and responses within the CUI. That may require new database talent as well as the data itself. How long will it take to generate this data? Is the current service even capable of it? What form does it need to be in? Can you buy off-the-shelf parts to construct it? Should you contract all of this out to a team to build it in Amazon's AWS bot architecture? This is why you likely need to bring on expertise just to identify the capabilities needed to offer new products, services, and other experiences.

Once you have your list of capabilities, you now need to research internally and externally how those capabilities measure up to other organizations. It's critical to understand how far ahead (or behind) you are on being able to deliver.

Also, remember that you may have defined several market segments with different offerings in each. You can combine all of the offerings together, unless you need to divide them between different teams or divisions in your organization, but you can't forget to account for any.

Once you have a list of the capabilities you need, including current ones and new ones you've identified, it's time to rank them in importance. You may not be able to ignore any of them but, at least, you need to prioritize them. You can't do everything at once.

Market Offerings with Related Capabilities Needed

Market Offerings:	Rank:	Operational Capabilities Needed:	Rank:
Generative AI	10	In-house AI Expertise, inc data science	10
		Partnership with Claude.ai or ChatGPT	10
Conversational UI	10	CUI Designer	10
		CUI Engineering Team (in-house or out-of-house)	9
		AWS Account and/or Partnership	9
Enhanced Security	10	Experienced Security & Privacy Chief	10
iOS Mobile App	10	Mobile Front & Back-end Team (or vendor)	10
Quick-start Tutorial	9	CopyWriter & Information Design resources	9
One-Click Setup	8	50 hours Engineering	10
ApplePay Integration	8	160 hours Engineering & Product Management	9

Setting Priorities Competitively

Now that we have a list of capabilities needed, with rankings for each, it's time to compare these against our competitors (the same ones from the competitive analysis in the previous Market sequence. While the previous step was done market segment-by-segment, this time, you have the option of doing it the same way (each market segment separately) or combining everything and considering them all together. It doesn't make a lot of difference unless your organization is already so big that different teams or divisions focus on different market segments.

Also, as before, Competitor X is important. It represents what competition might currently be lurking in the shadows, not quite ready to reveal itself to your customers and their competitors.

As before, this is a focusing exercise. When you're finished, you should have a ranked list of the most important capabilities you require to deliver the offerings and the value proposition you planned in the Market sequence. This makes up for not doing the traditional SWOT process. If you remember, people often combine market and operational strengths and weaknesses but discount one or the other, as they shouldn't ever be compared against each other. One set belongs in market strategy and the other in operational strategy—in this case, right here.

You can evaluate your needed capabilities per offering or not but, at the end of this process, all of the capabilities you've identified will be ranked in terms of priorities. It's unlikely that you can do everything. These priorities are just that (and critical). However, if you're more comfortable keeping them separated (perhaps, because they live in different teams or divisions of your organization), that's fine.

Also, as before, the operational strengths, weaknesses, opportunities, and threats are calculated automatically, based on the relative rankings. This is to prevent people from just picking the things they're excited about. Of course, they could always go back and fiddle with the rankings to make the capabilities they want become high priorities, but then at least it's conscious, deliberate intervention. What this process tries to mitigate is the unconscious, inadvertent bias that creeps into all of our work. I won't tell you not to fiddle with the process to get the results you want but if you do, then don't blame the process if it doesn't result in a winning strategy.

These rankings often need to be determined with internal experts. Your tech team may have capabilities you don't realize so instead of making assumptions, why not involve them and ask? The same goes for all of the other internal teams and divisions that have a specific perspective on some part of the organization. The more diverse the expertise, the more accurate the rankings—hopefully. If your offerings are brand new to you, the expertise needed to identify capabilities and rank them may require outside experts, as well. This is a good time to engage your advisors, if you have them.

As with all research, you need to be a bit careful. Organizations can be fraught with covert and overt politics. You may think your culture is open and straight-forward—and it may be for you—but it may not be for others. We'll talk, specifically, about culture inside a company and how it can be evolved strategically, but for now, realize that just like when conducting customer research, you can't always trust the literal answers you get. You'll have to judge for yourself, or compare answers from a variety of people, to identify any issues with what you find. Just remember, even if there is no subterfuge, it's possible to get the wrong information when people are, consciously or subconsciously, trying to give you what they think you want.

The competitive aspect to setting your priorities helps you define what may be most important to act on quickly. As said above, you may not be able to ignore any of these capabilities as they may all be required to build and offer what you intend. However, the ranking will tell you which capabilities are more strategically critical, thus you can act accordingly.

The last part of setting your operational priorities is to define an internal positioning statement. This isn't something to be shared outside the company but it reflects your internal strategy for the organization you want to be.

The process is the same as for the market position. The highest-ranked opportunities will help you focus on what you can build and deliver strategically, better than your competitors. It will help you differentiate your organization and may identify where you need to develop a new division or team or spin off an opportunity.

Ranked Offerings & Capabilities in Competitive Analysis (Setting Priorities)

Top Capabilities:	Rank:	Your Company: Your Offering:	Competitor 1: Offering:	Competitor 2: Offering:	Competitor 3: Offering:	Competitor 4: Offering:	Competitor 5: Offering:	Competitor X: Offering:	
Generative AI	10	10	4	7	2	8	4	9	Strength Opportunity
Conversational UI	10	10	7	8	8	8	7	10	Strength Opportunity
Enhanced Security	10	8	1	5	9	7	5	10	Strength
Quick-start Tutorial	9	8	1	9	3	5	3	9	Threat
One-Click Setup	9	8	10	10	7	8	1	4	Strength
ApplePay Integration	9	9	4	2	4	1	10	7	Strength Opportunity
iOS Mobile App	9	3	5	0	1	0	5	8	Weakness Threat
Android Mobile App	8	3	6	0	1	0	8	9	Weakness Threat
Web App	8	7	10	1	8	8	8	8	Strength Threat
PostgreSQL Database	8	8	6	8	3	3	2	9	Strength Opportunity

For example, Amazon was originally an online bookstore, then a marketplace for all kinds of products held in inventory in their warehouses. Then, they identified the opportunity to leverage the marketplace they created for others to sell directly to their customers, too. This was a comparatively simple evolution on the customer-facing side but required new capabilities on the operational side to make it work. They had much less control over other merchants and the number of factors that were to fall outside their control (shipping, packaging, quality, messaging, customer service, etc.) exponentiated for so many merchants. They had to add a lot of capabilities to realize that opportunity, which they did, of course.

Later, they identified a strong capability they had already built on the operational side: the ability to build and maintain servers for digital services. This was especially the case since so many server and hosting services for small and large companies alike varied greatly in quality and reliability. Their competitive operational strength became an opportunity for a new offering. So, this capability became a new offering, opening new revenue streams. However, it's a very different business than their online marketplace so they spun these capabilities and offerings off into a new division: Amazon Web Services (AWS).

Later still, as they built their Alexa conversational agent, they also realized that the quality of the service and algorithms they built were highly competitive compared to the few other CUIs available—Apple's Siri, for example, a roughly comparable CUI that was not available for use by others. Amazon recognized another operational strength as a new opportunity and built an offering around it: anybody can write programs that harness Alexa's CUI. You may identify the opportunity to do something similar.

It could also be the case that you realize that some capability you've spent a lot of time, money, and other resources building just isn't competitive. In this case, it may be better to relinquish the effort and close or sell it off and, instead, purchase these capabilities from a qualified vendor. Your goal should be to focus on what you're great at and what you can differentiate your organization on, not to try to do everything yourself. However, it should be obvious at the end of this process which capabilities are truly strategic and for those that are, perhaps keeping them in-house is more advisable than trusting them to a vendor or partner.

The Threat Matrix

Now that you've done this for the highest-ranked capabilities, you've set your priorities. However, you cannot forget about the lowest-ranked capabilities—your biggest operational threats. Before we lease this step, we need to make a list and prioritize the worst threats, then build an action plan to address them. This, too, may require collaboration with those inside your organization and outside, it too. Trusted partners might be invaluable in creating the action plan for addressing your threats.

Operations Strategy

Now that you've unveiled your priorities, it should be clear to you what new capabilities you need to build and which existing ones you need to strengthen or leverage. This allows you to begin planning how to implement these changes. This is when you build an operations strategy, detailing the tactics you'll take to achieve these: specific goals, the timing, the costs involved, the expectations, who will be responsible and who involved, and what metrics you'll use to assess success.

Operations is most of an organization's activities, internally, so this may be a big plan that covers most of the organization. This is why COOs (Chief Operating Officers) are paid the "big bucks" and often become the next President or CEO of an organization—they're overseeing nearly everything, already (think about Tim Cook replacing Steve Jobs at Apple).

This is also one of the most important points where business strategy impacts the company. While questions of "what business should we be in?" and "what should be offering the market—and to whom?" are critical about an organization's direction, how it deals with the answers to these questions is almost all about operations. If these two pieces aren't in alignment, this fundamental misunderstanding could shake a company apart and is highly predictive of failure.

- Once you've identified your market offerings, you can evaluate your capabilities to create, distribute, and maintain these, and then prioritize them. Many of these will include non-market influences, such as trend and stakeholder decision-drivers.
- Honest assessment of your capabilities will reveal your best priorities and should be set with the input of your entire organization. These are automatically validated via the market positioning, customer decision-drivers, and opportunities you identified from the Market sequence.
- Your capabilities should be compared to your competitors and their offerings in the same way you compared your customer decision-drivers in the Market sequence. This represents the second part of traditional SWOT and competitive analysis but synchronized with your best market offerings and position.
- You may have different capabilities required as well as different priorities set for each of the different market segments you serve. These need to come together into one set of requirements and priorities for your organization.
- As with positioning, you can opt to create an operational threat assessment to accompany your market threat assessment. This, too, will prioritize the capabilities you need to build, expand, or partner for.

Chapter 6

Your Partners & Resources

No one builds a successful organization alone. The larger the company, the more others are involved. And, it's one thing to consider employees but too many leaders never consider external stakeholders— other than seeing them as either customers (friends) or competitors (foes). You will vastly increase your chances of success by forming partnerships and cooperating with others outside your organization, to mutual benefit.

Now that you have prioritized your capabilities, built a plan to both strengthen your weaknesses and capitalize on your opportunities and strengths, that plan needs to be considered in terms of what key partnerships and resources will be required to build, use, and maintain those capabilities. You may not be able to build everything yourself, either now or in the future. So, consider what partnerships might help you build faster or better. The same is true of resources. You may find that you need a specific kind or quality of manufacturing tools, like Apple did when their industrial design and engineering got really sophisticated. They found that in order to build what they envisioned—things that only they could build—they needed to invest in their manufacturing partners to a new degree.

It wasn't enough for Apple to pay their manufacturing partners in advance so that they could afford to purchase new, expensive machine tools. Apple actually purchased these machines themselves, both to ensure they were dedicated to Apple's needs and, in addition, to make sure they weren't available to their competitors for a time. This was their defensive strategy. They realized to make the most compact mobile devices, they needed tooling processes that were, at the time, rare (like 3nm fabrication tools for the smallest possible microprocessors). They even realized that they needed to design their own chips if they were to better compete and open-up their opportunities (like their A and M series processors).

This integration with and investment in their partners is critical to their current success. They purchase key resources, often years in advance, to make sure their supply chain is stable. When they discover a technology to be absolutely critical to their future, their strategy is to first corner supply and access to it, and then often to bring it in-house so they can own it completely.

Partnerships are Mutually Beneficial

Too many businesspeople look at others only through a lens that sees their own benefit. Others are there only for their own success. This is the worst outcome of a business culture built primarily on the idea that competition drives business. It misses the fact that cooperation is as important to complex systems (and successful ones) as competition is to driving innovation and better solutions.

Because of this, most never bother to investigate whether they can involve others in their mutual success and merely follow the industry or company conventions they've grown accustomed to. Perhaps every non-profit looks for corporate sponsors in a specific industry? Perhaps most companies in an area look to partner with a local organization to support schools? These aren't bad but they're not considered deeply and they miss the connections and opportunities that thinking across the entire system might provide.

/Competition vs. Cooperation

It's worth talking briefly about the phony schism between competition and cooperation. While the business world has overstressed competition for over a hundred years, the reality of healthy systems is that nothing can be built on a playing field that is only competitive. Without a balance of cooperation, competition retards innovation, standards, and growth. Why? Because it is cooperation that allows us to build higher-level playing fields upon which we can compete. Otherwise, we'll always be fighting in low-stakes markets for low-stakes value.

Consider the considerable standards in electronics, even power outlets. If we didn't have these standards (and in fact, it often feels like we have too many), we couldn't have the diverse ecosystem of devices, accessories and services we do today. If every manufacturer had a competing power requirement, plug, and cable type, we would be competing at that level. We could only buy those products that fit those plugs and requirements and no market would be big enough to support more complex offerings. Instead, by collaborating on a few standards (at least regionally for power), manufacturers can turn their attention to fulfilling more complex and interesting needs and desires.

Without that collaboration, competition stalls much lower down. This is why it's important to consider stakeholders you might otherwise scoff at. They may represent an opportunity to deliver much more interesting value if you cooperate on the less interesting—and often less profitable—value.

Chapter 10 describes stakeholders and the larger potential ecosystem of your organization. In particular, it describes how to map value across these stakeholders to see where you already have important connections, as well as where there may be holes and opportunities to make new ones. If you do this correctly, it's clear where value of different kinds flow and where it may not be mutual value (that's nearly always the case with Nature—while we derive a lot of value from Nature, we rarely provide much value to Nature).

This is the point in your strategy where you should consider the value you've mapped and what you can do to amplify it. If your success depends on others, your plan better involve them! The same is true if your success can be increased by involving others— or if it might be endangered by others.

You can approach this in two different sequences and it doesn't matter much which you choose:
1. You can create a complete stakeholder value map first.
2. You can start here with the partnerships you already have or can imagine

Regardless, you'll likely need to go back and forth a bit and you absolutely will need to evolve both, over time; the market ecosystem is dynamic and always changing. So, too, should your strategy (to some extent) and your partnership strategy be.

Also, you can approach partnership strategy as a whole or in parts. Your different market segments may require or emphasize certain stakeholders to partner with. So can your list of priority capabilities, as can your list of offerings. However, these are mostly related if you're followed the strategy process in this book. Your priorities are the result of the offerings you've chosen to focus on, which are the result of the decision-drivers you prioritized within each of your market segments. This represents the power of this process as these things are all related and internally consistent (as well they should be).

I suggest that If you have more than one market segment, you should probably approach each separately in terms of partnerships and when you're finished, compare the overlap between them to set partner priorities. If you only have one market segment, then this suggestion is moot.

But remember that ***partnerships are inherently bi-directional.*** If they aren't, they eventually fail, often with bad feelings or lawsuits on one or both sides. If you can only articulate why someone should partner with you (to your benefit) and not why it's valuable to them, you haven't done the real work yet. Partnerships that are predatory or based on threats (such as if a non-profit threatened to expose a company's behavior unless they're given money—that's called "extortion," by the way) don't usually last long and certainly aren't healthy, long-lasting, or strong. You should be able to make the case for partnering with someone that they would make internally.

This is yet another step in which you should involve others in your organization—particularly those with outside connections (salespeople, customer researchers, customer support, buyers, etc.). Partnership strategy is external strategy so those in your organizations who regularly work with external actors have unique views and experience that will help you.

For each market segment, the stakeholder map may change slightly. That's perfectly fine. This is one of those explore > focus steps. It's common that you will identify more partnership opportunities than you can achieve so the process should give you context and help you focus on the most important partnerships.

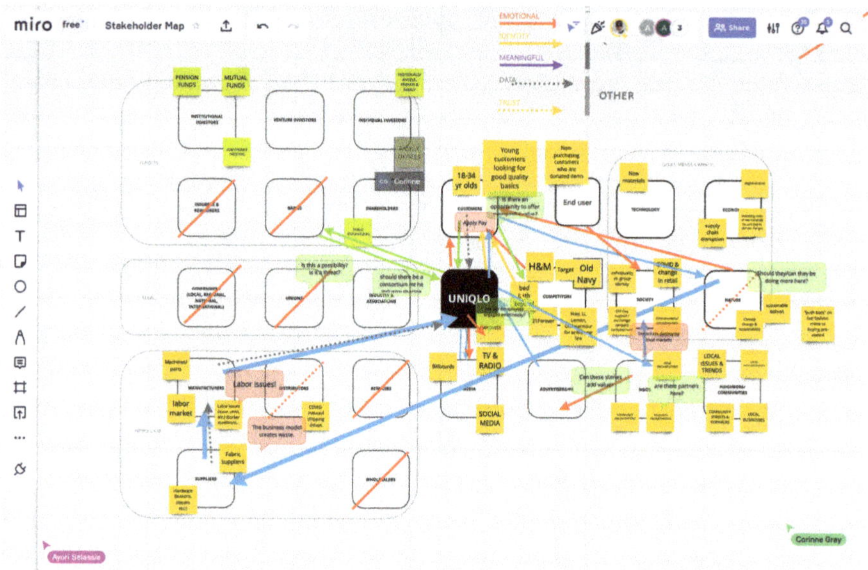

Identify Key Resources

After identifying key partnerships, it's time to do the same for key resources. Unfortunately, this isn't as standard as it is across a generic stakeholder ecosystem. As such, I can't give you a standard set of resources that you might peruse and pick from like I can with the stakeholders. So you'll need to identify this list yourself.

Start by looking at your expenses: what do you spend the most on, both in total and per vendor or stakeholder? What are the resources that most often defeat your timetables for production or delivery? Which are most vulnerable to outside price or availability pressures? Which are those directly responsible for your prioritized capabilities, partnerships, offerings, and decision-drivers? Which is your value proposition or position based upon? Which facilitate the connections with your customers?

Your key resources may also suggest key partnerships—if these haven't already been identified. For example, if you need a certain kind of microchip, a special kind of cacao, or bolts made a specific way, those may be great partners to deepen your relationship with. Perhaps, you've gone remote for your operations but you still need to meet up face-to-face as a company from time to time. That likely represents a lot of hotel and flight costs. Perhaps, you can partner with an airline or hotel chain to get a discount every quarter (as a start) but there may be deeper benefits you both can share, as well, depending on what your organization does.

Ideally, for your most important partners and partner opportunities, you'll delve more deeply into the motivations, values, and goals of those partners. Understanding your key partners on the same level as your customers goes a long way toward providing mutual value and building strong partnerships.

These may even result in acquisitions.

/Highlights
- Partnerships with others outside your organization are critical to your success.
- A stakeholder value map will help you identify both potential opportunities and threats for partnerships.
- Include others within the organization when identifying and evaluating potential partnerships.
- You may have different partnership needs across your different customer segments.

Chapter 7

Your Finances

There are so many potential pieces to your financial strategy. Undoubtedly, this is the most detailed area for most businesspeople—especially those that are business school-trained. However, numbers can be deceiving, as it's just as easy to measure the wrong things, make the wrong predictions, and be overconfident about both. The two most important parts of financial strategy are:

1) Your cost structure (where and what your costs are)
2) Your revenue structure (how you make money)

There are plenty of ways to slice and dice these two things and accountants and quant-types are great at tumbling the numbers into different configurations in order to identify different aspects. But, at its core, you need to both understand 1) how much money you need to operate (this includes both startup costs and revenue over time); and 2) how much revenue you can **reasonably** expect to earn from your activities (product sales, service revenue, event and venue sales, licensing deals, advertising revenue, etc.). If the first exceeds the second, you won't be in business for long and the first rule of sustainable business is: "You can't do good if you aren't still in operation." The same is true for non-profits (and, for that matter, government agencies). If your non-profit isn't raising enough from grants, donations, or other revenue sources, your good-doing days are numbered. If your tax base drops (or just as critical: your ability to collect), your government agency is also not long for this world. This is the reality of business.

Cost Structure

Since this isn't a general business book but one focused on strategy, I won't get into the details of business finances. However, in order to build a successful strategy, you need to accurately predict the financial impact of the future activities you envision—and choose the paths forward that lead to the best possibilities.

If you have an existing business, you should turn to the financial data available to you about your current expenses. Where are your greatest costs? How cyclical or seasonal are they? Which activities or customers cost the most? How many unexpected costs do you incur regularly?

The answer to all of these may signal opportunities to change your strategy in some way to minimize these expenses, negotiate lower costs, eliminate them altogether, develop partnerships that change your cost structure, or acquire companies (or even sell off assets) that would result in lower costs.

Be careful, however. It's not uncommon for businesspeople to look to short-term cost-cutting to improve today's "bottom line" while simultaneously eroding long-term revenue or even endangering the business completely. The "bean counters" often look only at the numbers (which is to say, only Financial value) and ignore the other four forms of value in the system. General Motors lost tremendous amounts of revenue, brand equity, and lifetime customer value because they cut so many corners during the 1970s that their products were mostly clones of each other that were neither durable nor interesting to consumers. Just because you can easily measure money doesn't mean you've measured everything important!

You also need to appropriately predict what your costs will be to develop, deliver, and service the new offerings you've identified in the Market sequence. Hopefully, you have a few alternatives, so costing them out can give you options that differentiate which might be better than others.

To do this, you may need to consult experts inside your organization or look to outside sources of data if these are new kinds of activities. You may need to bring in consultants who better understand these offerings or new, markets so that you have a more accurate view of them. Potential costs include (but aren't limited to):

- equipment (from employee equipment to factories)
- real estate (new offices, warehouses, factories, kiosks, etc.)
- salaries (and in the USA, this includes healthcare costs)
- vendors of all types (credit card services, janitorial services, consultants, IT support, marketing, etc.)
- development costs (research, development, prototyping, testing, etc.)
- licensing fees (patents, intellectual property, etc.)
- capital costs (investment or loans, interest rates, deposits, fees, etc.)
- don't forget taxes (if you're a for-profit corporation)!
- or inflation, over time!

The more detailed you can be, the better, but you shouldn't expect to nail this exactly. You need to account for the most significant costs (as well as identify those largely out of your control), even they're fairly rough. The only way to accurate identify real costs is to actually build and pay for the offerings in your strategy. You'll only know how close your estimates were when you're finished. The second-closest will be when you actually request quotes from vendors for the resources and services you'll need. For now, however, you want realistic approximations (those are guesses).

Revenue Structure

The most important things to focus upon are the best opportunities and offerings for you to meet and exceed your expenses. As such, you should look for potential offerings that, obviously, pay for themselves (at least). In addition, there may be sources of revenue available that you haven't considered. For example, there is direct revenue (sales), but also licensing, rent, grants, and interest on savings, investments, or endowments. Hopefully, your revenue is continuous, forming a revenue stream that you can mostly count on. Even non-profits and government agencies must get their money from somewhere. Often, this isn't thought of as revenue (in the classic sense) but it is, nonetheless. Once you see and understand the ecosystem your organization functions within, particularly that of the many stakeholders it touches, you may see new opportunities for revenue that were previously hidden.

Is It Still Worth It?

When you have figured your costs and your revenue, you can now compare them to determine which of your strategies are best. However, remember that just because an offering projects higher returns, doesn't mean it's the only or best option for you. This is especially true for government agencies and non-profits that aren't aiming for profit but merely covering their costs. Some offerings may not generate as much profit but may generate more overall value for the organization. Some may even not be profitable themselves at all, but generate larger revenues elsewhere. These are called loss leaders. One example is the rotisserie chicken at COSTCO, which they sell at or under cost because it brings people into the store, where they buy other things with a higher profit margin.

There are so many ways to measure this. The most common are:

- ROI (Return on Investment): how efficient funds are at generating revenue/profit
- Payback Period: how long it will take to recoup expenses, in months or years
- Breakeven Point: where and when revenues cover expenses
- ARR (Annualized Recurring of Revenue): how much continued revenue will result over a calendar year for a subscription purchase or service or
- ARR (Annualized Rate of Return): specifically for investments, revenues expected on an investment for each year
- CAC (Customer Acquisition Cost): how much you'll spend (costs) to acquire an (additional) customer, and so many more..

There is no end to what you might measure to determine whether one offering or opportunity is better than another. And, to some extent, it doesn't matter as long as you're using the same comparison across all and you're adequately including all of your costs and potential revenues. Some of these metrics might be more appropriate for different markets, industries, or offerings (like products vs. services vs. events, etc.).

In most cases with new offerings, you may need to look further into the future to best understand the return. Truly new products and services often take time to find customers and grow market share. Killing them off too soon may purposefully doom an otherwise great offering that just needs more time to be successful. This is incredibly common. Many companies end product or service lines before they're successful, ensuring that they become a self-fulfilling prophecy. Many otherwise successful offerings are killed before launch when short-term projections visualize them as unsuccessful or taking too long to succeed, even before the come to market. Being realistic

Now that you've set your priorities, your budget should reflect these. Everyone in your company should be able to tag and connect every budget item to your strategic priorities. This is why they need to be so clearly communicated. If the organization is spending funds on things not connected to either market or operational strategy, perhaps, those items aren't as necessary as everyone assumes? Budgets that correspond to strategy tell a story of focus and responsibility.

about how long it will take to be successful is key. Most new companies won't "break even" (become profitable) for 3-5 years as they build sales. That's normal and seasoned businesspeople know this. The benefits of the other four kinds of value may also take time to develop, as well.

One component of all of these is comparing them to not doing anything at all with your money. Instead, how much would you make if you put that money into a market investment, instead (such as the stock market, a money market account, a bank account, a government bond, etc.). Again, this is only a measure of Financial value but if the profit on your opportunity (what's left over of your revenues after all of your costs) is lower than simply putting that money in a Treasury Bill for the same amount of time (let's say 4.5% return over 3 months), why not just bank the funds and earnt he interest? This is sound financial advice but I'll, again, remind you that not all value is financial (see Chapter 1). There are still reasons, sometimes, to still invest in the offering and make less overall—especially if you're a non-profit or government agency—but you should still go into this decision with your eyes open, knowing the expected outcome and its alternatives.

Raising Capital

When you can't fund development of new offerings yourself, you need to look for investment. Your strategy may require outside investment to start up, develop, deliver, and support. For-profits look to venture investment (small, large, established, "family and friends," corporate investments, etc.) while non-profits look toward grants or donations.

Raising capital of any kind is a book unto itself. You may need to bring on an expert to help you as well.

If you're looking for venture capital of some kind, you can be sure that those investors are looking very carefully at "the numbers," meaning, they're looking almost exclusively at Financial value. They will discount or ignore all other kinds of capital. Even internally, the finance people in your company may do the very same thing. You'll need to make a clear case for a financial return on investment (and likely a hefty one) to pique their interest. Now, investors are definitely looking at other things (you team, your offering, your position, etc.) but if the financial don't make clear sense to them, the rest won't make up for it.

Nathan/ You combine product experience with financing experience. What do you wish people would know or do or prepare before they contact you? What are the questions you really want to engage with?

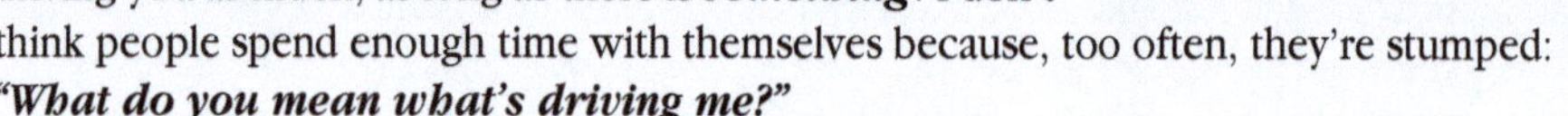

Spectra/ I want people to be clear about what's driving them, regardless of whether they're an investor or a funder. Why are you doing this work? It doesn't really matter what's driving you as much, as long as there is ***something***. I don't think people spend enough time with themselves because, too often, they're stumped: ***"What do you mean what's driving me?"***

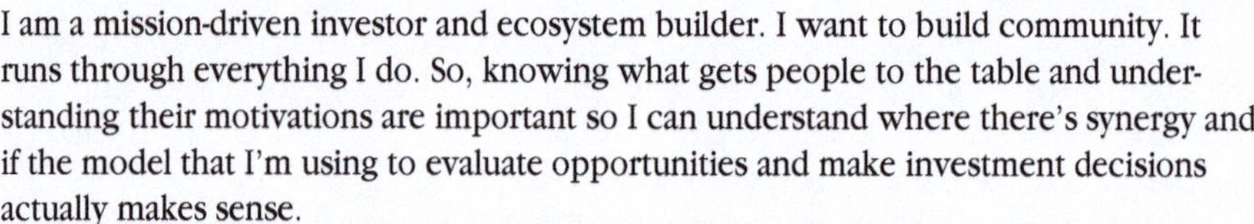

I am a mission-driven investor and ecosystem builder. I want to build community. It runs through everything I do. So, knowing what gets people to the table and understanding their motivations are important so I can understand where there's synergy and if the model that I'm using to evaluate opportunities and make investment decisions actually makes sense.

I was referred to a cybersecurity company the other day and I didn't understand why we were having a conversation. I took it because it was someone I knew but they clearly hadn't done any research about me or the fact that I invest in mission-driven businesses and that I don't really care about cybersecurity. So, I think being clear about who you are, is essential. And, when people spend time being clear about who they are and what drives them, it makes them curious about what drives other people.

Why aren't all investors mission-driven?

You know, that's complex. It feels like it could be. It really depends on where you come from. I'm from Nigeria and I have friends from there who didn't grow up with a lot of money and had hard lives. We've all had lives with varying degrees of difficulty in various axes.

I grew up with these two different figures. My dad was more of a traditionalist, climbing the ladder in finance. And my mom, was a stay-at-home mom but also a philanthropist whose business supported a large ecosystem of merchants where I grew up. Every year, if a deal didn't come in, I'd hear her say, "Ah, this person was depending on this." So, I grew up with that. It's in my DNA. As a result, I've never seen business and caring at odds with each other.

There are people who work in the same environment that I do that didn't grow up with my parents or my context; who see the accumulation of wealth as a way to honor their parents. They're not mission-driven in the same way that I am. I think everybody is on some sort of mission but their missions may just be different.

How would you describe to someone to align their values, their strategies, their goals with their finance and funding strategy, day to day? What does that look like?

For me, it's breaking everything down into questions and keeping top-of-mind, honestly in my heart, as to what really matters to me and the questions that I should be asking myself. Those questions come naturally, for me. For example, I care about doing good in the world, so when I become an investor, it was imperative to simply ask "What kind of investor am I going be? What does 'doing good' in the world mean?" This is combined with the way my brain works: I've always been someone who sees opportunity or made connections that are not always obvious to others. I intersect so many things so I see many things and care about things others don't.

What does it mean to give people money? When I started investing, everything was new to me. I had to learn about cap tables and so much more. I quickly came to the conclusion that the systems and paradigms we use today and inherited from finance haven't necessarily served the world well and are clearly antithetical to equality. So, if I'm going to play in this space, what does that mean for me? The point I got to—which many people get to—is to invest in people that ordinarily wouldn't get access to capital because of systemic discrimination. Because even when people are trying to be objective, they're not taking into consideration who gets it, systemically.

My paradigm is to actually invest in things that are going to make the world better—not just underrepresented or marginalized people, but anyone who is making the world better. That quickly led to the question of: "What are the problems of the world? What are the biggest blockers to prosperity for the most marginalized people?" That's how I came up with the thesis areas that are guiding me today. These questions beget more questions that beget more questions, and I follow my own North Star of what I want to do in the world. I try not to be afraid when I run into roadblocks or an absence of playbooks to guide me. This is where being a product person is very helpful, because that's a paradigm for figuring things out. At the end of the day, what are we trying to get done? I'm suspicious of current solutions because if they were working we wouldn't have these problems.

So what do you ask for from the people and companies that approach you. How do you come to understand where their values are and what they're trying to accomplish?

Because I've been a product leader who has worked in tech for about 20 years, I'm usually approached by early stage founders who are looking for advising on one of a few areas: product, go-to market, product positioning, clarifying value proposition, hiring, etc. I've been very loud about exclusively hiring and building teams that are high performing. I ask everyone the same question: "What are you building?" Just that simple question reveals a lot. Some people will start with their origin story. Some people will recount their elevator pitch. But, then I ask "Why are you building it?" which is really the question I'm trying to get to. That tells me if they're in it because they really want to make a difference in their customer's lives—if it's really for others or if it's just for themselves. That is a very strong signal.

I'm likelier to invest in people driving diversity in clinical trials than the person who's building a cybersecurity company because they won a competition.

Read the entire interview at www.nathan.com/whole-new-strategy

Grant and donation funding for non-profits might not look for return on investment but will likely take a lot longer to secure. You will also likely need to document more than merely the financial return. Your social and ecological returns may be just as important as being able to show that the offering is viable financially.

Finance Strategy

Lastly, the offerings and capabilities you prioritize will require some form of financial plan. These are the tactics for your financial strategy. How will you fund your strategy? How much funding do you need? What are you offering in return (equity, debt, discounts, etc.)? Equity is stock, debt is a loan. When do you need the funds (in total or in installments)? You'll need answer to these questions in order to realize your strategy. What metrics (financial and otherwise) will you look to in determining success?

Your financial strategy will also include how you manage the funding during design, development, deployment, etc. You may need everything immediately so you may want to keep the money making money for you in a bank or investment. But, we're clearly getting out of the strategy area and into tactics. Your organization's goals should be the guiding principles for both financial strategy and tactics.

At this point, you have all of the elements required for your business plan: who your customers are, what value you plan to offer them (and in return for what), what your offerings are and how they differentiate you from your competitors, what capabilities you need to build to successfully bring them to market, what costs you expect and what revenues you expect. Some of these may be a departure from how you're currently doing business and that incurs risk—something many businesspeople abhor. To mitigate the risk some will feel, you'll need to plan how to communicate and manage the organization (and the implementation of this new strategy). That's what the following two chapters focus upon.

/Highlights
- Your financial strategy needs to support the market and operational decisions you've made. These will prioritize your operational costs and best revenue streams.
- Your greatest financial opportunities will be those that are projected to pay for and earn the most money or, at least, pay for themselves in revenue. However, there may be reasons why an organization would prioritize operational costs that aren't profitable, such as during periods of venture development, high growth, or activities that support other revenue-generating activities.
- Remember, money is not the only measure of each of your organization's activities or priorities, even with a for-profit, but if you're unable to raise enough revenue or investment to cover your costs, you won't be in business for long.
- There is no single best way to budget. Each approach will have its positives and negatives. Your approach will impact the culture you create for your organization.

/Explore More
- *Financial Intelligence* by Karen Berman, Joe Knight, & John Case
- *Fixing the Game* by Roger Martin

Chapter 8

Your Teams & Culture

Once you have a viable business plan that includes all of the elements you need to be successful, it's time to get your house in order. One of the most important "tactics" for an organization is how that organization organizes its people for action. Of course, you can always just do this like everyone else does but, then, you could just adopt their strategies, too, and be done with the entire process. That's not a great, differentiable way to succeed.

People are never easy to manage—especially over the long term. Over time, goals shift, focus drifts, and priorities change. The world outside the organization is also constantly changing. You need to understand the activities, responsibilities, and actions needed for your strategy to succeed so that you can arrange your organization and communicate these effectively. This way everyone can pull in the same direction.

The standard way to organize people is into divisions and teams based on what they do: operations, HR, manufacturing, product development, IT, finance, etc. or by geography, market segment, etc. There's nothing wrong with this and it's expected. It may even be best for you.

However, now is the time to consider what might be better. Ideally, if you have identified specific market segments, those may be the best way to organize the people who focus on them. There may still be some core competencies (like HR or billing) to be shared across the organization, but building independent, fully functional teams or divisions to research, develop, and deploy specific offerings may be a more effective way to enact your strategy.

For example, the people in your organization who understand your teen market are likely very different than those focused on senior citizens. While they may use similar processes and tools, everything about their constituents, markets, competitors, and messaging is different. Rather than centralizing all of these functions so that everyone is a generalist (along with your organization), the specialization may be more important to keep contiguous.

This also goes for culture and not merely job responsibilities. Salespeople are famous for working very differently than other businesspeople (like accountants). Their jobs often entail much more risk and, correspondingly, more rewards. Their process is often non-linear and even chaotic to some. It's very relationship-driven and not usually standardizable. That's a very different way to work than quality assurance personal, those on a factory line or even those in accounting. Not acknowledging these differences can be disastrous for an organization's effectiveness.

Designers, too, often have a different way of working. For many decades, non-designers would marvel at designers' spaces (lofts, reconfigurable desks, unstructured space, everything on wheels, so many Post-It notes!) but not recognize that elements of these spaces and ways of working might work for non-design roles, too. If a space can promote creativity effectively, it can just as easily deter it.

When Teague, Boeing's industrial design firm of record for nearly 100 years, moved offices at Boeing's Everett plant (the largest factory in the world), they took over warehouse space off at one end of the factory campus. It you teleported into the space, you would instantly recognize it as a design studio (and a nice one, at that) without any knowledge of what lays around it. However, walking into the building from the parking lot, you pass through a cavernous warehouse, passing huge Rolls-Royce jet engines, cabin and gallery assemblies, and parts of all kinds. When you get to the Teague design studio, you immediately enter another world. The contrast is striking—so striking that when Boeing employees (engineers, project managers, etc.) visit their colleagues at Teague, they wonder why they can't have such nice offices (they can, but their facilities people can't envision it, even within similar budgets). They return to their uninspired cubicles and meeting rooms feeling forgotten and unappreciated. It's not helpful for people being their best!

Design firms are often facile at reconfiguring teams, as needed, for different projects and clients. Multidisciplinary teams working toward the same goals is often most effective even if individual employees officially report to other managers. Ford Motor Company famously did this when they created the Ford Taurus in the 1990s and it practically saved the entire company. They formed one team to research, design, develop, and plan every aspect of the car, pulling in people from all parts of the company and process: marketing, manufacturing, delivery, engineering, design, service, etc.

Unfortunately, they seem to have promptly forgotten how to do this once the Taurus shipped—the US automobile industry has a history of promptly forgetting successful strategies in favor of "business as usual."

The idea of scrums in modern Agile development also focuses heavily on multidisciplinary teams. These teams may disband once the deliverable is finished, moving to form new teams around other projects.

In my old consultancy, *vivid* studios, we had parallel lines of management. We organized multidisciplinary teams around projects but we had contiguous internal teams of similar functions (engineering, experience, admin, strategy, client engagement, etc.). Any given person in vivid might be one a few project teams but also have a clear person they reported to in terms of administrative management (sick time, vacation, performance, etc.) and a corresponding team of like-minded and related coworkers with similar interests and concerns (engineering, experience, etc.). Then, we also had two parallel management structures: administrative and subject-matter. I was the chief creative officer for the company so questions of quality of experience, as well as professional development and culture in this were my responsibility. If there was ever a disagreement over some aspect of client work on the front-end that couldn't be effectively resolved, it escalated to me at the end and I would make the call. The same was true on the engineering side with our chief technology officer.

However, I had a manager within the Experience group, too—just like everybody else in the group. Administrative decisions (hiring, firing, skill development, vacation time, reporting, etc.) were handled by this administrative structure and I hired my own manager to run it.

While this may sound confusing, everyone was clear about which issues were whose responsibility and where to go for guidance, when needed. All of this has to be considered. And, it may need to be reconsidered periodically.

What's important is that you consider the different functions needed within your organization and what they require to be effective. The tactics of your strategic plan become the strategy for each of these levels. For example, if one of your prioritized capabilities is to develop expertise in machine learning technologies, then the hiring department needs to develop a strategy to source, hire, and manage this talent. This might not be a big change for a large organization with an existing engineering group, but what if there's not even an engineering group, yet? That requires a bigger plan.

Each of the functions in the organization need to be consulted in context of the strategy and asked to create strategies of their own, at their level, to implement it. As with the larger strategic model described in this book, one of the important things about this list is just that you consider each function before discounting it. Too much of failed strategy stems from forgetting about something important and never even considering it. So many strategies fail within organizations simply because no one creating the strategy ever consulted some important part of the organization for their expertise, experience, and insights.

Has Manufacturing been involved with the strategic decision to outsource manufacturing to a new partner or location? Has Research & Development? Or Legal? Maybe someone should consult these before the final decision is made because it will be costly, if not a disaster, to find out later that you've overstepped the law or destroyed customer value or have a time zone or quality issue.

However, this chapter isn't really about organizational structure. It's about organizational strategy and, to a larger extent, the culture you build within your organization. However, each of the divisions or categories above will, ultimately, need their own strategies to prioritize their initiatives and focus on what they can and should deliver within the overall organizational strategy. These are the details that realize the organization's strategy at every point of operation and delivery and every action.

Setting Teams Up for Success

Once you have a structure that works for you, and you have all of the bases covered—for now, there are some clear tactics that help teams perform better than average.

A **team charter** is set of semi-formal agreements, created by team members themselves, that describe the kind of team culture and values they wish to work within. This should list the goals of the team, the responsibilities of each team member (both to the project and their peers), the roles they will play, the ground rules for communication and interaction, what metrics or benchmarks constitute success, and what defines accountability. I know this sounds like a lot to cover but each section doesn't have to be onerous. Each could be just a few, clear sentences, as needed.

The point is for everyone to clearly understand their place in the team, what the team expects of them, and how to succeed. In addition, it helps teams recover from missteps and avoid misunderstandings that could lead to missed deadlines, unfulfilled tasks, and obstacles. A high-functioning team is resilient when obstacles appear. It quickly identifies challenges and moves to fix them while they're small.

The most common misfunction in a team is poor communication. These could be lack of clarity or a team hierarchy that is too rigid, or members misunderstanding who to raise concerns with. Often, business is rife with missing conversations: the discussions that could avert problems or fix them, whether these are between peers, managers and those managed, or strategy misaligned with tactics.

There are actually communication tools that consistently improve interactions between people. One is called Generative Communication but it's also known as Concise Communications, Conversations for Action, and a variety of other evolutions of what started as Neuro Linguistic Programming (NLP). My own version of this is an evolution of what learned at business school and it's based on a clear definition of common business terms in order to distinguish their essential meaning in a way that everyone can speak in a consistent way. It's not necessary for people to use these, specific terms (though the work has already been done to define them), but merely that everyone on the team, or in the organization, knows what they are and how they work.

For example, when someone agrees to do something, they don't equate it with a promise, which has a very personal connotation. Yet, that's exactly what they're doing. Understanding it in that context helps some people take it more seriously. My mentor, Bob Dunham, who I learned this from, told a story about his team at Ford Aerospace after instituting this tool. They went from being the worst preforming team in the company to the best, in under a year. They could hold five minute meetings (or less) by simply asking "Is anyone in danger of breaking any of their promises?" If the answer was "no." then everyone could go back to work as they all trusted the others to know the details of their commitments. If the answer was "yes," the knew the steps to discuss what and changed and how to react (counter offer, commit-to-commit, etc.).

This tool also helps identify when there is misunderstanding. For example, if you've ever heard someone exclaim "Someone should look into that." Ask yourself: who is looking into it? The answer is no one. "Someone" is no one. Knowing these definitions allows you to quickly notice when something is not going to happen, and why.

Another example is *trust*. So many businesspeople talk about it as something they want to build but have no idea how to go about it. What are the components? What do you say to build trust? These tools have a succinct definition: ***Trust is the result of Sincerity, Competence, Reliability, and Tolerance for Risk.*** There. Now you know. There is nothing to say to build trust other than what supports your actions because the first three of these components are about what you do, how well, and how reliably (the last component is more about the person you hope will trust you).

I particularly like the definition of Leadership: ***Leaders clearing declare a shared future to which others commit.*** There are details to each of these, for sure. However, that's more clarity than most books on leadership describe. These tools are like a precision communication format similar to the precision that financial tools bring to financial data. Humans aren't entirely quantitative, of course, so there is a little more at work here than merely publishing clear definitions and coming to agreements about them. But, this is a far more effective way to improve team communications and function than any other tool I've found.

"Culture Eats Strategy For Breakfast"

This is a famous quote from Peter Drucker, one of the fathers of strategy and it speaks to how important culture is but doesn't even begin to address how difficult it can be to manage. Every organization has it's declared rules and procedures… and then there's everything else. That's culture. Think of it as an organization's personality, or the sum of the state of mind of all of its employees.

Culture is the unwritten (and sometimes invisible) customs and styles of the people within it. When it's great, it's easy to maintain and when it's bad, it's notoriously difficult to fix. Little is unfixable but everything is unfixable if it's not identified and addressed. Therefore the most important part of culture is simply acknowledging it exists and understanding its reality (which is often not what leaders think it is).

And it effects everything: relationships within and without the organization; how challenges are approached, successes are celebrated, difficult or missing conversations are discussed; how it expresses itself, supports innovation, deals with change, rewards effort, and attracts talent.

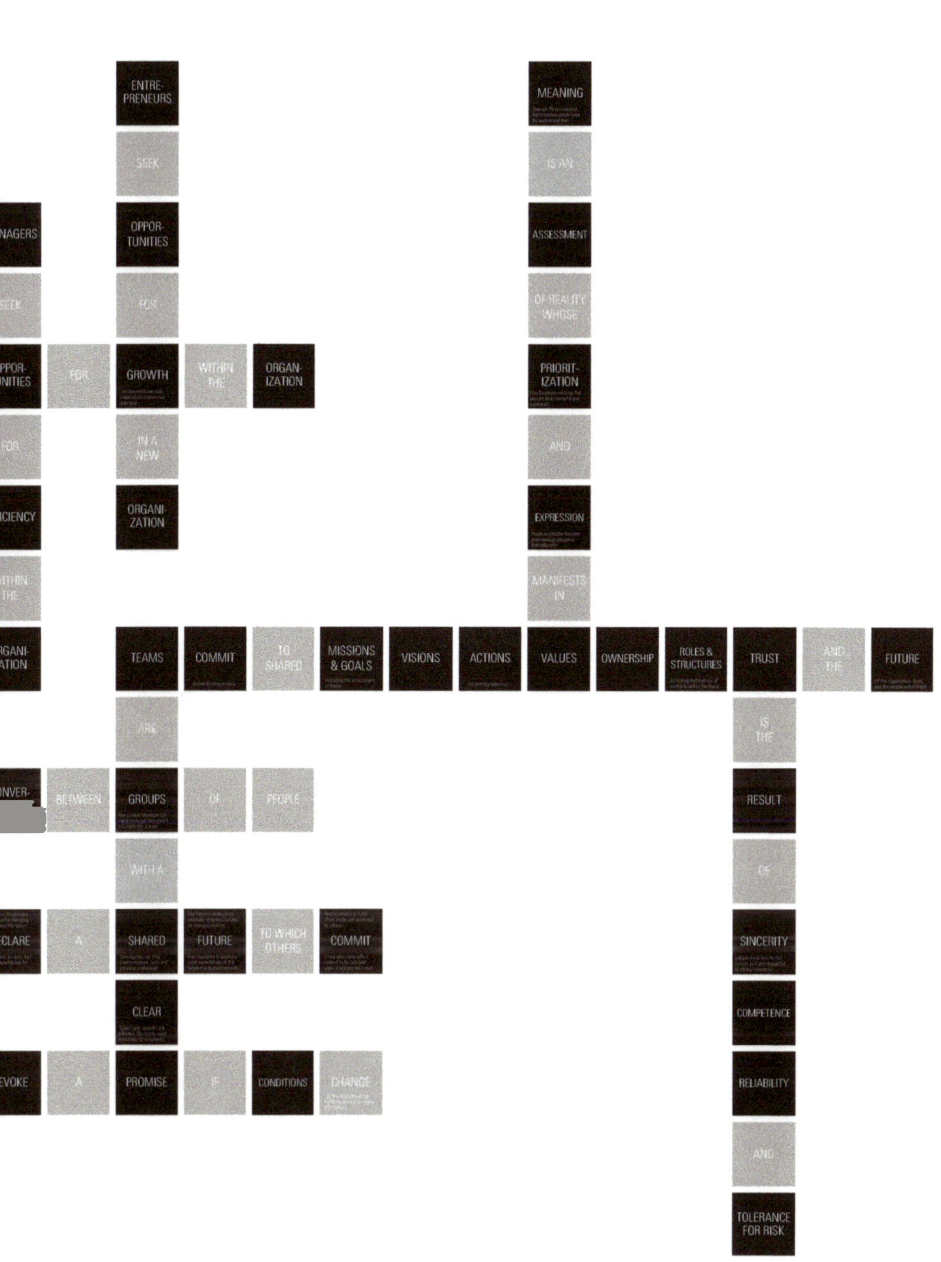

Strategically, culture is reinforced from the top of the organization even if it doesn't originate from there (culture happens everywhere). When leaders are engaged and considered, they can drive tremendous change by inspiring everyone to enact strategy where they are in an organization. Steve Jobs famously made sustainability a priority

within the company and made it clear it was his expectation for everyone to enact it wherever they were in Apple. The result was probably the most dramatic transformation of any global consumer company. Every aspect of the company thought deeply about reducing energy and material impacts. It resulted in a new design strategy that emphasized clean lines and lack of ornamentation and, along the way, reduced packaging, product design, eliminated toxic materials, improved energy efficiency, more seamless services, etc. Even something as simple as the power adapter that plugged into a power outlet was radically redesigned to be much smaller and more efficient than those of their competitors while eliminating vampire power and radically reducing toxic materials.

Steve Jobs didn't specific each of these changes. He likely oversaw and made choices about the options but he allowed his employees to enact the strategy wherever they were and find things he wouldn't have identified.

The Components of Culture

There are several ways to slice and dice culture. Some categories include: shared values, communication style, decision-making processes, workplace relationships (these extend to external ones as well as internal ones), and responsibilities. The challenge with most of these is in being honest about the culture. I've never found a company whose stated goals were to make the world a terrible place, be dishonest, be annoying, make it difficult to deal with them, or hurt people. Yet, too many companies do these things regardless. It's easy to list off the expected values, for example: honesty, integrity, collaboration, service, etc. but another thing entirely to make them so real that everyone inside the company would list those as their experience, when asked.

Likewise, it's easy to say "we have such a collaborative culture!" But, in my experience, those who jump to this when describing how they work are often the least collaborative people I've worked with. So, we need to delve more deeply to understand how to make culture successful.

My colleague, Josh Levine, has thought about and consulted upon culture for decades. He describes culture in seven parts:

Purpose: how we inspire employees and communities
Values: guardrails on our decisions and authority
Behaviors: our actions and (official and unofficial) processes (and their output)

Recognition (and Rewards): how we measure, reinforce, and reward behaviors
Rituals: how we build & strengthen relationships
Cues: how we keep people connected to our goals (digital and physical reminders)

Feedback: how we react to and address behaviors we don't want and reinforce those we do

This feels complete to me and a terrific list to focus upon. He emphasizes that there's really no such thing as a "good" or "bad" culture, just what's appropriate to any particular organization and the people within it. I'm not sure I agree and I'm sure he would admit that a culture that constantly demeans or threatens people isn't a good one. But, his point is that what works for some organizations doesn't necessarily work for others, and that's OK. His book, **Great Mondays**, describes culture in detail and how to develop, change, and manage it.

The same is true about other aspects of culture, like innovation culture: there is no single right way to innovate. Different companies have different approaches. Research from Cheskin outlined five different innovation cultures:

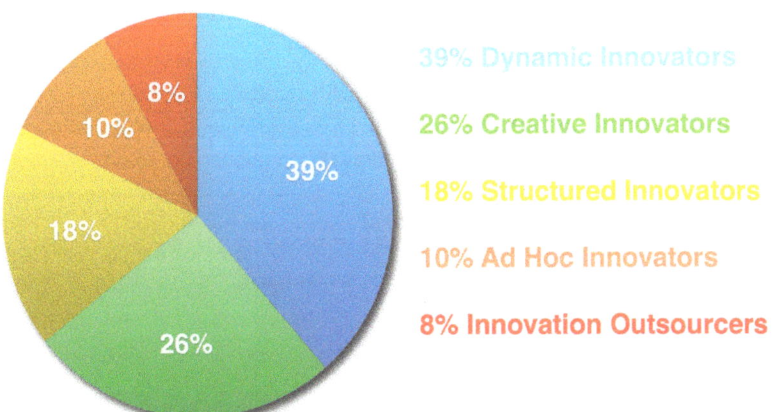

Some cultures integrate innovation throughout the organization and support at all levels. Others are simply unable to support innovation and their efforts nearly always yield nothing, for a variety of reasons: they evaluate success too early and decide to kill innovation projects, they only evaluate in terms of money, they don't support risk-taking or hire the right kind of leaders and managers who are comfortable with risk,

Nathan/ How do you define "culture" and how does it relate to strategy?

Josh/ Culture is the cause and effect of every decision you make or gets made in an organization. It's about choices, both those you make and those you enable everyone else in the organization to make. Strategically, you need to create a structure and framework for the right culture to take root and grow.

Why is it so difficult, in practice?

It's mostly due to lack of alignment between the organization's goals and values and those of the people in that organization. Everyone in the organization needs to be not only be aligned but understand the intent of the organization and where they fit into it, as well as how they contribute to it. The more people there are, the more difficult that gets.

Few organizations ever have a unifying theory of culture because they don't even know they should have one. And, just because you don't specify, create, and grow one, doesn't mean one doesn't exist—it means it's there without any consideration. In that case, which is most companies, the culture isn't a healthy one. It's not conscious, tended to, or watched so people are usually left to competing interests. ***Culture isn't usually even recognized as a business tool*** but some sort of other thing that, sometimes, some people pay attention to. But, there's always a culture there, regardless.

Then, even if leaders recognize the need for a considered culture, few have experience building one consciously. It's usually not a responsibility in anyone's job description. When it is, it usually falls to HR, where it's sometimes treated as a set of trainings and rules, not a living, evolving, pervasive, and embodied thing. If all of the leadership isn't part of the process, it's not likely that any culture is going to be cohesive throughout the organization, nor tied to anyone's responsibilities.

The culture is the sum total of all of the actions within the organization. It's lived every moment by everyone in the company whenever they do something.

How do you help businesspeople manage the qualitative aspects of measuring culture?

You have to measure both quantitatively and qualitatively. The latter is easier than the former, as you know. But, both are critical. The quantitative aspects you can get from surveys, pulse checks, and reports of the various business activities—actions —within the organization. That's fairly straight forward (though not always done well). That tells you a lot about what's happening in the organization, and, to some extent, who is feeling what.

However, you need to be more indirect to get to the real why behind people's actions. It's difficult to see all of the choices people make—all of the behaviors. Without the qual, you don't really see how everyone understands the company, and whether what they are trying to achieve lines-up with what you're trying to achieve.

Ultimately, it all comes down to prioritization. What do you want to prioritize and how are you going to communicate that so that other people will act on that same prioritization. That's what makes it strategic and why it has to absolutely needs to tie to the organization's strategy.

Where does culture live?

It has to live everywhere and it has to be aligned to everything but it also has to be driven from the top. Growing a great culture is nearly impossible if leaders aren't on board. If different business units are building different cultures, it's going to be a mess—and likely unsuccessful. And, leaders may not even realize this is the case, especially in really large organizations. Even now that business changes a lot faster than it used to, the same basic ideas still apply.

What are the components of culture then?

There are six components to the framework I created, plus one. ***Purpose*** defines how you inspire your employees and communities—even those outside the organization. Then, there are ***Values***. These are the guardrails of your actions. What actions are in-bounds and which are out-of-bounds? Third, are the ***Behaviors*** of your organization: these are the actions, themselves. How are you going to achieve you goals? What are your employees actually doing—and allowed to do? How will they do these best?

Perhaps, one of the most important, one that lots of leaders miss, is ***Recognition:*** How do you reward the right behaviors? It's one thing to say you want everyone to do "the right thing," but if you never define what that is and then you never actually reward it, you can't expect people to act that way. Worse, is when the organization says one thing but rewards the opposite. Sometimes, this is people being promoted, given bonuses, given new titles or raises, even just being called-out in a company meeting for some kind of success but at the expense of the stated values of the company.

The fifth component is ***Rituals:*** How do you build and strengthen the many relationships within and outside the organization. This needs to be deliberate and not accidental (as it so often is). Rituals are the synapses of culture and they're difficult to create and enact when people aren't together. This has gotten more difficult with so many people working remotely, now. It's not easy to develop true trust when you don't have a lot of experience working with people.

The last component is ***Cues:*** How so we keep people connected to our goals? What are the digital and physical reminders of everything above?

Read the entire interview at www.nathan.com/whole-new-strategy

they're afraid of cannibalizing their current businesses and sources of revenue, etc. Many companies are only capable of innovating by purchasing innovations from others, either through consulting or acquisitions.

Jeanne Liedtka and Robert Rosen showed in their book, ***The Catalyst,*** how successful intrapreneurs were most often successful by doing things within their organizations that could get them fired. Because too many organizations' cultures are so rigid and focused on financial performance, they don't allow new, innovative initiatives to thrive if they need time to grow into a successful business unit or might cannibalize their existing business at the start. They found that successful innovators within existing organizations often hid budgets, work, headcount, etc. and didn't stop working on projects after they were cancelled were common tactics that led to success in many organizations. These companies are usually the bottom three categories above.

Like Josh Levin's observation about culture, neither generating nor purchasing innovation is inherently "good" or "bad." What is bad, however, is not understanding which innovation culture your organization is imbued with, which will waste your time (and everyone else's). This is especially true of leaders who believe that their culture is one thing when it's something else entirely.

Strategic leaders need to perform the same kind of "customer" research within their organization as they do outside. You should know the decision-drivers of your employees as well as you do your customers and use that information in the same way. It will become the basis of setting your internal cultural strategy (which includes everything to do with human resources and people management): hiring, firing, promotions, assessments, incentives, rewards, communication, etc.

Changing an organization's culture is a book (or more) unto itself. There's not enough time in this chapter to describe everything involved—Josh's book is a great place to start. However, you should recognize that change only happens where people are incentivized to interact with each other differently—hopefully better. And, those incentives may need to be individualized to employees—particularly for your most talented and key employees. This can be a difficult juggling act. Different people have different needs in their lives and respond to different incentives and types of compensation, but you can't always give something to one person that you don't make available to others. If you have an open, humane culture, your employees should be able to understand this reality, particularly if they're extended the same opportunities to have incentives that work best for them. However, the typical (and easiest) approach is that everything needs to be fair and, therefore, everyone should get the same thing. This idea of parity is often misplaced and leads to a nit-picking culture where everyone scrambles to scrutinize what everyone else does and gets, breaking trust and creating suspicion that will, ultimately, take over the culture. Fair is still a goal but in the context of what works for individuals.

Operational Strategy

Every function within an organization (including those not yet in existence but are nonetheless required) should impact the strategy while it's under development and each needs to develop its own corresponding strategy once it's set. What's critical is that these activities are related and not decoupled. If the divisional strategies aren't in service of the overall organizational strategy, you're off target (and you would be amazed how often this is the case). A sales strategy that isn't using related messaging for the offerings being prepared is going to be selling the wrong thing. Incentives for specific performance that doesn't achieve the goals of the strategy is, obviously, a recipe for disaster. Simply coordinating the communications and plans among these teams is half the battle for success.

Your operational strategy will include those plans, actions, and metrics for everything under it: manufacturing, development, research, deployment, customer support, finances, HR, facilities, IT, etc.

Specifically, the team and employment strategy will need to include those elements for identifying needs and matching them to people who are responsible for them. It includes planning for growth, hiring, managing people assessing performance, and consciously managing the culture. As with every other element of an organization, this must be someone's responsibility or it won't happen.

/Highlights
- How you organize your teams of employees impacts how they work together, as well as the culture you create and support for your organization.
- There are best practices for organizing teams.
- Culture is the result of seven categories: purpose, values, behaviors, recognition, rituals, cues, and feedback.

/Explore More
- *Great Mondays* by Josh Levine
- *The Catalyst* Jeanne Liedtka, Robert H. Rosen, and Robert Wiltbank
- *Rise of the DEO* Maria Giudice & Christopher Ireland
- *Changemakers* Maria Giudice & Christopher Ireland
- *The Team That Managed Itself* by Christina Wodtke
- *Innovation Culture video:* www.youtube.com/watch?v=HqTUThYBm7U
- *Innovation Culture article:* www.nathan.com/tool-innovation-cultures/
- *Generative Communication workshops* by Bob Dunham generateleadership.com
- *Conversations for Action & Collected Essays* Fernando Flores & Maria Flores Letelier
- *Powers to Lead* by Joseph S. Nye
- *Difficult Conversations* by Douglas Stone, Bruce Patton, Sheila Heen, & Roger Fisher
- *A General Theory of Love* by Dr. Thomas Lewis
- *The Power of a Positive No* by William Ury
- *Concise Communications* by Nathan Shedroff (2024)

Chapter 9

Your Messaging

Congratulations! You've just completed your strategy! It's not that there isn't more to this book or more you can explore, but you've completed both the Market sequence and the Operations sequence and that is the complete path through strategy. You should now have a great, detailed understanding of what drives your customer decisions as well as your best opportunities to offer them products, services, and other experiences of value. In addition to these offerings, you also should have an in-depth understanding of what it will take to deliver those offerings and what resources and partnerships should help you. Above all, you should have a focus on your goals and priorities.

The rest of the parts of strategy (and book) are enhancements to strategy—important ones. But, you've completed the basic process.

What enhancements are there? There is a greater understanding of the context for your customers, competitors, industry, and organization. There is the consideration of various trends that impact your business and those around you. There are various stakeholders you can understand on a better, deeper level. And, there is an understanding of the future and what forces it applies to your business.

All of these are important but you should think of them as modifying the rankings of your decisions within the Market and Operations sequences: the core of strategy. One of the most important is how you communicate your strategy and to whom. The best strategy in the world won't be effective if the people required to enact it don't understand it. You would be surprised how often an organization's leaders spend time, effort, and money on devising a great strategy… and then only tell the top people in the organization about its details. Too often, the rest of the organization, all the way out to those who directly build relationships with customers, constituents, and partners, are never included in the grand plan—or any of its details.

Yes, you need a strategy to communicate your strategy. This is true externally, to your customers, competitors, industry, and market but more essential internally: to your employees and partners. When planning your communications, you should take another look at your stakeholders—particularly, your key ones. How does the message need to be modified for each of these stakeholders? How does it interest and motivate your various partners? Does it need to soothe some and excite others? What parts of your strategy need to be confidential at different levels? You don't need to tell everyone in your organization every part of your strategy but all will need to know the parts they're expected to act upon. Plus, there may be influences they have on even parts of the strategy you don't expect! So, don't be stingy about sharing.

At the very least, your messaging needs to be clear! There should be no confusion on anyone's part what the priorities are. Jan Carlzon was famous for turning around SAS, the airline of Scandinavia, in the 1980s. His communication of the company's new strategy was simple and clear:

1. Safety! No plane takes off if there is any safety issue.
2. On-time! If the plane and passengers are safe, nothing else should interfere with the plane being on schedule.
3. Comfort! The customer experience should be exemplary—but not at the cost of the first two priorities. This means that if not everyone gets a meal or has their favorite drink, the airline will determine how to compensate passengers for that later.

With this strategy, Jan Carlzon turned SAS around financially and made it Europe's top business airline. It catered to what business travelers needed most: to get where they wanted to on-time, even at the expense of vacation travelers (who aren't, typically, the most lucrative customers anyway). Regardless, he not only ensured that the message was simple, clear, and communicated to every employee regardless of position, he followed it up by empowering customer-facing employees to make decisions, as needed. As long as they were following these three priorities, they didn't need to check with managers (or managers' managers) every time something unusual or unexpected happened. So many leaders extol their desire to have customer-facing employees do this but never actually give them the authority to do so.

Your messaging needs to consider who the various audiences are (internally and externally), how they will be reached, and who is responsible for the messaging to be delivered:

Key Messages	(what you want your various stakeholders and segments to understand about the organization and is new activities, priorities, foci, and offerings)
Target Audiences	(who those messages need to reach (and how the messages differ, as needed)
Channels	(how those messages reach others: newsletters, social media, internal memos, email, press-releases, interviews, etc.) and in which geographies
Timing	(before, during, and after key actions, new offerings, changes in policy, etc.)
Feedback	(how you will hear back from your stakeholders and any metrics you'll use to evaluate success)

Tech companies (and others) have implemented OKRs (Objectives and Key Results) and KPIs (Key Performance Indicators) in the past two decades as a way of implementing clear instructions, accountability, goals, and metrics. I applaud the clarity but have seen these tactics fail often because the OKRs and KPIs don't cover everything desired from a person or team. In particular, there are often either hidden, unspoken OKRs and KPIs (like personal conduct, team values, etc. that set parameters within which the work gets done),or ignore any objective or result that is qualitative instead of quantitative. Often, this tool is used as just another quantitative metric to make management simpler but performance, value, and customer experience worse. Simply having OKRs and KPIs doesn't fix many business challenges. Likewise, simply issuing them and checking in frequently (important though it is) doesn't bring success if the OKRs are the wrong tactics or don't align with strategy. Great management isn't that easy. If the OKR or KPI doesn't connect directly to the organization's goals, value proposition, and strategy, it's likely a distraction that will not only measure the wrong performance but one that will direct the organization away from its strategy.

In addition, ***communications are always omni-directional.*** Not only are they two-way (from leaders to front-line and back), communications run across organizations and throughout your ecosystem in many ways—some often unexpected or unintended.

/Teens in Sports

Back near the start of the Web, I had the opportunity to work for one of the biggest sports equipment and clothing companies in the world. We were their Internet "partner of record" and developed several online experiences for their customers via the website, as well as their specific strategy at the time. This was a very different time, long before social media, commerce platforms, SaaS platforms, etc.

Our strategy was to counter their big messaging in television, print, and outdoor (billboards) where they could have big, exciting, brash, and short messages (what the traditional media excelled at) with more personal, quiet, and meaningful interactions online (what the Web and other digital media excelled at). The company could do things online that it could never do in previous media: in particular, listen to their customers' stories, ideas, and desires. The Web was the first global medium (channel) that allows companies to hear from their customers in deep ways (as opposed to customer feedback surveys).

I remember sitting in a meeting of their global marketing council with all of the heads of various marketing touchpoints around the world (all regions, all channels, including those in charge of working directly with sponsored athletes). I and the global head of marketing were trying to explain the purpose of this direction and the opportunities allowed, particularly for hearing from their most staunch customers: those between 15-21 years of age. Note that these are usually the customers that drive style and sales for many mega-popular brands. One of the council's members at this level replied indignantly "what the Hell do I care what a 15-year-old wants to say to me?" That pretty-much summed up the inexperience and misunderstanding of this new medium.

Of course, from the 21st century, we clearly see the impact two-way (and more) communications channels have in giving critical and even inspiring feedback to any organization. Back in the late 90s, too many traditional businesspeople couldn't see just that. Sadly, that attitude permeated much of the global marketing organization.

If parts of the messaging are confidential and not to be shared with others, that too needs to be clear, but consider this only in the most extreme situations. They more your teams and people know what the organization is trying to accomplish, the more they'll be able to use their skills, experience, and opportunity to make that so.

Your internal and external messaging also needs to relate to each other. Often this is called being on-brand. This doesn't mean that you have to share everything externally that you do internally nor that it needs to be shared in the same way. However, there needs to be a relationship between the two—they can't contradict each other or you're going to confuse your stakeholders. The best technique to test this is simply to share your messaging with key representatives of different stakeholders—especially employees—while they're being developed. We've all seen the disasters different organizations have created with new messages, logos, or other aspects of their expression that fell flat, failed to have the intended impact, or even created ridicule.

Your messaging needs to match your brand attributes, which need to also match your organization's values and mission. All of these are interrelated and need to work together—internally and externally.

Actions speak louder than words

Remember, that no matter how carefully crafted and poignant your messages, if they're just words and aren't reflected in the organization's actions (and the actions of its employees), they're merely empty promises. Often, it's better to say nothing at all than to make grand statements about the future and then leave your stakeholders disappointed in reality.

Your messaging needs to clearly describe a vision toward something your customers desire (hopefully reinforcing those decision-drivers). What's the path to reaching their goals and how are you going to help them get there? What are you asking them to run toward? How will they know when they arrive? Why should they trust you to help them?

One of the ways to accomplish this is to identify reinforcing statements: those messages that help various stakeholders "see themselves" in the messages of your organization. It can be as simple as "we're just like you" or "you're the kind of person who…" as long as its authentic.

How will you measure the effectiveness of these messages in terms of awareness and, more importantly, action? How will you know which messages resonated with which audiences (and which weren't)?

- There are a several kinds of messages (both internal and external). However, all should communicate the value your offer to your various stakeholders.
- Internal messaging is a vital part of your culture and speaks to (and reinforces) the values, behaviors, and responsibilities you want to inhabit. It does now, however, take the place of internal actions and behavior.
- External messaging might be directed to your customers, competitors, industry, or partners and should clearly reinforce the value you provide through your offerings, partnerships, etc.
- External messaging includes advertising and public relations, regardless of medium.

/Explore More
- *Moments of Truth* by Jan Carlzon

The World Around You

In Chapter 1: Your Customers, we discussed how organizations need to be more focused on their customers than themselves—an all-too-familiar issue in many organizations. Similarly, too much of strategy is focused on the company and too little on the outside world.

There are only so many things any organization can do to control their circumstances. It's difficult enough to devise, implement, and manage a strategy at all. Adding the forces outside the company makes this a truly difficult feat. But, by better understanding the world around us, we can better prepare for the things we cannot control—which is most things in a market, industry, or society.

The Market and Operations sequences are the core of strategy. If those are all you do, you'll be doing better strategy than most. Trends and stakeholder analysis identify issues that may not surface in these two sequences and allow organizations to better respond to even more variables. While this is supplemental, it's also important as it can identify weaknesses that can blind-side an organization.

This is, essentially, *systems thinking.* Your organization lives within a complex ecosystem and the more you understand that ecosystem, the more you can address in your strategy. Sometimes, simply mapping the system at all provides immediate insight into new opportunities—or threats. But, the more you delve into your stakeholder ecosystem and the trends that flow around you, the more nuanced your perspective, the stronger your potential partners, and the more prepared you are.

Chapter 10

Trends & Stakeholders

It's one thing to have a good understanding of your customers, competitors, and the market they represent. However, there are other factors that impact your strategy and performance. The world around you is rife with change and noise. Consider how much news and other information you hear about every moment of every day: politics, society, the economy, the environment, the latest and greatest somethings that don't have anything to do with your company, your market, your industry, your customers, etc. A successful strategy needs to take some of these into account—but which?

This is where strategy can grow complex. There are so many things to consider and it's impossible to know or investigate them all, plus not all of them are relevant anyway. In addition, some will impact the market (and your customers) more and others will impact your operations (like the supply chain, your partners, or your employees). So, here is a way to keep them straight, explore them quickly, and integrate them where they most impact your business.

Trends

Let's start with the categories of trends: Nature (the literal environment), Society, the Economy (which is a part of society but a special part), the Legal/Regulatory System, your Industry (because different ones have different trends), and Technology (because the advance of technology creates special pressures and opportunities). That's only six categories so these shouldn't be too taxing to explore.

In each category, you need to ask "what are the most important trends." You might find this from your ongoing customer research, from trend reports and other news, or from talking to experts outside (and, sometimes, inside) your company. Your job, here, isn't to identify every possible trend but those that have the most impact on your business. There is no light that goes on when you have them all—or even the most important ones. But you'll certainly know when you miss one later as you assess your performance in the market or within your operations. If you get side-swiped by a competitor's new offering, a collapse or rise in prices, a new regulation, or even a hurricane, you've likely missed a trend or two. Let's explore them more deeply.

Nature

Whether you believe in climate change or not (and you really should), there is scientific evidence that the planet is getting hotter and the weather is getting more extreme. This might mean that your operations need to prepare for difficult or disrupted supply chain management, higher energy prices (like for air conditioning in the summer), disruptions in natural resources (like certain crops), or more flooding in low-lying areas.

Are your warehouses in places that will get flooded? What about your data centers? Are your offices or other facilities at risk from storms, tornados, floods, or tsunamis?

Additionally, the effects of climate and weather are but one type of Nature's impact. Pandemics erupt from Nature and, in the case of COVID-19, have completely transformed work, school, and society in countless ways. Was your strategy prepared for these impacts? Is it prepared for the next one? The one after that? COVID-19 changed everything, with some companies winning big and many others losing even more. Imagine if your strategy had identified this possibility and had contingencies on-hand and ready just in case. Your agility and resilience, your ability to change, and your responses would have put you in a better position to succeed than if it had never occurred to you as a possibility.

Are your customers concerned about the environment, whether it's the climate or the fate of pandas, harp seals, or dolphins? Are they concerned with threats to endangered species or even access to drinkable water for themselves? What are your customers and partners hearing in the news or from their neighbors that weigh on their mind (and drive their decisions)? Some of these are things that impact your business, so your first step is to identify them.

Society

Society is always in flux. Some of these changes are trends that will flow for some time, others are fads that won't last long at all. Depending on you're the time horizon for your strategy, you'll need to differentiate the two in real time. If you're in a fad-driven industry (like toys, fashion, or teen anything), you may need to research, plan, and implement much more quickly. But, there's no metric to say whether a change or evolution in culture or society is going to last or not. We can hope about some (like recognizing injustice or teaching more critical thinking skills) but there are no guarantees and you're going to have to assess these changes yourself.

Someday (soon), when strategy is more easily manageable, it may be realistic to perform, implement, and evaluate in near-real time. Let's call that Continuous Strategy. Until, then, it will always be a judgment call.

The worst approach, however, is to ignore societal trends altogether. They can sideswipe your business more than any other kind, because economic, industrial, and policy trends usually have early indicators, as most of them don't change overnight. Even Natural and technological trends show precursors, but, societal ones can seem to come out of nowhere.

Consider the mobile phone industry in the mid-1990s. While the industry was focused on antenna frequencies, bandwidth, protocols, phone plans and rates, and trying to lower the price of phones, what temporarily destroyed sales were none of these. Instead, worries of brain cancer from antenna radiation swept industrialized countries and these worries depressed sales for a few years. The mobile industry was caught completely off-guard and had no response prepared. Had they been watching people and talking to potential* customers about buying decisions—decision-drivers—they might have foreseen at least the possibility, and prepared a strategy to respond more quickly and effectively than they did—or even nip it in the bud. Those fears are beginning to rise again, with new research. Will mobile phone companies get caught again in the same predicament?

Even today, it's still inconclusive whether or not this concern was warranted at the time (and the technology has changed drastically since). But what was the most significant trend to impact that industry for these years? It wasn't technological, economic, or policy; it was societal.

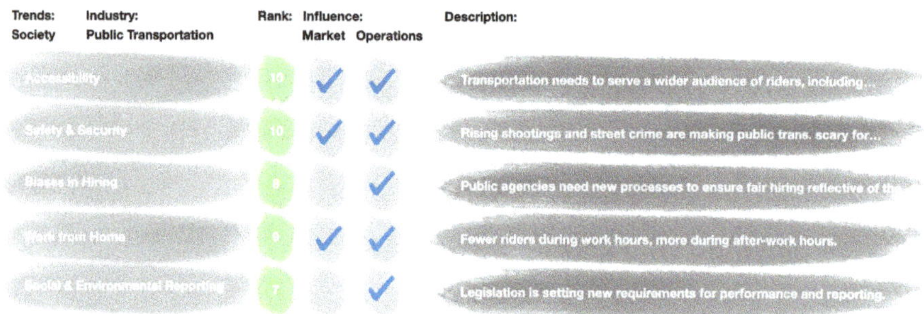

And, it's just as possible today as it was before that Societal trends can sometimes be the most important ones to follow.

So, just like with Economic trends, you need to be close to customers and markets and look for the changes that seem significant, especially if they touch or change decision-drivers. When you start a strategic process, you need to list, rate, and integrate them into the Market sequence alongside everything else you identified about customers, how competitors compete, and how they help shape your best opportunities. Many of these will impact the Market sequence but some may also impact the Operations sequence. If so, you should integrate them into both.

Economy

We all know how the economy impacts people's buying decisions. If you recall Rick's story in the introduction, however, you also know how these impacts can be overstated (compared to other factors). Some economic trends impact buying decisions (and, therefore, the Market sequence) while others impact costs within your organizations (the Operations sequence). If so, separate these accordingly.

Economic trends are often easier to watch, partly because they're quantitative so they're easier to measure* but mostly because most of the business world is so hyper-focused on them. Market reports and data abound, nearly everywhere you look. However, don't think that these always tell the entire story or capture all of the trends

*Talking to current customers, by the way, would not have likely uncovered these concerns among buyers. Most current customers would have already "bought into" their phones, whether it was the convenience, necessity, or even status these phones afforded them. Current customers were the least likely to express these concerns.

at work. It is likely that you'll need to supplement what you easily find from the typical sources with your own on-the-ground research, either as part of your customer research or alongside it. Remember, you're looking at this process a little differently and more holistically. You will see things others don't and ask questions that never come to mind for many industry experts. That's a feature, not a bug. Don't ignore your intuition but verify with actual data.

Policy

These days, you can get whiplash following the legal system, as well as governmental legislation. Sadly, it feels like everything is politicized and that the assumptions made about how laws work and, more importantly, how they're implemented, make little sense. This seeming chaos means that you can't always rely on the assumptions about your market, industry, or surroundings as much as you think.

For example, the classification of drivers for Uber and Lyft was such a fundamental assumption and part of their business model that when government regulators started talking about classifying them as employees instead of independent contractors, both companies (and a few others) leapt into action to stop these moves. The entire business model for these companies was already dubious* but this would have radically changed everything about their companies, potentially so much as to put them out of business.

Suffice it to say that there is a world of laws and regulations that pertain to your business (and your customers) that you should keep on top of, as well. As with the others, these need to be integrated into the factors your consider in your strategy, both in the Market and Operations sequences though, for this category, more likely in the latter.

Industry

Every industry has its separate issues and impacts. Some may bleed into others but most are specific and unique to an industry, at least once you focus to the most important. How do you uncover these? Well, if you're already in business or if your business has been around for a while, just like with the economic trends, there are many sources of industry trend data, predictions, and analysis. You can start with industry associations and their associated journals and conferences. There are myriad publications that cover most industries, whether independent or tied to associations or research firms. There are often reporters and journalists who focus on particular industries as well, depending on their size and how common they are (think about healthcare or digital services sections in some business newspapers). For other industries that are fast-moving or poorly covered, you may need to turn to consultants and other experts to tell you (for a price, usually) what they see and why.

However, you uncover these trends, as with the others, it's critical that you consult outside sources. People inside your company are experts mostly in that company and then their expertise starts dissipating the further away from that company that the

* https://americanaffairsjournal.org/2019/05/ubers-path-of-destruction
  www.economist.com/business/2019/04/27/can-uber-ever-make-money

Nathan/ You work with corporate clients, nonprofits, and especially government agencies. How do you talk about foresight in the context of strategy?

Jake/ So much of foresight work is pre-strategic. There are always subtleties in different organizations, but this work is more about shifting mindsets. Sometimes, you need to use the strategy hammer to pry open minds, address culture, worldview, and ideology. Strategy often gets signatures on a contract, but if the will or mindset isn't there, the project may be doomed to failure. People have a lot of the biases and in the short-term many are only looking at a narrow band of things that are really just planning.

People usually have a narrow view of alternative futures and possibilities. And, the usual focus on business in in the near-term, so we need to stretch their timeframes—at least 5-10 years out. When you truly look at the long-term, there are so many more plausible opportunities but that needs to nest in a framework that makes sense. That's what strategy foresight is. Sometimes, this work feels slippery, especially the further out you looks. But, the tools are much the same as strategy, just with that longer perspective. You still need to look at trends and forces, stakeholders and other actors in the ecology. We have tools to look forward that far and then point you in the right direction. Strategy often opens-up that process and gives permission to ask these longer-term questions.

How do you go about finding trends and signals and then identifying which are important?

These days, finding trends is not hard, from government reports to boutique firms, we can get them from many places. We know the demographics that are heading our way. We have data that backs it up. These big trends are sometimes called drivers or mega trends. I tell my clients, don't spend all your time on that. It's just your baseline. Now, looking for the signals of change, like weak signals (sometimes called emerging issues), maybe completing a horizon scan, those are more difficult to make sense of because they are so early stage.

We don't know whether this protest movement is going to blow up into something big. We don't know if this new patent will be transformative to our lives, but we're looking for those things. There's a lot of noise out there and, for futurists, it's a habit to look to our digital streams and consult early adopters, to find where the edges are, where the weirdos are, where the fringe is. That could be in technology, politics, society, art, etc. We're always keeping our eyes out for those signals. They are, now, a lot of automated tools that give me a list of the latest things going on out there. But, I've been around long enough to know that the human intelligence, sense-making, and interpretation is still critical. That can't be automated much. Of course, we have tools, techniques, and templates that really help us structure our thinking systematically to make sure that we're looking carefully at each issue. And, there is also a space for creativity and speculative leaps, It's a mix of rigorous, systematic thought and intuition.

How do you help people differentiate signals from noise and then evaluate which signals are worth attending to?

Because the present is so noisy, it's usually easier to see 10 years out. The tools we use have an effect, too. Each tool or cognitive partner creates a different mental ecology. Thinking with a computer produces different results than with paper and pencil. Now, with AI, it's different once again. Part of this is technical, yes, but part of it is aesthetic and cultural, and nobody wanted to be talking to somebody. It's not a coincidence that a lot of us come out of social science and anthropology. We try to be holistic and look at the layers of shifting dynamics. When a new force or technology enters the system we look to how that may change the dynamics, looking at that. It's important to discern the forces behind something from the surface effects we see, the phenotype versus the genotype. Pokémon Go was a huge deal many years ago but it isn't top-of-mind, now, even though there are still thousands and thousands still playing. So, what can this speak to, currently, about augmented reality or location-based gaming? What's happening at the deeper levels and is it something that still deserves attention?

It sounds like you could almost simplify this into a question: "Okay, this thing exists. You've found the signal. Now, can you imagine that signal in 5 years, 10 years, 15 years, or 20 years?" If you can, than it's likely an influential or important signal.

Yes, and what do people going to use it for? Thinking about real use cases, consider all of the hand waving around blockchain and its importance. You need to listen to your gut. While some of the blockchain uses look important and stable, NFTs (Non-Fungible Tokens) felt like bullshit from the start. Can you imagine them in 20 years and, if so, what do they look like? Now, consider AR/VR/XR googles: Are people really sitting in rooms with these things strapped to their face in 20 years? You can use your knowledge about human behavior and economic power. How does it impact the system and how does the system react? You have to question your assumptions, but you also need to play-out the possibilities, then choose the ones that feel more likely. But, it's all systemic.

Most people look for trends but few ever consider all of the stakeholders, so, they miss things. How do you help clients identify their ecosystem, who's in it, and then who they need to pay attention to versus maybe who's not really consequential to them?

And, these days, everything is everywhere. There are few industries that aren't impacted. You're a car company, well, you're actually a mobile computer company. You're also part of a public safety community. We need to expand the aperture of what an ecology or system means and who stakeholders are. A you a credit union? Well, guess what? Amazon is your competitor, as is Apple. And, these are all moving targets. We're used to thinking only of people as the agents of change but when we look at the whole inventory of actors in the system, the interaction with environment matters and, then, new things emerge that interact for X amount of time. You may be seeing things that are close to happening now, but they're really part of a much bigger cycle that you need to take a step back and consider.

Read the entire interview at www.nathan.com/whole-new-strategy

questions get. It's easy for even experienced professionals to miss important trends because we simply cannot see, understand, and express everything. And, as in everything else, often the staunchest experts are the ones with the biggest blind spot(s).

Nearly all trends in your industry will apply to the Operations sequence. It's not uncommon for them to only apply to the Operations sequence, in fact. Don't worry if this is the case. It's because most customers have little connection to the industry's inner workings of the industry—and rightly so.

Technology

I'm sure few readers these days would think that technological developments can't impact their strategy. Many assume that their strategies already take into account technological change. And yet it's not uncommon for an established industry to be just as sideswiped by a startup bringing a new technology to market they had discounted didn't foresee.

I remember consulting for a large publishing company in Australia having been brought in to redesign their classified advertising to increase relevance and, ultimately, revenue. It was a fun project and thought it was focused on their print ads, my report implored them to look at the Internet (this was 1996). Evolving their print ads was a smart strategy (albeit one they ultimately did nothing about) but it was imperative that they move into online ads. It wasn't because I was brilliant but I lived in San Francisco, which was 5-10 years into the future versus much of the rest of the world at that time. I mean, Craigslist was already eating away at classified ads in the USA. Yet none of these managers cared about the Internet, or digital technologies, at all. While they would be the first to say that technology was important to their business, they meant printing technology. So, in this case, they might have identified and considered technology trends, rated them accurately but still completely missed the technologies that were going to eat their lunches and destroy their ad revenue.

It's not always easy to separate technology fads from true trends. How many of your friends and colleagues (if you were of age in 2013) said that Google Glass was the future and we would all be walking around with AR (augmented reality) glasses in just a few years? Nearly ten years later, we're still waiting for this to be the case and the industry still hasn't found a "killer app" to compel regular people to do so. Oh, it's always on the horizon (sort of like "true" AI) but it never seems to get here. Even today, with the Billions spent on VR/AR/XR goggles, plus all of the advertising and promotion, it's still a maybe technology. We see it over and over in tech industries: hype about this or that thing. As of this writing, it's AI (which isn't really artificial intelligence at all), AR, crypto everything, and—shockingly—still flying cars.

Let me state this unequivocally, you will never have a personal flying car, regardless of the technological feasibility because it is not a technological problem. Largely, it's an economic one (but that's not even the big obstacle). Instead, it is an issue of product experience (for everyone but the flyer) that will keep them banned from nearly every community: the noise. Sure, in science fiction films, they're silent (or maybe there is a slight whir) but, in reality, they are really loud. Think about how noisy drones are already and then magnify that a hundredfold. That is why you won't have a flying car. Every community will ban them nearly immediately as a nuisance (as many have already done with drones) and the wealthiest communities will do so first! So, choose your technological trends carefully and plan your strategies wisely.

Once you have identified your technology trends, rate the most important and focus on them. These, too, will likely apply only to the Operations sequence but, sometimes, they impact customer buying decisions— particularly for "early adopters" who look for the "latest and greatest" when they buy things. Be careful here, however. Early adopters are often a small segment that is not always representative of the rest of the market. And, as with the flying car example above, sure lots and lots of people want flying cars but that doesn't mean there's a realistic market to sell them for all of the other reasons.

Ranked Choice Trends

Now that you've identified 5-10 trends under each category, rate each from 1-10 (with 10 being most important). Like with Customer decision-drivers, if everything is a 10, nothing can be important. The point of focusing is to start wide and then narrow your focus to the most important things. It is the same here. Will you be dropping some trends altogether? Absolutely. Should you put them on a follow-up list to address later? Great idea. But, for the purpose of strategy, not everything qualifies for an equal amount of attention. Narrowing your focus is mandatory.

And, there is another calculus we should apply. While we only looked at customer decision-drivers in the previous Market sequence, and we should have uncovered the most important factors, it's worth taking a look at these trends for a moment to see if we missed anything before. In this case, we should address whether any of these trends effect customer decisions and the market, as opposed to impacting the organization's operations. In some cases, they may impact both.

So, besides each one, we should label them Market, Operations, or Both. Anything tagged with Market or Both should be put back into the previous sequence, starting at the Market Segmentation step. Do these specific trends override any of the previously ranked decision-drivers? If so, then it's worth recalculating the Competitive Analysis and anything that follows. However, if you're in a rush, you can wait and do that the next time you run through this sequence (don't wait 3-5 years to do so).
Ideally, yes, we should do this Trend sequence before or simultaneously with the Market sequence. However, I'm trying to clarify the process here for the purposes of teaching. Technically, there may be some other things to add in form the Stakeholders, too. So in the future, do these steps as part of your initial research and fold them all together. For now, however, it's not the most important thing to worry about.

The rest of the trends, plus the stakeholder analysis we'll cover in just a moment, should be folded into the Operational sequence coming up in the next chapter. That's where they will have the most impact.

There is another aspect to consider and that is the level at which the trend impacts your business. For example, Climate Change is a trend everyone should be working into their strategy. However, that's too vague and unspecific to your organization. Is it the theft of extreme weather you need to consider? Rising costal waters? More frequent and more severe wildfires? Bleaching coral and the collapse of ocean fisheries? There are so many. You will need to dive into these complex trends to understand how they may impact your business. You may need to consult experts to do this well. Ultimately, your responsible for interpreting these trends and integrating them into your strategy. This includes their rank and whether they impact your market (customers and competitors), your operations (resources, activities, and priorities), or both.

All of this is systems thinking as applied to business and strategy. Too few organizations take a system approach and consider the full ecosystem in which they operate. One of the objectives of systems thinking and mapping is to identify and leverage the points within the systems and its stakeholders that represent the most effective and efficient change. Where should you focus your efforts for maximum change. There are usually places to act in a system that result in the greatest change, compared to others. Those are the pressure points to build your strategy around. Perhaps, those connections or stakeholders impact many others or cascade into other system effects? Often, they lie in parts of the system that most businesspeople never consider (like regulation, academia, industry alliances, etc.). This is why they form the basis of a partnership strategy. Your stakeholder ecosystem map should highlight stakeholders that can help you leverage your efforts for mutual success.

Stakeholder Strategy = Partnership Strategy

For way too many years, the only people who are seen as important to serve in a business were customers (often, reluctantly or disparagingly) and shareholders. Shareholders are those who own the company. They might or might not work in the organization but they get a share of the rewards if it is sold (or even of the ongoing profits if the organization pays a dividend each year). Business went along like this for over a hundred years with no one seeing a problem—except for everyone who was left out of this reductionist frame.

More commonly, we use the term stakeholders now, to refer to those who are involved or impacted in some way. The reality is that there are many stakeholders of different types and there always were. Each of these is an opportunity to strengthen or weaken the business any good strategy should be looking at the entire system, not just a few parts of it.

Some of these stakeholders may be competitors or impediments (or simply seen this way). For example, many businesspeople think of NGOs and government agencies as adversaries to what they're trying to accomplish. But these same stakeholders might be the key to a strategic alliance that shifts the value proposition in an organization's favor. Or it might secure a needed resource that is hard to find. It might represent an opportunity to share key intellectual property or level a regulatory playing field to make it more fair. Each category of stakeholder should be considered in this regard to understand how the organization can be more successful.

As discussed in Chapter 8, cooperation and competition are both important forces in both stabilizing systems and evolving them. One is a force of convergence and the other of divergence and both drive a healthy ecosystem.

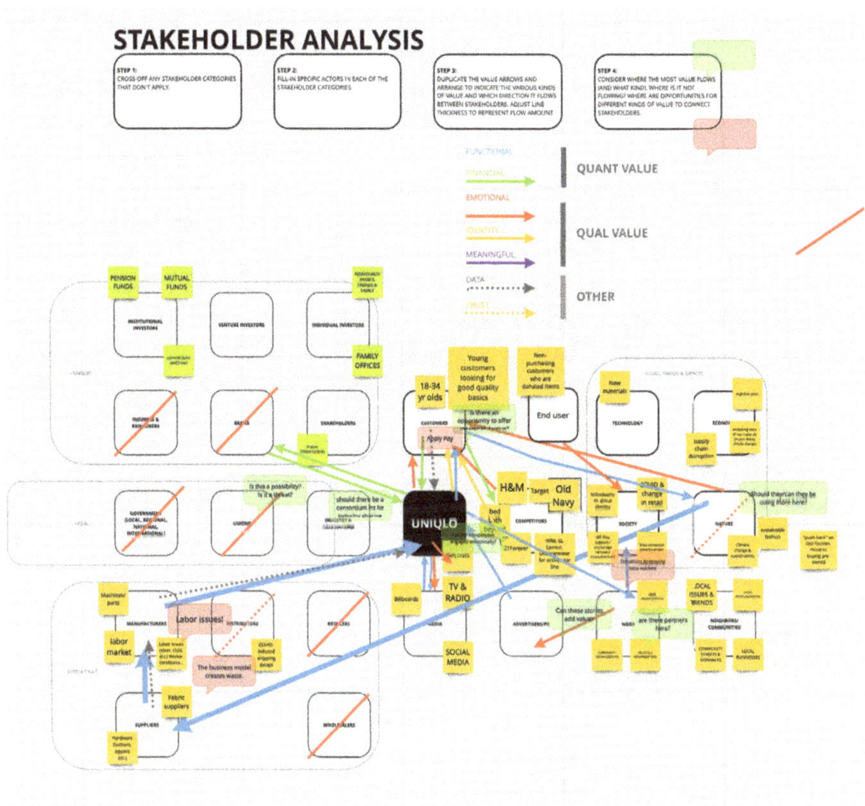

While all of this seems like a lot of work, it's really only as much work as you want to make it. Even considering each of these categories for an hour and what impact they have on your business is a worthwhile hour—and, certainly, compared to being shocked when a competitor outmaneuvers you because they bothered to do this work.

Not all stakeholders impact all organizations but there are likely some in this diagram that hadn't occurred to you or your colleagues. Consider it a superset of stakeholders you should consider. Again, whether you're a for- or non-profit, it doesn't matter. All of these represent players on your field and actors in your system. Even though it doesn't have a leader behind it, Nature is a stakeholder too. It makes resources and valuable ecosystem services available while also creating potential threats to your operations (like extreme weather or infectious diseases).

Each of these categories represent industries of their own which might be fairly complex. Note that these are all external stakeholders. We'll talk about internal stakeholders in Chapter 13. Once you identify the specific actors in each that might have an impact on your business, you may want to dive deeper into understanding what motivates them. More on this in just a bit.

The worst way of performing stakeholder analysis is to not perform it at all.

Mapping Value (and More)

Stakeholder analysis is a process of mapping value and identifying opportunities, not unlike the Market or Operations sequences. Like the Trends sequence, the results of this process drop into the Market and Operations sequences with important, high-value content.

The first step is to identify the stakeholder categories that impact your business. These will always include customers, competitors, and Nature. Always. It's also likely that government agencies, some NGOs, and Media are in your system, as well. If you're a digital services provider or many kinds of consultancies and NGOs, you may not have any physical supply chain (and, therefore, no manufacturers, distributors, wholesalers, retailers, etc.). That's fine; it makes your system a little simpler but it makes the other stakeholder categories that much more critical.

In each of the categories above, cross off the ones that simply don't apply. But be careful. It's easy to discount a stakeholder you haven't considered before when they may just be one you've never engaged but should. Every business has a bank, but is the bank a strategic/systemic partner? Can they be? Or, are they just a place you have an account? Only you can answer this. For many, insurance companies (and, even more so reinsurers) aren't a systemic partner. It's something you need to do business but they simply don't play a notable role in your business.

However, for others, it may be a significant source of revenue, expenses, or regulatory oversight. In the quest to reduce climate change, for example, many NGOs and activists are discovering that these are the very companies who pay the most when climate-based disasters hit. This is why insurance companies and reinsurers have begun to exert so much pressure in the last decade. The impacts of climate change and extremely costly for them. And, they're not the only ones. Restaurants and grocery stores pay much more for food when supplies are constrained or crops wiped-out. These are already low-margin businesses so they have an elevated reason to act. And there are so many more that have the most to lose from climate change and the most to gain from correcting it. They are now seen as important leverage points in the system that can exert influence on reducing climate change. That's very strategic. The point of this exercise is to explore the opportunities and value in your system because there may be hidden gems like this one.

Once you've eliminated the stakeholders that don't apply, it's time to be specific about the ones that remain. Make a list of individual organizations in each of the remaining categories. If you have a parts supplier, list them. If you're looking for promotional partners, list the ones you're considering. If you work with a retailer (or several), make sure you call them out, specifically. You don't want to forget an important stakeholder—especially if they're one you're already working with.

/End Users

All organizations have customers of some kind (perhaps, they're called constituents?). Often, these stakeholders aren't the ultimate source of value, either to provide or to reap. While you have customers, your customers almost always also have customers and these may be your end users. B2B, specifically B2E customers officially have other customers. While you're investigating your customers' needs, desires, and values, you usually get to the point where, in order to serve them best, you need to help them better serve their own customers. But, often, they don't really know their customers/constituents that well because they aren't using the research tools and methods that you are. In essence, in order to provide your customers with value, you have to do their work for them and determine how best they should be serving theirs. I know, this is a drag. You have enough work on your own plate without doing others' work. However, most consultants know this situation well and it's just part of the job—if you care about providing the best service you can.

The next step is to map the value you exchange with the remaining stakeholders. This is a good place to involve others from within your organization. Bonus points if you involve external stakeholders, too, in gathering this data. The more eyes and perspectives on this process, the better.

Refer back to the five kinds of value described in Chapter 1. You'll want to consider all of these kinds of value. For some stakeholders, the value might be functional or financial. If money goes either way, that's easy to acknowledge and represent. The same is true if some product or service is exchanged. However, the qualitative value may be more difficult to track simply because it's often ignored (and not measured) in many organizations. And, as we learned in the stories in Chapter 1, sometimes these are the most important (and valuable) kinds of value!

Using lines or arrows, show what value is exchanged between which stakeholder. If you can represent the amount of value (perhaps, through line thickness or color?), all the better. But, it's important to represent everything you can, however you can. Be sure to look at bi-directional value. For the most part, if one kind of value is going one way, there's likely some kind of value going the other (in exchange for that value). If there isn't, something odd is happening. Perhaps, that value comes back through a series of stakeholders? Or, maybe it's funded from another source (like an NGO or government agency)? Really, the only stakeholder that has value only coming from it (and usually none benefiting it) is Nature. Ask yourself: what role does this stakeholder play in the system and how are they resourced to act?

You'll likely see lots of concentrations of value in a few, key places. What you'll also likely see are large parts of the system lacking exchange of certain kinds of value. Who isn't rewarded financially? Who isn't engaged emotionally, meaningfully, or via identity? In other words, who could be more engaged with different kinds of value. These are all opportunities for strategic relationships—and creating new value.

Data, Trust, and Communication

Now that you've mapped the five kinds of value, there are some other important things to map. In particular, how Data, Trust, and Communications (of any kind) flow between stakeholders is critical to understand. Too often, these are afterthoughts, meaning they're rarely designed well nor attended to. Not realizing when two stakeholders don't trust each other (or not understanding why) can be a point of failure in a system (or an opportunity for those who correct it).

Likewise, not understanding how data flows within a system, and to and through whom, is absolutely not optional anymore. Privacy and security are so fundamental that, in some industries (and increasingly more), they're regulated by laws.

Lastly, communication of all types flows the same way throughout organizations. Data is only a specific (and critical) kind of communication. It's imperative that you see and know what flows to whom and through where. Otherwise, you don't see this important leverage point in the system you're trying to succeed within.

All of this is true within the organization as well, and when we address this in Chapter 13, the same exercise and process works there.

This mapping exercise gets better the more it's considered. The more you uncover, the more opportunities identified. But, even if you only have an hour or so to consider it, that's better than not doing so at all. When you really dive into it, though, important relationships and opportunities can emerge.

When you're finished, you should have a rich, visual record of your organization's external system. This value map should visually show who you work with and where, how, and what kinds of value flows. If you want to understand these relationships better and refer to them more easily, the next step is to create profiles for each of your key stakeholders.

Just like the profiles you created at the start of the Market sequence, the same template can be used to capture your understanding of what motivates your stakeholder's decisions. These should have a direct correlation to the value you've identified, as well as the opportunities or threats you may have just uncovered.

If and when you find important ones, these should be rated and integrated into the Operations sequence at the first step (described in the next chapter). This is a focusing step within this process. You may have uncovered a lot of interesting things but only the most important should be carried over to the next step. Documenting these opportunities is crucial and should be shared, in detail, with those in the organization responsible for the relationships with these stakeholders. That might include sales people, marketing people, researchers, or managers of finances, manufacturing, or distribution. Ideally, you've leaned on them to help create this map, in the first place. And, even though only some of the most important items will move on to impact business strategy, all of these findings can be used tactically by these departments so that they can better perform their roles.

These profiles, just like your customer profiles, can be living documents you come back to repeatedly, share with others in your organization, and evolve over time as new information comes to light (or something significantly changes in the system). This helps you quickly modify your strategic outcomes rather than starting from scratch next time you need to. Imagine your stakeholders as personas the same way you imagine your customers, and track their changes as such.

Mapping Trends and Stakeholders to Strategy

Once you've identified trends and stakeholders that are critical to your business, ranking them in importance, what do you do with them? How do they relate to the Market and Operations sequences?

Each of your trends impact either your market, your operations, or both. For example, the fact that more people are concerned about mis and disinformation in news impacts their buying decisions and, subsequently, your market conditions. They may have no impact on your operations, whereas a tightening supply chain or more costly labor impacts your operations without impacting market demand. Therefore, you need to direct those trends to the appropriate sequence. Trends that impact your market should fold into your competitive analysis because you want to consider how these trends

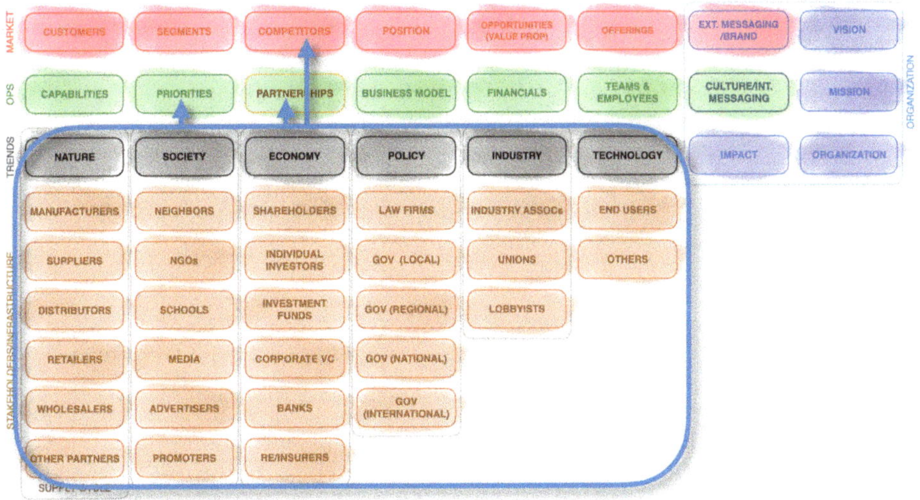

change your competitiveness. High ranked trends (such as those ranked 7, 8., 9, or 10) may outrank customer decision-drivers you already identified if those decision-drivers are ranked as highly—and, that's exactly what should happen. These trends are more important to focus on than lower-ranks decision-drivers. Remember, these steps are all about focus.

Trends and stakeholder decision-drivers also impact your Operations sequence and she folded into that work in the same way, but at two points: when you set your Priorities (which is also in a competitive context) and when you address partnerships.

Top Decision-Drivers:	Rank:	Your Company: Your Offering:	Competitor 1: Offering:	Competitor 2: Offering:	Competitor 3: Offering:	Competitor 4: Offering:	Competitor 5: Offering:	Competitor X: Offering:	
Wonder	10	10	4	7	2	8	4	9	Strength Opportunity
Community	10	10	7	8	8	8	7	10	Strength Opportunity
Hates conflict	10	8	1	5	9	7	5	10	Strength
Climate Change	10	5	1	9	3	5	3	9	Threat
Artificial Intelligence	10	5	10	10	7	8	1	4	Threat
Likes working with...	9	8	4	2	4	1	10	7	Threat
Excited by new chall.	9	8	5	0	1	0	5	8	Strength
Feels successful whe.	8	9	6	0	1	0	8	9	Strength Opportunity
Feels relief when thin.	8	3	10	1	8	8	8	8	Weakness Threat
Wants clear instructi.	8	3	6	8	3	3	2	9	Weakness Threat

Of course, some trends impact both the Market and Operations sequences so they should be addressed in both (at the same places as described above). Climate change, AI, and health concerns often fall into both categories. For example, climate change is changing people's priorities in buying and using all kinds of products, services, or attending events or traveling to specific places. It is changing the nature of decisions in most markets. And, it is also impacting organizations' abilities to deliver what they currently deliver.

When you process trends and stakeholder concerns in this way, you cannot miss their importance in determining your strategy. The appear right where they have the most impact. Of course, you can always fail to identify a trend or stakeholder concern or mis rank their importance. Nothing about this or any other process is foolproof. But, this process makes it much more difficult to miss something important.

/Porter's Five Forces

One of the most famous models for business strategy was created by Michael Porter and published in Harvard Business Review in 1979. He describes five force that companies must counter:

- The bargaining power of *suppliers*
- The bargaining power of *buyers* (customers)
- The threat of *substitute products and services* (competitors)
- The threat of *new entrants* into the market (competitors)
- The rivalry among *existing competitors*

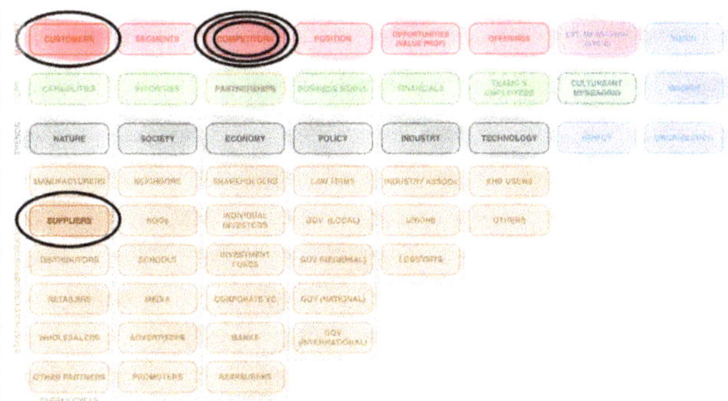

These can be powerful forces and, ever since this realization, businesspeople have paid particular attention to them. None of them are particularly new, of course. Businesses know they have competitors (the last). They know that new competitors might arise (either startups or existing companies creating new offerings. Businesspeople know the other three, as well, but they get complacent and don't pay enough attention to them. Often, because they don't think from their customers' perspective, they don't realize that customers have choices that might not be in the same category but that might still satisfy them (like reading a book or watching television instead of going to a theater).

The bigger issue is that there are so many more forces than these five. If we look back at the trends and stakeholders in the model (as described in Chapter 10), there are at least 33 other places where disruptive forces might come from! It should really be the 38 Forces if were being realistic about what businesspeople should be looking at. Of course, not all of these forces apply to every business. But, as proof, consider the force that COVID applied on every organization for 2 years or the force that the EU government exerted by requiring companies to protect their customer's privacy (GDPR) or requiring all electronics manufacturers to switch to USB C charging plugs and cords. These forces are at least as powerful as any of Porter's five.

The point of this strategic model is that these forces are always visible. You have to work to ignore them. Using this model, it's much easier to automatically address all of the forces, not merely the ones popular in HBR.

Partnership Management

Understanding your stakeholder ecosystem to this extent gives you all of the information you need to identify and manage current and future relationships with a myriad of partnerships. This also applies to identifying threats within your stakeholder ecosystem from partners that may move against you somehow. While it's not stressed enough in business, it's crucial to understand that it's not possible for any organization to succeed on its own. Every organization requires cooperation with many others just to develop, source, create, distribute, sell, and support their offerings.

/Highlights

- The most important part of strategy is context: understanding the market and other conditions around your organization and their impact on it.
- Trends are issues that impact your business. Most are out of your control and influence but you still need to respond to them. Ignore them if you like but better strategy carefully assesses which can be an opportunity or threat and what to do about either.
- There are six categories of trends: *economic, social, Natural, policy, technological,* and those specific to your *industry*.
- All trends are always constantly evolving. You should always be looking toward these trends. The faster you can respond to them (or prepare), the faster you can react and succeed because of or despite them.
- This biggest trend from Nature is that of climate change and this may show up in many different ways, from shortages of certain materials, higher costs for resources or environmental services, to flooding, droughts, and pandemics.
- Social trends come from many sources in society and from different levels. Fads are usually too short and fast to be part of organizational strategy. But, longer-term trends, especially those that impact buying and investment decisions should cause you to prepare and evolve your strategy accordingly.
- Economic trends, like fads, are longer-term changes in the economy. These might be due to government or banking changes, economic swings in value (and, therefore, the behavior of money markets), or impact customer buying behavior. In this way, some trends are interrelated between the six categories.
- Governments, at every level, make and change laws, setting legal policy. These may impact your business in several ways but especially its operations. Whether these changes impact employee rights, employment law, materials and your supply change, reporting, investment, or technology, every aspect of your organization's functions could potentially be affected.
- Every industry has its specific trends. You should be tracking those in your industry the same way you should track other trends. Industry associations and publications are good sources of these trends but their impacts are for you to assess and integrated into your strategy via both the Market and Operations sequences.
- Technology has emerged in the past several decades to be a source of major, dynamic

change, shifting industries overnight and in some cases, even eliminating them. Staying abreast of current technologies and their ability to impact your markets and your operations is critical. Like Nature, some of these trends are more easily trackable than others while some can seem to appear overnight. Understanding technology is nearly as important as understanding Society, Nature, and the Economy.
- Once you have identified the trends in each category, you should rank their importance to or impact on your organization and markets. The highest-ranked trends should be integrated right into your Market and Operational competitive analyses.
- Each stakeholder category may contain specific stakeholders that could be partners or threats, but you won't know which without performing a stakeholder analysis: how each makes decisions and where/how value flows in your industrial ecosystem.
- Tracking all five kinds of value throughout your network of stakeholders can identify opportunities where most value can be traded or where a type of value that is absent can be added.
- Mapping Data and Trust is an important, though optional, addition to the value mapping exercise in stakeholder analysis. It can highlight additional concerns and opportunities for your organization to address and integrate into your strategy.
- Essential to stakeholder analysis is the concept that both cooperation and competition are important to any healthy ecosystem. Neither is better than the other and both are dynamic. However, cooperating on lower levels is what allows competition at higher levels. As such, cooperation is the only way to both develop and maintain a sophisticated market and operational ecosystem and the only foundation for more complex offerings.
- Porter's Five Forces represent threats and opportunities from only three types of stakeholders: two from customers, two from competitors, and one from suppliers. However, the same forces can come from any of 42 stakeholders so, really, there are 42-44 forces you should address periodically.
- Not every stakeholder will impact every organization. However, never addressing the complete set ensures that you will likely miss an important opportunity or threat, as well as significant partnerships that can help you be more successful.

/Explore More
- *Thinking in Systems* by Donella Meadows

Your Organization

Whether for-profit, non-profit (and there are many different types of both), or government agency (as well as extra-governmental organizations), the organization itself, is a thing that needs creating, managing, and designing.

How the organization is arranged, its form, culture, resources, activities, and people are all deliberate decisions made by its leaders. Arranging them one way makes some activities easier and others more difficult. Arranging them another way emphasizes some intents and purposes over others.

How you organize your organization makes all the difference in how it runs.

Chapter 11

Your Mission & Goals

I've taught many students: in degree programs, certificate programs, and workshops, in both a for-profit and non-profit context. I find that there are many assumptions people make between these two worlds. Because, ***traditionally***, non-profits come from a different intent: their goals are not only different, but their values and expectations. And those expectations are often centered around assumptions about charities: sacrifice, poor management, low pay, and a altruistic mission. Likewise, the assumptions about for-profits are mostly about making money—usually as much as possible!

The reality of these two forms is that they should be only minimally different. Whereas people in and working with non-profits often have expectations of poor management practices and low pay, there is nothing about the corporate form that requires or even suggest this. There are gigantic non-profits in the world with equally gigantic budgets and well-paid employees. In the USA, AARP (the American Association of Retired Persons) is one of the biggest non-profits in the country; its staff is very well-paid and they have plenty of money to run any program that comes to mind. Up until 2015, the NFL (National Football League) was also a non-profit and their leadership was paid extravagantly. Both are exceptionally well-run organizations that use state-of-the-art management practices. Even many charities are nothing like the image of charities where employees are expected to sacrifice every hour and ounce of energy for the cause (think of the American Red Cross or American Cancer Society). Of course, these organizations are not just run professionally, but they have solid business models with real, stable revenue streams.

Most for-profit companies are expected to be focused on revenue (and profit) and little else. While the tech sector for the past 30 years has been known for sometimes extravagant compensation and perks, these have always been expected to return steady profits and value to their investors. A few have declared corporate missions that reach beyond financial targets but it's well understood that money is a key driver of decisions. However, there is nothing preventing for-profit companies to ignore having more goals than a mission to make money and, in fact, they should.

All organizations, in both of these categories (and, to some extent, government agencies, as well), should be run very similarly: professional management practices, reasonable expectations of employees and compensation, accurate understanding of the value to be provided to customers, constituents, and stakeholders, and a mission that focuses on more than just making money. Any organization that doesn't meet these requirements runs risks of some kind—either Market, Operational, Financial, or Cultural.

What does that leave then as the difference between for-profits and non-profits? Very little, including: whether or not they pay corporate taxes, who "owns" the organization, and where they raise investment funding. That's really it. Now, I'm mostly talking about the USA here. Some countries don't even have non-profit organizations, some are quasi-governmental, and some don't even have fully for-profit ones. However, those are quite rare, so this is still a useful differentiation.

For-profit companies pay corporate taxes to the governments of the companies they do business in. They can raise this money by offering equity (ownership in the firm). They are owned by a combination of their investors, founders, and often employees. Investors might be private (venture capital, corporate venture investors, "friends and family," crowdsources in rare instances) or public, in the case of public companies that are openly traded on various stock markets. There may be different tiers of ownership with different decision-making influence but there is a co-ownership of the organization. Because of this equity, raising funds is often faster, easier, and greater because ownership is exchanged for money (and the hopes to make money later, as a result). So taxes and equity are all that really differentiate a for-profit from a non-profit.

Non-profits, on the other hand, have no equity. No persons technically own a non-profit. In some cases, the government it is registered under can be seen to own it, but that's a bit of a stretch. In return for not being ownable, non-profits are usually not required to pay corporate taxes, which can add up to significant savings. In the USA, that can be around 30% of income which is retained by company. Nothing prevents a non-profit from having lavish offices or salaries (well, except the wrath of funders if they think the expenses are too lavish for the organization's mission). There are many non-profit institutes who pay fantastic wages, have lovely offices, etc. but do not turn a profit. Most are even allowed to make a little profit if it's rolled back into the organization. The trick with non-profits is if getting one off-the-ground requires funding, it's got to come from someone who doesn't expect to be repaid. For example, grants are common. This means that the mission of the organization needs to be clearly something those granting it money care about and it must show progress toward that mission in order to keep getting grants.

So, if there is so little difference between these two kinds of corporations (and non-profits are corporations, too, in the USA), why is there so much difference in how these two categories of organizations are run?

The main difference is cultural; it has to do with expectations and intent. That's it.

This is a long way to discuss how important intent is. The intent of the organization is a rallying cry for those in and around it. It attracts and retains funders, employees, customers, and other stakeholders. It provides a goal that transcends Financial value, and opens up possibilities for other kinds of value to flow into, through, and out of the organization. This is why a clear mission is so important.

An organization that has no other intent than to make money isn't necessarily a bad one, but it's a limited one. It will attract *only* people who care about money and will focus only on a limited view of Financial value. This means that your investors will only care about their returns and will be upset with any spending that doesn't maximize their returns (meaning, the company's profit). And, often, this is a very short-term view. The same is true for employees. If they're only engaged on a financial level, the moment they find an opportunity that pays more, they'll leave for that opportunity, taking with them the institutional knowledge, training, and convenience (among other things) that you rely on to function. That's a costly move for most organizations, but if this is where they're engaged, it's what you should always expect.

The same is true for customers. If they are only engaged because your prices are better than your competitors, they'll stay happy as long as that doesn't change. That's all they expect or want, so the moment someone can offer a lower price, your customers are no longer yours and there is little you can do but lower your prices, if you can. This has been Walmart's strategy for several decades in the USA (and a few other countries). They engage their customers only on the level of Financial value. That's been great for their business because of their relentless drive to lower costs any way they can to offer the best prices to their customers—often only a savings of pennies per item. They've been safe doing so because they've been able to negotiate and manage their operations in order to offer these low prices. But, the moment a competitor can, those customers are gone.

Don't think this is possible? Here's a scenario. Chinese (or maybe other) manufacturers decide to open their own retail stores in the USA or other countries. Unlike Walmart, they are the manufacturers of their merchandise. In fact, they manufacture Walmart's merchandise so they can easily undercut Walmart's prices. This is how they beat Walmart at their own game, and there is little that Walmart can do because they don't engage their customers on any level but price: Financial value.

Customer loyalty is based on offering value beyond and in addition to Financial value. It might be Functional value, like convenience or unique features. It could be Emotional Value, like making customers or stakeholder feel heard, happy, or excited. It might be Identity value, like customers feeling the company understands and cares about what they do or behaviors like they do. It might be Meaningful value that delivers the experiences customers, investors, and other stakeholders care most about in the world. This is especially true for non-profits that rely on attracting customers, investors, constituents, and partners that have the same goals and intent.

Regardless of the additional value, if there is none, the organization's mission doesn't offer a lens with which to understand customer behavior and value nor employee, investor, and stakeholder values. Without a mission beyond money, there's nothing else to measure, care about, or engage others upon.

This is why your mission is so important and why it sometimes takes so long to formulate a clear one. It requires a conversation among more than the leader or leadership team. It requires an understanding of the intent of a range of stakeholders and that requires conversations with each of them to understand what drives them. It requires understanding the nature of these relationships. It requires collaborating with employees and constant, clear communication with them. I realize that sounds like a lot of work but this is how an organization creates Functional, Emotional, Identity, and Meaningful value (and, ultimately, greater Financial value).

Your Mission is More Than Money

Here are some mission statements from some well-known organizations:

Google's Mission:
To organize the World's information

Nike's Mission:
To bring inspiration and innovation to every athlete* in the world.
*If you have a body, you are an athlete.

NAACP's Mission:
To achieve equity, political rights, and social inclusion by advancing policies and practices that expand human and civil rights, eliminate discrimination, and accelerate the well-being, education, and economic security of Black people and all persons of color

That last one might be a little long but it is clear and descriptive. A mission statement need not be a tagline.

All of these mission statements are aspirational (as well they should be). Some are more aspirational about the organization (Google) or more about the customers (Nike) or the constituents (NAACP) but they all communicate something more than "make a lot of money." They engage different stakeholders in different ways. Nike's is more than aspiration because they are looking to convert those who don't see themselves as athletes (their customers) into people who do. That's a lot of aspiration but it's a great goal.

Your mission should be what drives you (and hopefully others around you). It's why you get up in the morning and go to work here as opposed to somewhere else. It's what you decide to do with your limited time instead of something else. If you're great at clearly communicating it and it's something others care about too, it's just that much easier to find and keep employees, customers, investors, partners, and other stakeholders.

So, what does motivate you? What are you hoping to achieve with your organization (other than making money or getting bigger and more influential)? If you can't answer these questions, you have some soul searching to do. If after that search, you still can't, that's a sign that you may be on a solo quest that won't gather much support from others.

Perhaps, if your company is really just a feature—and many tech companies (for example) are—then this isn't an imperative because you expect to sell the company quickly to another company. In this case, the organization is just a vehicle. So be it. But if that's the case, you shouldn't be expecting world domination or even prominent growth.

And tech companies aren't the only feature companies. There are many operational companies, in every industry, that are feature companies. They exist to build and prove a specific technology, process, market opportunity, or generate important intellectual property that was always intended to be acquired by a larger organization in the industry.

Meaning is the Best Mission

This is where core meanings become essential. Not only are they something to understand about what drives your customers' decisions, they're just as important in understanding what drives the decisions of the rest of your stakeholders. This a job for Meaning Strategy, that investigates alignment of meaning drivers across customers, organization, and employees (at the very least) and, often, partners of other kinds and stakeholders.

If you read Chapter 1, Your Customers, and the section that described the five kinds of value, you know that Meaningful value is the deepest, most stable value that you can deliver and exchange with anyone. This makes it particularly well-suited to mission statements since this engages the organization at the deepest levels, too. If you can align stakeholders on this level, you can build the greatest, longest lasting value there is. It's the point of highest impact.

This requires investigation, of course. Perhaps, you've already researched your customers' Meaningful value. If so, you have an idea of the core meanings they prioritize highest. If you can duplicate this process for your employees (or specific teams or divisions) and your company's brand, you have an easy way to look for overlap. If you can do this for some or many of your competitors, you can look for ways to differentiate at this level, as well. Regardless, the same research techniques, such as laddering,* will be the main way to uncover these core meanings. The rest is fairly simple.

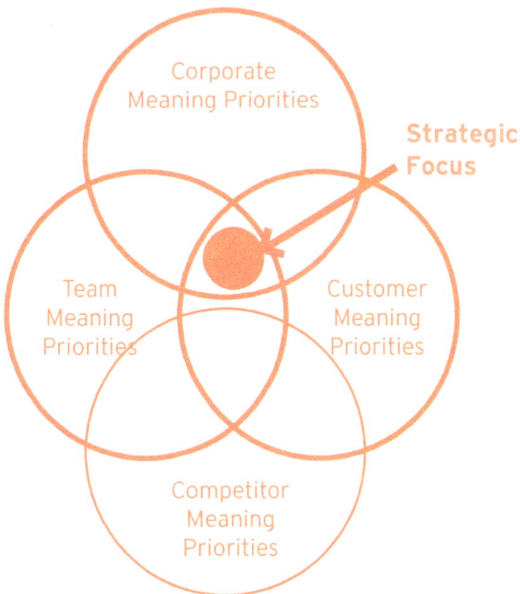

*Laddering is an interview technique used in qualitative research (such as design research) where deeper, meaningful value is uncovered through a series of questions.

15 Core Meanings:

Accomplishment	*Enlightenment*	*Redemption*
Beauty	*Freedom*	*Security*
Community	*Harmony*	*Truth*
Creation	*Justice*	*Valdiation*
Duty	*Oneness*	*Wonder*

Now, what about the opposite: what if there's little-to-no overlap? Well, this isn't the end of the world but it is a clear signal that you're attempting something difficult, if not impossible. If there's little-to-no overlap between your customers and company, it means that your customers just don't see your organization that way. They don't have trust that you can deliver meaning (or, perhaps, any value at all), they don't expect it from you, and they don't look to you for it. This doesn't mean that you can't surprise them and develop a relationship on this level, it just means that it's going to take a lot of time, energy, and resources to do so—and you should prepare for that. It's an early signal that this will be an uphill battle.

For example, I and a colleague once had a meeting at Warner Brothers about licensing the Batman brand to other companies. Our initial advice was to look at what Batman meant to their customers (Batman fans) and how that overlapped with those companies they were looking to license to. Right off the bat, there were some obvious opportunities, like Security and Justice. At the heart of the Batman brand, these core meanings, along with Duty, seem to be obvious signals. Of course, if we had continued with Warner Brothers, we'd have wanted to do the research and verify what was actually at work.

So, consumer security products were an initial opportunity. Perhaps, Batman branded home security systems (cameras, home alarms, car alarms, even window stickers) would make sense. Certainly, this would be a better fit than Batman refrigerators, wallets, and art supplies. I know this probably sounds incredibly obvious, but it wasn't to those we met with.

We also advised them that the value of the Batman brand was so high that they needed to think beyond merely slapping Batman branding onto various devices. Painting a Honeywell home alarm black and putting the Batman logo on it wasn't enough if they cared to maintain the high value of the Batman brand. The product, (a home alarm in this case) needed to feel at least a bit like Batman's would, even if it were just a better display or higher quality. That would require more of a partnership with Honeywell (or whomever they engaged) and not the same agreement they would have with a phone case or t-shirt manufacturer. Ultimately, they decided it was too much work to do something valuable in this space and the risk of souring the brand was too great for the minimal amount of time and energy they wanted to expend. That was a great strategic decision.

Now, what if there isn't much overlap between your customers or teams and the company or brand? This means that you may not have the right people working for you. It means that they aren't engaged on a deep level and may find it difficult to deliver or communicate the company's mission throughout its operations.

I'm reminded of a friend who worked for Microsoft at the launch of their broadband group and MSNBC, in 1993. He interviewed a brilliant engineer for a job after many colleagues had already done so (you were always lucky to make it to the afternoon interviews at Microsoft if you attended the morning ones). This person made it through at least eight other interviews throughout the organization. My friend's first question (that no one previously had thought to ask) was "tell me some of the television you watch most." The answer: "I don't watch television, I hate it." My friend further asked "then, why do you want to work at MSNBC?" In effect, the answer was: "So I can make it easy to turn off." This is not an employee well-positioned to fulfill the goals of the organization on any level, but particularly at the top. As it turns out he was perfect for another group within the company and they hired him.

Now, not every employee needs to be engaged at the deepest levels. I'm certainly not arguing that every person drink the corporate Kool-Aid.® However, if you have a lot of employees that don't understand or care about the mission—or actively are against it—you also can't expect to get very far very quicky. These people will resist and work against what you're trying to build, even if only by apathy.

Of course, this is more critical for those in some parts of the organization: sales, customer service, marketing, communications, development, etc.—those whose job it is to understand and serve customers. Many others don't need to engage on this level (although it doesn't hurt). Bookkeepers, quality engineers, manufacturers, HR, etc. can do their jobs well without feeling the company mission (although, again, they will be more valuable if they do).

Imagine your yoga studio not having instructors who can speak to customers on the level of their meaning and values—who can't engage in something so crucial to the experience. They don't have to agree with customers or even like the studio but they can't build the experience both you and your customers are expecting. Now, imagine an environmental NGO working to reduce climate change with employees who mainly don't think it even exists.

Not everyone who works in a religious organization, such as a church or religious school, needs to be of that religion. Many parents, for example, send their children to religious schools that aren't their religion for a variety of reasons. Perhaps, it's a better school than others in their area. Perhaps, they want their child exposed to other cultures. However, if a staff or faculty member in one of these schools actively behaves or espouses values that are contrary to the organization's values, you can see where that might become a problem. It's not that they can't work in this organization nor that the organization can't succeed, but it will be more difficult and require more work to do so.

This speaks to the last area of overlap: between employees or teams and customers. As with the other places of overlap, if there is a lot in common (2-3 similar core meanings), it means that these customers understand and can serve those customers more easily. If there's not much overlap, it means that these employees or teams will find it much more difficult to do so. They will need more time, training, exposure, experience, verification, and even attempts to get it right.

Lastly, what if there's great overlap between all three groups but that this overlap is on core meanings that your competitors also share? In other words, what if Nike and Adidas both share ***Accomplishment***, ***Beauty***, and ***Oneness*** with their customers and employees? How do they differentiate?

This is where communication and design really matter. The differentiation between these two companies can still be strong, based on how they communicate, which I call triggers. These are the design choices that trigger core meanings. There are many ways to communicate to customers (and employees, too). ***Accomplishment*** isn't only communicated (triggered) by images of runners crossing a finish line or players scoring a goal. Video doesn't have to be active and chaotic, as if it's shot running alongside an athlete. There are more colors, typefaces, cinematic styles, music, and scores of other design attributes that can communicate Adidas' approach to ***Beauty*** differently than Nike's. This is where design can be the crucial differentiator between companies. However, design can't do this without understanding what lies at the heart of that differentiation.

I remember a time in the late 1990s when Nike's television advertising had a specific fast-moving style. It was fresh, authentic, and very successful. You knew a Nike commercial within the first few seconds of it starting. Soon, there were imitators, and not only from other sports equipment companies. There were these other ads that followed the same format, even similar color palettes and video styles but as the ad came to a close, there was no Nike logo; it was a Gatorade logo. Gatorade at the time effectively built upon Nike's brand equity with visual and other messaging that espoused the same meaning and, therefore, aligned with the very same customers as Nike. Think of this more as strategic homage rather than all-out copying. If it were any other sports company in the same product categories as Nike, it would probably have been received negatively—by Nike as well as their shared companies. But it wasn't, because Gatorade wasn't seen as a competitor. Now, had Adidas done this, I imagine that it would have been a failure. Not only might Nike take legal action but customers would be confused and, as a result, would not build trust with Adidas as easily.

In short, there is always a way to differentiate your organization even if there is a lot of overlap between the value you provide and that which is promised by your competitors. The more plentiful, clear, and meaningful the differences are, the easier this is. But you always need to follow your customers and not try to engineer differentiation where there is no clear path to its success—and this is true in ***B2B***, as well.

All of this speaks to the organization's mission. The intent must be clear and must be clearly communicated throughout the organization. And it must be a message that easily transcends the values and goals of all three groups. Again, this doesn't mean low overlap automatically leads to failure, but neither does it mean that it will create greater effort, time, and resources to succeed.

Communicating Your Mission

It's not enough to have a great mission. Too many companies go to great lengths and expend time and resources to create what they feel is an apt, motivating, and engaging mission…and then sit on it. If they communicate it at all, it's almost always controlled to such an extent that it shows up quietly on a website, in an annual report, or in a strategic plan, or it's shared only with the highest levels of management. Employees, customers, partners, and everyone who might benefit from knowing the mission are an afterthought in communicating the mission. This renders the entire activity mostly ineffective, if not worthless. In turn, the lack of results or impact from the mission convinces leaders that it was a waste of time and those resources, self-fulfilling their expectation and making it an activity that will not likely be repeated.

/Highlights
* Fundamentally, there are few differences between for-profit and a non-profit companies: where each gets investment/funding and whether or not they pay corporate income taxes. Otherwise, each should be well-run, have sustainable sources of revenue, and have a mission that goes beyond simply making money.
* Having a mission that customers understand and support gives your organization an advantage as customers will be more loyal.
* Missions should be concise and clear, both externally and internally. It's essential to communicate your organization's mission throughout your organization, to partners, and to customers or constituents.
* Meaningful value is the deepest form of value and, because of this, can form the basis for more effective missions.
* Meaning strategy analyzes alignment between customers, employees, and the organization using core meanings. This can also define differences between competitors' core meanings.
* Even when organizations have similar core meanings prioritized as their competitors, they can differentiate via different design triggers.

/Explore More
* *Blind Spot* by Steve Diller, Nathan Shedroff, & Sean Sauber

Chapter 12

Your Organization's Organization

I remember being in a meeting in a small, dark room in 1995, when the Web was first growing. We were meeting with our client, Karen Shapiro at Bank of America. In this meeting, we were trying to define how to organize everything the bank offered to its many different customers onto their website's homepage. This was a very new thing for them. They had a simple placeholder on the Web but it wasn't much more than that. We were working alongside our colleagues at Ketchum Communications (a PR and advertising company), Tim Bruns and Susi Watson. The challenge was that Bank of America was an enormous company that offered a lot more than checking and savings accounts for people. They worked with institutions of all kinds, including domestic and foreign governments and the World Bank. Their divisions and departments alone each required a separate directory and it was an old institution that had grown organically and somewhat esoterically. We had to communicate all of that in a clear way to those who found themselves at that one page.

After grouping and categorizing and regrouping and recategorizing for a few hours, we had an organizational structure we thought could quickly funnel people through to where they needed to go, along with a brilliant visual metaphor that still communicated that it was all one, multifaceted institution (thanks to Tim). There was much more behind the top level but that didn't need to be revealed immediately (and in some cases, not revealed at all). As a consultant (and therefore an outsider) to Bank of America, I represented these customers and neither knew nor had to respect the sometimes byzantine structure and politics of the organization that Karen had to.

At the end of the meeting, I turned to her and suggested, "you know, ultimately, how we've organized the breadth of Bank of America on the website will slowly start to reorganize the company itself, over time."

Karen responded, almost pleadingly "Don't tell me that, I can't think about that."

But, that's a very real possibility. How you conceive of your business plants the seeds for how that business best operates. There are many ways to slice, dice, and rearrange an organization but the way you choose emphasizes one aspect over the others. In a very real sense, the organization of your organization determines how you deliver value and the promise you make to different customers. It does this in that it makes it easier to deliver some value over others or some promises over others. Now, it doesn't prevent you from delivering value; poorly configured companies do this all of the time. But some do it at great cost with significant internal confusion and disorganization. It doesn't have to be that way.

This is at the heart of a service mentality, meaning, that the needs and desires of those being served (internally) take precedence over those doing the serving. You know those organizations. They make their HR and accounting systems easier to administer but, by doing so, make it extremely difficult to submit reimbursements or generate reports. Their IT decisions are based on making their purchasing and administration as easy and inexpensive as possible but the ramifications for those who uses these products and services often outweigh the value saved. You've undoubtedly worked for a company or know someone who has, the computer and other equipment options are few and don't work for everyone—and there is no recourse. It's not uncommon for people to leave otherwise good organizations because the very organization of the company make parts of it very difficult to succeed within, that an otherwise good culture, coworkers, or compensation notwithstanding.

So, consider how your organization might better function if it were configured around the value you deliver or the meaning you generate. Perhaps, organizing geographically isn't the best way to group customers or serve market segments (especially if those segments aren't arranged around geographies). If your mission is to deliver Community, Wonder, and Beauty, why isn't your organization organized around those three core meanings? You can see how, at least, that might make both the quality of those meanings and understanding and delivering offerings around them easier over time.

Regardless of the arrangement you choose, to prevent silos and disfunction you'll also need to build cross-communication to counteract competition between groups and increase collaboration. Even though all of your employees work for one organization, it doesn't mean that everyone is pulling in the same direction or with the success of the whole in mind.

Consider a typical medium-sized corporate org chart:

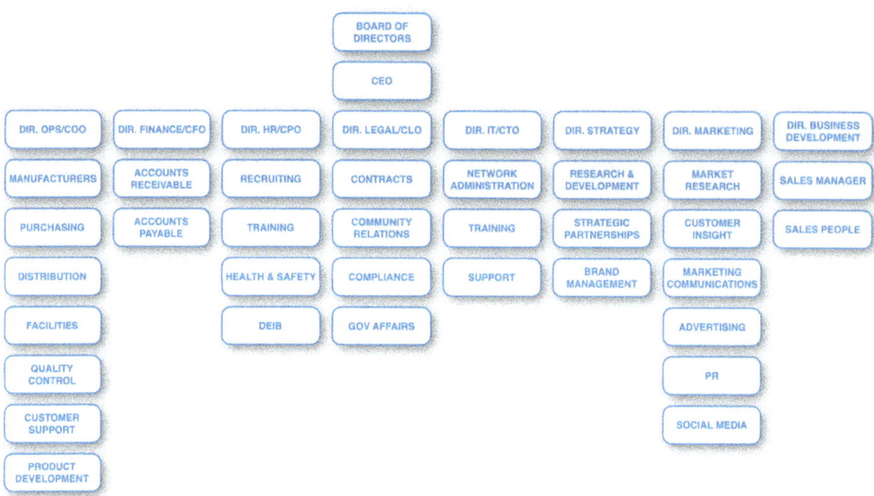

When it comes to authority, most businesspeople imagine that they are to "govern" those below them. Instead, managers in the healthiest cultures understand that their job is to service those they're responsible for, even if that means protecting them from the rest of the company. This is what's meant as a "service culture." Instead of decrying policies that make their own jobs easiest, managers, divisions, and departments should be asking those in the rest of the organization what their needs are, with respect to their functions so that they can devise the policies and imperatives that make everyone's job easier. For example, it's common for Information Technology groups to want to standardize on software, services, operating systems, and hardware because it makes everything easier to manage. However, often, this makes everyone else's job in the country more difficult when these decisions don't enable them to do their best work. A service culture would see managers researching their peers' needs and finding a way to fulfill them even if it made their management a little more difficult. The result is a better working organization for everyone, rather than an easier management job for a few.

This means that the natural impulse to create layers may create unnecessary blocks in action and communication, For sure, a large company is going to require extra management but the 1980s adage "managing by walking around" met a big counterpoint in the age of COVID-19 work-from-home. It turned out, that for many companies, their layers of management weren't providing a lot of value. The litmus test you should use is this: "Does that layer or that management role help those they manage be more productive? Does it provide value to others?" If not, it shouldn't exist.

When I ran the Design MBA program at California College of the Arts, I knew that I had to serve my faculty in order for them to serve our students. My job was to make their jobs easier, wherever possible, and to clear the way for them to focus on teaching, rather than paperwork. I couldn't do all of the administrative work for them but I could find ways to make it as clear and efficient as possible, even if it meant more work for me or innovating the process.

"Parity" is often a term used to denote equality and, sometimes, it does. But one thing that was clear when I was chair of the program was that different students, faculty, and programs had different needs at my institution. What one program required, my program might not need at all (like private studios for each student). But, we had other needs they didn't (like unique alumni or job placement services or monthly dinners). The administration always pushed back on anything that didn't fit the "template" of other programs, even if it meant hurting revenue or the success of the program. This is another example of oversimplifying operations and reducing innovation to cookie-cutter services and procedures. It's a management challenge but the tactics of the organization need to make room for uniqueness, as long as it aligns with the organization's values and strategy.

Ultimately, most of the 18 components in the Market and Operational sequences, the Organization grouping, and the internal components could use its own strategy. They all flow from the overall strategy for the organization and they all represent tactics of that strategy but they all need detailed strategy of their own, to direct how they should function.

/Highlights

- How you organize your company sets the stage for how it functions. And, how you express that to customers and partners matters more than how you divide responsibilities within the organization.
- The best organizations adopt a "service mentality" in which everyone in the organization understands the stakeholders around them, even internal peers, and makes decisions that work across the system, not merely in their own interests.

/Explore More

- *Guide to Organisation Design* by Naomi Stanford

Chapter 13

Your Plan & Business Model

Once you have an idea of your financial model, it's time to integrate everything together, both in the Market sequence and the Operations sequence. (Remember, the trends of stakeholder influences should be integrated right into your Market and Operations sequences.) Together, these form your business model. There was a nice—not so long ago—when your business model was a choice between the two or three prevailing models in your industry—basically, you chose what one of your competitors was doing and maybe tweak it a bit. However, today we have better options—we can create custom business models with more opportunities that better respond to opportunities. One of the tools that most impacted this process is the Business Model Canvas. It's been the way business models have been taught in business schools for over a decade and it's used more and more by businesses of all kinds.

While innovative in the past, the Business Model Canvas is definitely showing its age. It doesn't account for many things: trends, all stakeholders, Nature, society, all kinds of value, etc., though some of these can be wedged into it if you try. But, it's ripe for improvement and evolution. Before this canvas, the prevailing way businesses chose their business model was to choose from the few currently in the market,. There were usually 2-3 already in use by competitors. People would tweak these in minor ways on an ad-hoc basis. The Business Model Canvas made it possible to develop a custom business model from the many elements of business. Instead of merely picking and tweaking, the canvas allows people to build one up from elements, innovating at every part. The result was often a much more considered business. This said, the results often fell into some larger categories, such as:

- Products: selling products and content (sometimes, servicing of these products is free, other times, for a fee)
- Services: selling services (sometimes, including free products)
- Freemium: Free basic products or services with for-a-fee upgrades of functionality
- Advertising-supported: publishing content that is free to customers with advertisements alongside or embedded
- Open Source: Free products with suggested donation or support
- Platform: offering a platform for others to sell and charging them a fee
- Distributor: charges a fee to connect and manage transactions to special channels
- Broker: negotiates deals on behalf of others, for a fee

Some of these may feel different in different markets or channels. For example, music artists are in the product business—they make something and sell or license it to others. Increasingly, they may sell directly but traditionally they sold to music labels who acted as distributors. When we hear the word "product" we more often think of physical products, like food or furniture, but digital products, such as a game, are products, as well. Events and places, like a concert or a theme park can be thought of as a short-lived service.

Of course, there can be many combinations of these. Apple is a huge company with several business modes: they sell products, digital services, and offer free software. They also run several stores for others to sell applications, games, music, movies, books, etc. (and charge 15-30% fee to these sellers). And, they offer a bit of advertising in places, too.

Disney runs a myriad of business models in various channels. The sell movies to consumers and distributors, alike. They sell services as events and in theme parks. And sell products, services, and other events within these places. They sell advertising and product-placement space in most of their channels. They license real estate and their intellectual property. Smaller companies don't often offer as much of a mix of business models. It's all they can handle to do one well.

You've likely heard of companies who "give away the razors in order to sell razor blades." These services with free or low-cost products that make use of the services. A retail store is a kind of platform. Some sell only their own products, like the Nike Store, while others sell a variety of other company's products (sometimes alongside their own), like a grocery or department store.

Ultimately, it doesn't matter if the business sells physical or digital products, services, events, or places. It's only important that you investigate the alternatives and decide what's best for you and your organization. Your business model is a function of your activities, resources, team, and those you serve. Your team is more than just those in the company. They include the partnerships you make and rely upon to succeed. That's all there is to a business model. It's just people, resources, and activities. It's not a secret key to success, nor does it have to be set and never change. To the contrary, it should always be evolving in small ways to stay on a successful path. That's why it matters to strategy, and why strategy should be continuously evolving.

Your strategic story

At this point in the process you have more than enough to complete a strategic plan. The most important part of this plan will be the story it tells—even more than the data and decisions that went into it. By all means, these decisions and the data that validates them are important and should be included but on their own, they will not convince anyone of the plan's success.

Your strategic plan is a story about the present and future that must be clear, concise, and motivating. You plan should be clearly organized so that anyone can find the parts that apply most to them but the story should be front-and-center and organize all of the work. Different readers will look for different things. Some will scrutinize your plan for "proof" that your conclusions are correct. Often, this means that they will only trust quantitative data that underpins your decisions. That's OK. Even though some might adamantly demand that they're not swayed by "fluff" and are "hard-numbers" folks, they too need to hear and believe a story of potential success, just one told mostly in numbers.

By all means, you need to include metrics that you'll use (or others will use) to judge your success. But, don't fall into the trap that numbers alone will tell that story nor that they represent the most compelling parts of the story. Depending on the audience, some will look for quick successes, even if they're only short-term. Others will take the long view. Some investors are looking to get their money out in 3 years or less (a very difficult thing to do) while others will look for a longer strategy that includes continued growth from deploying more and more services to capture more and larger markets.

Ultimately, you will have several versions of the story, for different purposes. Each will summarize or elaborate in more or less detail, with more or less supporting materials. The "elevator pitch" is the shortest statement that describes what your strategy intends to accomplish. two to four sentences is all you can afford, so they need to be concise, clear, and inspire the listener to hear more. That's your first story.

Your strategic plan is a much longer story that goes into much more detail and is intended for many people within an organization, from the board of directors to senior leadership to various levels of management to all employees. You will need an abbreviated version to share with external partners. But, all of these have to support the same story, even if not all parts are disclosed in each.

A good outline for your story is no different than any other kind: a film, a novel or short story, etc. It needs to have a beginning, middle, and end. The most interesting stories have a twist, where the goal changes or unfolds and expands. This is an advanced move, however, and I don't recommend you try this unless you have a lot of experience or some very talented storytellers involved.

The beginning: describe the current state of your company, your industry, and you customers. Where is the pain? What is the conflict? Maybe things are currently fine, or maybe things are failing. This is all about context. Everything in Chapter 10 could be used here. Are there trends that require you to make changes or stakeholders that are disrupting business-as-usual?

Stories have ***characters***, who are yours? Is it your customer or constituents (new or current)? Is it the organization, itself? Is it the story audience, such as an employee, investor, or partner?

How are your customers impacted? How are your competitors reacting? What will happen if you do nothing? Describe this change in context and the potential result in both quantitative and qualitative ways (hint: the qualitative will provide greater emotional imperative, and the quantitative will validate the qualitative).

The middle: describe how you got to your response (the strategic process and steps you've used to get to a better plan). What did you investigate? Who did you talk to? Move through this quickly because few people like to cover process trivia. You can always come back later for more detail. However, get right to the insights you uncovered. What are the pressure points inside your organization or in the ecosystem that you can press to make the best change? These insights are both tension and release. What was surprising about what you found? Perhaps, you discovered that customers' requirements were not what you expected or have changed significantly. Perhaps, something changed (or is about to change) in the industry because of changes in Nature, technology, society, or policy? If this is something only you see (insofar as you can tell), that's exciting and promising, but you need to describe why you're able to see it before others do and validate that what you see is in fact real.

The end: describe your response: what's the specific plan to make change and what do you expect the outcomes will be? This is where you should plan the most detail (at the appropriate levels, of course). How will you make change, what changes will these be, how will you ensure success, and how will you know when you've succeeded? Then end with the new state you expect to be in. What will the organization look like once you succeed? What will your industry or the world look like?

How does the strategy impact different departments or divisions? Does it help them by making their jobs easier? Will they need support?

Use visuals at every step to help you tell this story. These include not only photographs, but diagrams as well. You can tell a story much faster with a detailed diagram that makes clear the important insights while preserving the supporting detail than you can using endless columns of numbers or paragraphs of text. This doesn't work for everyone but it really helps many understand without having to read the fine print.

One helpful exercise is to write an ***article*** about your business for a magazine or website of your choice. What are the headline, pictures, diagrams, pull-quotes, hashtags, etc. from the article? Assume it's written by the most flattery journalist (but still, a serious one). You might list help from a real writer, too. The interview process for the article, alone, would be a worthwhile experience for those in your company (and for you to see who can clearly explain the organization's goals, vision, activities, etc.).

Does your article have a narrative that tells a clear story? Or, is it merely a selection of facts? Does it help your reader learn something interesting about the world or themselves and not only about the organization (the best stories do)? Are the most interesting or key characters referenced? Does it set the context for what came before the

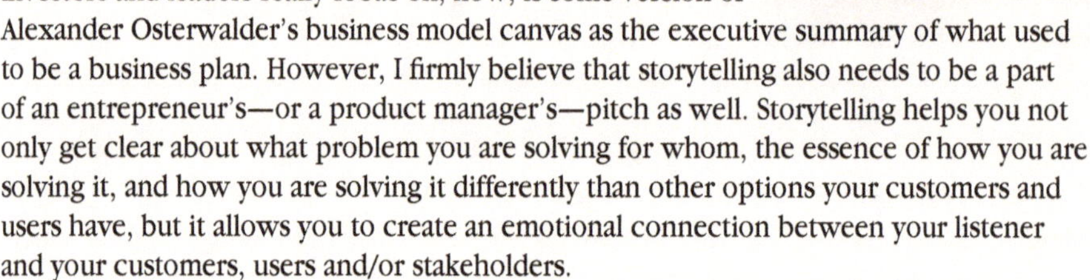

*Nathan/*Twenty-five and more years ago, in order to start a company or even a major new initiative in an existing one, you needed an 80-page business plan. That was the expectation. Not even 10 years later, it was down to a 14-slide deck, at least if you're in the tech world. What would you say the requirement is today?

Sara/ From the people I speak with, it seems like what investors and leaders really focus on, now, is some version of Alexander Osterwalder's business model canvas as the executive summary of what used to be a business plan. However, I firmly believe that storytelling also needs to be a part of an entrepreneur's—or a product manager's—pitch as well. Storytelling helps you not only get clear about what problem you are solving for whom, the essence of how you are solving it, and how you are solving it differently than other options your customers and users have, but it allows you to create an emotional connection between your listener and your customers, users and/or stakeholders.

I spend a lot of time with product managers through our Product Management Programs at UC Berkeley and observe a widespread problem: They struggle to get to the essence of the story that captures the experience they are creating for their customers or users. These challenges show up in several ways. Sometimes the person has trouble getting to the heart of what the product does and starts listing myriad features of their offering instead. Other times they struggle to get to the core of the problems they are tackling, instead providing a laundry list of the challenges customers might be facing. Overall, they struggle to articulate a coherent story arc: We are helping this person, who really wants to achieve these outcomes, but cannot do so because of some conflict, with our value proposition (that resolves the conflict, thus facilitating the outcomes). Our offering works in the following ways (e.g., it collects data, analyzes data, and provides personalized reports), unlike other ways the customer has to solve the problem.

I imagine it changes a lot based on whatever the culture is within the organization.

Yes. Culture, organizational design, reward systems all make a difference in the extent to which an organization can work in a customer-centric fashion. Data from thousands of product managers across a wide range of industries, for example, unsurprisingly shows that sharing of information across functional silos in their organizations is a significant impediment to actively innovating customer and user experiences. Years ago, Jay Galbraith wrote a book about organizational design as an information processing model, meaning that we structure organizations to optimize flow of information. As information flow has been simplified, obviating the need for hierarchy to manage it, we are now arguably faced with a new challenge of creating meaningful and targeted information sharing.

Some would say that it's just data, not information.

Absolutely. That's an important distinction. We have mountains of data now, so we must be smarter about asking well-considered questions of that data, employing "backward market research" as it were to thoughtfully query the data available to us. How do we get meaningful insights from that data? How do we move beyond focusing on functional performance of our offerings to see their emotional or meaning-based effects on customers and users? (Hint: the Net Promoter Score is not the answer.) How do we remember to take a step back and ask "why?" when we find interesting and unexpected correlations in data? How do we exploit both qualitative and quantitative research to discover meaningful opportunities? Who should be doing this exploration?

It is much more common today for people to ask, ***What problem are we solving for our customers?*** so at least that behavior is more ingrained in some organizations. Unfortunately, the answer is often something along the lines of ***"we give our customers these features,"*** so we still have some distance to go in embedding problem-focused mindsets in organizations. Organizations remain overly focused on keeping the "feature mill" fed and regularly lose track of the outcomes those features will facilitate for customers.

Of course, there is always someone in class who suggests that this mindset doesn't apply to B2B businesses. My question in return is "Do you not have any feelings at work? Do you not care about the social dynamics of your workplace?" I had a great example in class a few years ago from a product manager who worked for an anesthesiology equipment company. He shared that his team had done interviews with anesthesiologists and heard regularly that they the equipment to be "more modern." In trying to understand what that really meant, they had to ask more questions. It turned out that the anesthesiologists felt that they played second fiddle to surgeons in the operating room. What they really wanted was to have the surgeon be a little jealous—for the surgeon to look over and say, "Hey, what have you got over there?" Of course, the equipment still had to fulfill its functional requirements. But, if it also considered status and creating jealousy, anesthesiologists would select that equipment and convince the procurement people to pay just a little bit more for it. There are more than just desired functional outcomes, even in the B2B world.

Right. This equipment was heavily researched using the typical market research methods but I was adamant about also visiting customers to see their experience. It was like pulling teeth to get the engineers to visit a customer site. They saw no value in it. But, it finally happened and right as they walk into the customer's lab, they immediately see this expensive piece of equipment sitting on an office chair. It's meant to sit on a counter, of course. They ask the researcher, "What is this doing on a chair?" They answer, "It's so expensive that we can only afford one in the lab. But, we all need to use it. So, whomever needs it wheels it around on the chair to their workspace." It was a revelation to the engineers because, of course, they didn't have a shortage of them and could never imagine how they might be used differ-ently than intended in the field. They went back and designed the next version to be on wheels.

subject of the article (the state of the market, customer challenges, the origin of the organization, etc.)? Does it have a satisfactory conclusion? Does it describe what comes next?

It's also never a bad exercise to do the opposite. What's the most scandalous, scathing article that can be written about you or your company, while still being truthful. That ought to be a threat you start mitigating immediately!

I remember a quarterly board meeting when I was on the board of Teague, the design firm that has designed the interior of every Boeing jet since the 727. I was the junior person on the board, and still fairly new to the aerospace industry. Teague had several studios, both in the US and abroad, and focused on different industries. The CEO was taking us through "the numbers" for each studio and I remember having trouble following the details of the contribution margin for each and its overall impact on the company as a whole. I remember thinking I was likely the only one until the chairman of the board spoke up: "Can you please give us a one or two sentence summary of each studio?" I was relived to find out I wasn't the only one unable to put together the story of the studios' performance. And, just like that, in two sentences for four studios, we got a succinct, clear story of what was happening. The rest—all of the numbers—are just support for that story. It was a revelation to me and extremely common in these kinds of presentations.

If not part of the main story, the detailed stories for various divisions, departments, or teams will need to be described here as well. What are the tactics that will form the strategies for each level lower than the overall organization? What are their specific goals that will contribute to the larger ones?

The addenda: what are all of the validating details that quickly but completely back-up your insights and decisions? You can plan to have a lot of material here, but that material is outside the story. Every strategic plan emphasizes the organization's mission, vision, values, goals, etc. They usually make these prominent and often the first and most highlighted parts of the plan shared. Personally, I'm not swayed by this and feel that it dilutes and diverts from the story. Yes, you should have a mission (which is itself another mini-story of your organization's strategy), vision, values, etc. but as discussed in Chapter 11, these are often inauthentic and regardless, are borne out of action, not words. They have far less weight than most leaders think and often provide groans and eyerolls from employees who live a different reality. Instead, stick these at the end or in the appendix. Your goals can be in the middle or end of your story but the rest are the least important parts of your strategy.

Here is a template for organizing your strategic plan in different ways. You can also find it online here: URL

Strategic Plan Outline:

Market sequence:
- Who is the protagonist of the story? What can you tell us about them? What is their context?
- What *value* are you currently creating and for whom?
- Why are current solutions and offerings not working?
- Customer Insights
- What *value* does your new strategy create, for whom, and how?
- Competing offerings (including from Competitor X!)
- What is your new strategy for delivery value, your sustainable position, your opportunities and your offerings? (this should complete everything important and insightful from the Market sequence)
- Why is this strategy going to succeed? What needs to be true in order for it to work?
- What are your biggest threats?

Operations sequence:
- How do you plan to capture value? What are your sources of revenue and estimates of both revenues and costs? (be ready to show your work)
- What are the changes you need to make operationally?
- What priorities do you need for building or evolving your capabilities? What key resources and partnerships will help you succeed?
- How will you measure success (both market-wise and operationally)?
- What to you need financially to succeed?
- What do you need to develop, deliver, and support your new offerings?
- What's your communications plan, internally and externally?
- Advanced: How do your offerings need to evolve to succeed with more customers or constituents?
- How will you understand the changes as they happen? What mechanisms of feedback are you building and who is responsible for them?
- How will you operationalize your goals over your entire organization?

Corporate strategy:
- How are you organizing your teams to effectively use this strategy?
- How are you incentivizing collaboration?
- Who do you want to be as an organization? (here, you can list your mission, vision, goals, "values," etc.)
- How might your brand need to evolve, and why?
- Will this strategy require you to acquire companies, technologies, resources, or intellectual property? If so, how much will this cost and how will you go about it? How does any acquisition create net value for you (of all five types)?
- Does this strategy indicate that you should sell off product/service lines or divisions of the company? If so, how, to whom, and what do you need to prepare? How will you know the right buyer when you find them?

- Are there other strategies that you investigated? If so, what were they and why did you choose this one, and why is it better than not altering your current strategy?
- How do you plan to measure, report, and monitor social and ecological impact? How are these metrics (qual and quant) integrated into your decision-making? Have you explored potential harms and how to mitigate them?

Consider the above a rough outline but one you should be modifying extensively to meet your own needs and tell your unique, important story. It's a reminder of some of the things you should consider addressing in the same way that the full list of stakeholders is a reminder (in stakeholder analysis) to consider some things you otherwise might not. It's not a requirement to include everything.

The multi-storyverse

As I described above, you may need several versions of this story (and plan). You'll need a version you can share with every employee. You'll likely need a different version (more detail here, less there) for each of your partners—especially any new partners. You'll need a version you can share with your investors—again, especially if you need new investment to accomplish your strategy. You may need a version for lawmakers—especially if you employ lobbyists. You may even want a version to tell your competition (as a warning, a challenge, or a manifesto)!

Each of these may reserve some organizational secrets or emphasize a different—but related—message. If you have different market segments, you already need different messages for those specific customers which emphasize the drivers of their decisions. Your employees that interact in each of these segments, and your partners in each, will need somewhat different stories. Each may build interest, excitement, or trust in different ways. Each may care about different metrics for success—particularly if their compensation is changing as a result or based on specific measures and milestones.

Each story should include some form of action plan. Once you've captured people's attention and excited them with the new vision, show them explicitly what they can do to make it a reality. Be prepared to evolve these with their input, too. People closer to customers, partners, and different aspects of operations know details you don't and will be able to help hone the plan to greater success.

The naysayers

You should absolutely prepare for the naysayers: those who will deny your insights, disagree with your decisions, and decry your path as leading to destruction. These are valuable people who are usually well-meaning (though not always). Some are simply uncomfortable with change-any change. Others see things you don't or have entrenched biases that make it difficult to accept new contexts or understandings. You need to have a story for them, as well (and, perhaps, one for each of their concerns). These don't have to be the main part of your story but these responses need to be ready to deploy if you need them.

Most naysayers are simply concerned about risks. Fair enough. However, there is no risk-free organization and you can definitely mitigate risk so much that you impair your ability to change, respond, or succeed. All actions entail some risk and the old adage "no rewards without risks" is true. Your plan should definitely minimize the risks you've uncovered and you should be prepared to describe how. It's likely, however, that you have identified every risk, which is one of the reasons to share your plan fairly far and wide. You want others' input, especially from those with a different perspective or experience.

Many lawyers see their jobs as eliminating all risk for their organizations and this is just not possible. It's also a recipe for never innovating at all and missing important opportunities that keep you competitive. The best lawyers see themselves not as risk cancellers but risk evaluators: what can be done to lessen risks while still moving forward? The question should be: which risks are worth taking? Those focused on risk need to assess them in the context of the market, society, and Nature, not just the context of the organization.

Instead, address your risks and threats head-on (one of the reasons why you should build that threat matrix from Chapter 5). This is a normal business function so don't let someone use it as a kind of "gotcha" to denounce your work or strategy.

There are also risks that haven't been part of "business-as-usual" but now need to be. Chief among these are social and ecological risks. It's no longer acceptable to simply go about business without thinking of the impact that strategy and those activities will have on others. Sure, pummel your competitors into the ground while taking your customers to new levels of delight, but not at the expense of justice, equity for others, or the world's ability to support life.

Risk mitigation

There are several kinds of risks you should consider. Most strategies look at financial risk as a part of traditional approaches to strategy. Some look at risks from competitors. Only a few consider future risks, as in scenario planning or other foresight techniques. However, it's one thing to look at risks to your business and yet another to consider risks to your customers, to society, or to Nature.

In the market sequence, you likely identified **risks** from competitors as part of competitive analysis or from your prioritization process in the Operations sequence. These are the threats, and to a lesser extent the weaknesses, that result from these SWOT-like analyses. They should be addressed almost as much as your identified opportunities. These might be legal, organizational, managerial, economic, or (internal) cultural risks. They may be risks associated with the business model, with scale, or with convincing customers to change their behaviors. All of this still falls into the rubric of traditional strategy.

But, there are risks we can no longer ignore. These include ecological and social risks. They aren't yet required or common but they should be.

When you identify social and ecological risks, even today, many traditional business leaders and managers choose to ignore them. They aren't experienced in dealing with these risks and many don't even acknowledge that they need to. But, that's no excuse. We can no longer praise organizations for their beneficial impacts while exempting them from the harmful ones. It is the responsibility of everyone in the organization to identify potential ecological and social harms, prioritize them, and develop strategies and tactics to mitigate those harms. To do otherwise is simply unethical. And, there may be a long list of potential harms. Just a few include:

Ecological Impacts:
Air Quality
Animal Cruelty
Biodiversity
Clearcut Logging
Climate Change
Genetic Modification
Hazardous Materials
Hazardous Waste
Industrial Farming
Land & Sea Habitats
Greenhouse Gases
Nuclear Power
Soil Health
Waste
Water Quality

Social Impacts:
Accessibility
Alcohol
Clear Labeling
Community Relations
Economic Impact
Equity in Employment
Equity in Leadership
Explicit Violence
Fair Compensation and Benefits
Fast Food
Gambling
Human Rights
Impact on Democracy
Mis/Disinformation
Privacy
Representation & Diversity
Safety Disclosure
Sexual Assault and Stalking
Sexually Explicit Material
Tobacco
Unethical Conduct
Weapons
Working Conditions

There are likely more, as well, but this is plenty, for now. In essence, you need to pause to contemplate how people might use your offerings to harm the environment or others. If the major purveyors of social media had done that 15-20 years ago, we would have had a chance to mitigate the impacts on democracy and voting, disinformation in the news, and teens' self-esteem (to name only a few) before they had such negative impacts. By all means, you should tell the story about how your offerings benefit people, the planet, society, etc. However, you would be hypocritical to only mention the benefits without at least considering the potential harms. Not addressing the latter in your strategic process also means that you will be caught off-guard when they come to light, and be unprepared for the consequences.

Real-time strategy

We're not quite there yet but you can start to see why it would be preferable to build strategy—and manage it—in real-time. If the market or your customers change, you would want to immediately see how it was impacting the insights and assumptions you used in making the decisions inherent in your strategy. Imagine having the ability to view your organization's performance in the context of its strategies. You could see where you were exceeding your strategy and where you were already deviating from it. All of your employees could contribute, in real-time, to the data describing the changing context (market and customer research, competitors' new offerings, etc.) and changes in the organization (new sales, sales lost, costs of goods going up, new partners, constraints on resources, etc.). The "holy grail" of business would be to have a real-time management tool for strategy. Strategy could become continuous instead of occasional, dynamic instead of static.

In the meantime, you can build parts of this vision yourself: empower or even require each team to tell a story about its performance and validate it with quantitative and qualitative evidence. Ask them to interpret the overall strategy in their own way and compare their understanding to yours. These should be written down somewhere others can see, comment, and contribute to (online or on a wall somewhere). I've worked with a major global clothing manufacturer who ran prominent advertising all around the world, localized to each country and culture. Yet, no one in the organization could see the entire external communications for the company. We suggested an online space where, at the very least, each ad was posted when it ran (not even in advance if it would slow response). We even suggested taking one room of its massive corporate campus and designating it as a real-time repository of current ads simply by hanging them in clear sleeves all around the space so that the global head of marketing could walk into the room and survey the entire company's communications in one place. To this day, I don't understand how they could function without something so simple (hint: a lot of trust and even more hope).

Where does your strategic plan reside and where are the elements that went into it? Who has access to them and how often are these elements, let alone the plan itself, refreshed? These aren't difficult questions to answer but you need to commit yourself to doing so.

- Your strategic plan is a story about the present and future that must be clear, concise, and motivating.
- There may be several versions of your strategic plan with different levels of detail but they all must be consistent.
- Where possible, a great strategic plan should include metrics for success, though not all metrics are quantitative. You should make room for qualitative indicators, as well.
- The plan should clearly describe the customer, market, partner, and organization's view of your strategy. It may even include potential reactions from competitors and industries.
- While your plan may not, specifically, address potential harms and social and ecological impacts as well as your plans to mitigate them (for legal reasons), you should definitely have these discussions and plans within your organization.

/Explore More

- *Business Model Generation* by Alexander Osterwalder & Yves Pigneur

Chapter 14

Your Impact

Worrying about unintended harms or impacts other than financial ones are definitely not part of traditional strategy (which is a big reason why they're such endemic problems in our lives). This is just one of several ways in which traditional business strategy and "business as usual" has failed us—and why new approaches to strategy are required. You should consider it a mandatory part of your strategy—everyone should. We have new tools, processes, and understandings to make impact strategy easier and more manageable. But, it certainly isn't easy.

The biggest issue regarding impact is traversing the many, many kinds of impact that should be addressed. I'll say, right away, that it's not possible to accomplish everything so you'll need to focus. But, before you can do that, you do need to explore a myriad of possible harms and benefits that your strategy could cover. Then, you can choose which ones appeal to you and your organization's values, intents, and goals.

Careful research

Because the best kind of customer and other stakeholder research is qualitative and focused on all five kinds of value and what drives the deepest decisions, it must get personal. However, this can also bring up potentially traumatic memories, experiences, and current circumstances. When you ask someone about their most valued possessions, the most meaningful events in their lives, and the opinions and understandings that shape their worldview, aside from merely being invasive and eliciting private emotions, you can sometimes trigger trauma. It doesn't really matter how well-meaning our intent is regarding the research we conduct and the ways we would like to help the constituents we design for. Instead, we need to be sensitive to their situations and the impact of our interactions with them.

Trauma-informed research techniques are a set of sensitivities and processes we can use to lessen negative impacts, increase the respect we show toward our research subjects, and discover more important understandings about the people we ultimately serve. This is because there are many communities who suffer a variety of conditions we don't and we can't ignore this context if we want to learn from them. It is also the tip of a process that leads from the hero researcher/designer/engineer to a more participatory relationship to people. Ultimately, we may serve people by handing-over to them the means to manage their own communities in unique ways or determine for themselves what they need and how to satisfy those needs. Think of this as the opposite of traditional colonialization that much of the world has suffered.

It's certainly noble to want to help others but the world
is rife with stories about savior-businesspeople who failed
because they didn't involve those they tried to "save"
and didn't even understand who actually needed
saving and in what ways. If you want to create impact,
this is a call to involve those you seek to impact into
the strategic process, rather than imagining that
you'll do it all for them and then deliver it as a
present. Roger Hart developed the Ladder of
Change in 1992 for UNICEF in order to communicate the various ways we can and should
involve our audiences into the strategic
process.

This is never an easy process and it can
be fraught with criticism from all sides
—often conflicting ideologies. Some
critics of participatory design claim
that it make those you seek to help
do your work for them. Others
proclaim the value of not assuming why people are in a particular situation. Critics tell us not to
learn off the backs of others or steal ideas
for solutions from their community while others convince us to enable communities to
find solutions for themselves. There are probably no right answers here, except to be
sensitive to those you research, approach, involve, and serve.

Developed by Roger Hart for UNICEF, 1992

Measuring impact

There are a lot of ways, currently, that organizations are measuring impact. None of
them are standards yet and all of them are evolving and probably still somewhat inadequate or incomplete. This isn't a reason to do nothing, however. Investors, customers,
partners, and governments are quickly adopting goals and even measurement models
to assess impact of the organizations they work with so it's only a matter of time before
you'll need to tackle these subjects in order to take advantage of the best opportunities
and, increasingly, stay competitive for customers, partners, and employees.

There are two broad categories of impact: ecological and social. The first, ecological
impacts can be approached mostly quantitatively (if your operations and their impacts
can be easily measured). The second, social impacts, will need to be approached both
quantitatively and qualitatively. And, while there are only a few categories of ecological
impacts and benefits, there are hundreds for social impacts and benefits. Take a deep
breath and we'll dive right in.

TOOLS: LEVELS OF PARTICIPATION

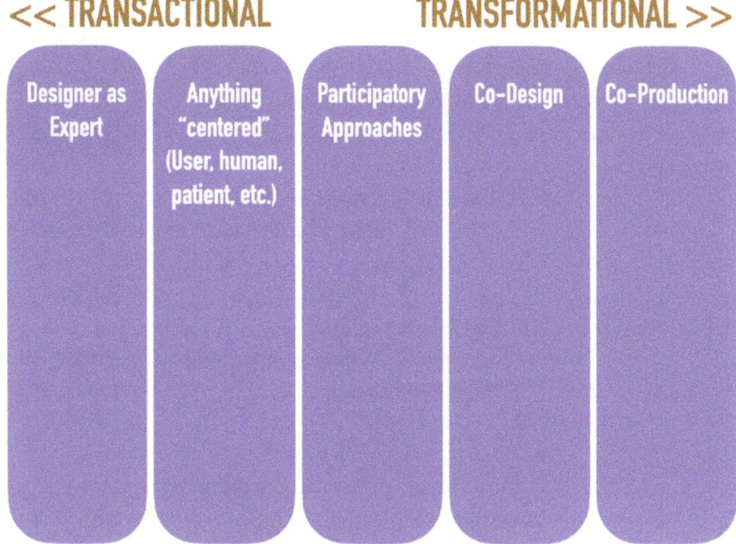

Ecological benefits include the following categories currently (they're always evolving): Air, Water, Soil, Biodiversity, and Carbon. Carbon Dioxide (CO2) is the most widely recognized and focused-upon component of Air but it's not the only one. There are many toxins that impact air quality, including dust, particulates, methane (CH4), and more. The same is true of water quality: trash, saline, toxic chemicals, etc. However, measuring these is usually straightforward. Often, when people get concerned about water, they usually focus on fresh water. This is for good reason, but doesn't account for the fact that the seas have become our global dumping ground and the problem is so pervasive that it's an afterthought for most organizations and individuals. You may not be able to measure air and water in real-time or entirely, but there are ways to approach identifying and measuring your inputs here and correspondingly, your strategy might change these to have positive benefits.

Every single one of us has ecological impacts, including organizations,. Even digital services that seemingly exist only in "the cloud" have ecological impacts, particularly electricity used to power servers, databases, networks, transmission, displays, etc. Much of this impact is hidden and surprising, especially the enormous processing power required for Artificial Intelligence (AI) that eclipses most other forms of computing. Even in our personal lives, we all eat, travel, use lights, heating, and cooling in our homes and offices. We cook, buy, use, and discard, and all of it has an ecological impact.

Nathan/ Your work is so much greater than just impact but your experience and journey have so clarified and informed impact for me, I'd like to ask you what counts as impact?

Minnie/ There are so many ways to define and measure impact, from the social context to so many broader contexts, such as the 10 versions of Capital: ecological impact, social impact, financial impact, etc. What I tend to focus on in my practice is the individual and the organization and the downstream implications of decisions we make as product designers every day. I start at the human level and then scale from there. It's important to get super granular: what are the *guardrails* we need to set up to be conscious of how an individual is going to be affected. In my work, we ask questions like, "what are the ramifications of mental health when people are using technology all the time." We know that there's negative impact on young teen girls, for example, when they're using social media but, why? What's the cause? If we can understand the causation, we better set ourselves up with the education and guardrails to prevent that.

So, I usually focus on the human scale, including *community impacts* and then scale to business implications from there. We can look at these other layers too, environmental impact or societal impact, but I wouldn't call myself an expert on the things that sit outside of the human condition.

How do you start that process inside of companies?

I always encourage people to talk about their *theory of change.* Historically, every socially minded organization has their theory of change. And I think we that that should be true for profit-minded organizations, as well. There should be an intended challenge to be solved and the outcomes associated with that *intervention*. A theory of change lays-out the series of *inputs* and interventions, the activities needed in order to support those, the opportunities, the *outcomes*, and the measurement. And I think by being really concrete about what, exactly, are going be the indicators of success, we can we see when change happens and what are we can do to revise the intervention when it doesn't.

It can be challenging both in-house and in the tech community—especially with smaller scale projects. If we don't know what, exactly, we're measuring and the outcomes we expect, we set ourselves up to lose sight of the impacts—especially the social ones. I also want to mention the *Ethical Design Toolkit.* It focuses on three core questions around measurements: one is *safety* of our users, two is *transparency* for them, and three is *autonomy* for them. So, I always ask these questions on every project.

In addition, I find *dichotomy mapping* really interesting, which is anticipating what could intentionally go wrong. We spend a lot of time considering how we're going to benefit our users but what do we anticipate by creating this product or intervention that what could be harmful. What are the downstream impacts? For example, ride sharing allows people to move around much quicker and easier. There's new infrastructure for transportation, now, and we're democratizing it, but what has it disrupted? Wages, traffic, equity, safety, etc. It's important that we think about all of these different tools as ways for us to really be conscientious of the impact on individuals and communities.

Theory of change is essentially strategy, right? Companies already have a theory of change in the market or in their sales, and that theory needs to be tested. When you work with companies, how do you go about testing and validating their theory of change for social and ecological impacts?

I like ***hypothesis-driven development*** because it's a great way to put a theory of change or a mission into practice. It's not dissimilar to the scientific method and I love the idea that the scientific method can create some degree of rigor in our industry. This idea has four stages. The first is the ***hypothesis***: what problem do we think we're solving, We have to be really clear what it is and not change that hypothesis throughout the course of the experiment. The second stage is the ***evidence***. You need to know that this hypothesis is or isn't working. If we think we're going to make our customers' lives easier by creating something, okay, how will we know that their lives are getting better? What evidence so we have for their current lives and what will we look to after our intervention?

The third is ***data*** and its collection. What kind of data do we need to measure? Is it quantitative, qualitative, both? How are we collecting it? Pre and post surveys, work product analysis, interviews, something else? They are so many ways we can collect data in this day and age but not all data is equal—nor their collection methods. Fourth, what is the ***action?*** How are we planning to use that data as evidence of our hypothesis working (or not)? I think this is a concrete way to look at something like a mission statement or a theory of change and to create these feedback loops to validate action You may need three or four hypotheses, but you have to have that degree of rigor for each and every one of them.

You emphasize the importance of ***trauma-informed research*** or "careful research." As a design researcher, you've had lots of experiences that has informed this. Can you speak about that journey?

Historically, in the time that I was learning the process of human-centered design, designers had a bit of an inflated ego about their process. We thought of design a sort of silver bullet process that was going to help businesses and companies innovate in the service of customers. Liz Jackson talks about "pathological altruism," which is the blindness that well-meaning people have in seeing the impacts of their actions, even if genuinely good. Basically, designers would go into a situation believing "We're actually talking to the people who use the products." But, sometimes, they were just stealing the ideas and things that already worked for those communities, selling them back to these giant companies and calling it "design thinking." Designers were inadvertently repacking local knowledge. And, sometimes, we're putting those customers in a really vulnerable place because we're asking very personal questions and we're not giving them a lot of context as to how the information they share with us is being used.

Read the entire interview at www.nathan.com/whole-new-strategy

However, we're only beginning to define all of the things we need to measure for healthy soil and biodiversity. These are just as critical for life on our planet as air and water; we're just further behind in identifying their components, interactions, and impacts. You should also address these in your strategy, as well. Climate is more complex because it's a factor of air and water. The more we impact air and water adversely, the more extreme weather we create and need to prepare for. In this category, your strategy should focus on how you plan to mitigate climate and extreme weather risks (bigger and more frequent hurricanes, hotter summers, colder winters, flooding, rising seas, etc.). Your insurance providers may already require you to address these. But, are your activities making things worse? That's what you need to assess and address.

Once we get into the realm of social impacts, things get even more complicated. This is because there are so many potential issues and impacts and also because not everyone agrees on which are important or what constitutes a benefit or a negative impact. People of different walks of life, cultures, religions, ethnicities, nationalities, and even families have different values and express their core meanings in different ways. They have different priorities and different ideals. That means you can't satisfy everyone—not every employee, nor investor, partner, government, or reporter. That's the reality. What you can do is explore the wide range of issues, focus on the ones you feel you can impact and those that most closely match your values (and that of your organization), and then plan for potential fall-out.

When Florida's governor came down against LGBT rights, driven by conservative Christian values, Disney changed it's strategy. The two administrations are locked in a governance war as their values collide and each maneuvers around the other. The same is true about #metoo reactions against organizations and individuals accused of misogynist behaviors, the #OscarsSoWhite hashtag calling-out lack of representation in film awards nominees and winners, and NGOs exposing working conditions in corporations' factories, lack of representation on their boards, and pay equity at all employee levels. While it may seem a minefield of issues to navigate, it's really not so difficult to identify those that are important to your organization. It's more a matter of not being able to please everyone, by definition.

Social impacts are everywhere: issues on equity, justice, inclusion, and a plethora of specific social issues: animal rights, LGBT rights, healthcare equity, fair pay, living wages, nuclear power, pornography, unions, renewable energy, alcohol, sexual and violent content and imagery, transparency, disclosure, gambling, human rights, industrial farming, genetic modification and experimentation, stem cell research and therapies, lobbying, and so many more. Each of these can be complex issues with five to fifty sub-issues—or more. Clearly you can't do everything. However, what you can do is make a good-faith effort to explore them and prioritize which are most important to you—and your customers and partners. Those running the Academy Awards may not have thought (or cared) about minority representation but their diverse stakeholders do and that's caused them to change, albeit slowly. You very well could have unseen or inadvertent issues in your own ecosystem, and you need to identify these issues and potential missteps before they happen.

/Gamification

In my courses, students often throw-out the term *gamification* in their desire to make their software services more successful. Often, it hides in the legitimate desire to make our designs as popular as possible, and to widen their impact and reach. However, the techniques of gamification can be damaging and are often disrespectful to those who use or are impacted by the things we design.

The elements that fall into gamification include "addictive" aspects of games, like competitive and public scorecards, loyalty programs, and some kinds of rewards (there are many others). All of these derive from *operant conditioning,* psychological techniques used to, among other things, train rats in laboratories.

Originally, the term tried to replace that of *game design*, a term that pre-dated this one, still exists, and simply means designing games (even when applied to things other than games). Now, the term means something very different. The tech world, particularly with tech investment, looks at it as "must use" aspects of software to make it difficult to stop using. Most of what has been deemed addictive about Facebook, Instagram, YouTube, and other digital services are the result of "gamified" features. None of these services are games. All of these are designed to addict us and thus command our attention, and the result has been harmful to self-image (particularly among teens), truth, and democracy.

When you hear the term *gamification* you should think "harming people." That's what it has come to mean in the tech world, whether those using it realize it or not. If people want to make something entertaining or "game-like" they should just use those terms. But, gamification has become a desire to addict and though addiction may be seen as strategically desirable, it is a short-term benefit that, in the long term, hurts customer and constituent relationships. It also promotes short-term emotional value at the expense of deeper kinds of longer-term value, and ultimately ruins customer and constituent relationships. In short, easy, short- term engagement comes at the expense of real, long-term value and loyalty. It's up to you to design strategies that create bi-directional, long-term (sustainable) relationships for your organization and this isn't the way.

Traditional business used to chant the mantra "the business of business is business," using it to claim that corporations had no business worrying about the issues I identified in the previous paragraph. It's so endemic in the way business is done in the United States (less so in Western Europe and Canada), that many businesspeople—particularly investors—still follow this approach or react negatively when they encounter it. However, gone are the days when organizations can sweep issues under the rug, and the power of social media can derail billions of dollars of value almost overnight—just ask Uber, Tesla, Nike, and so many more.

Nathan/ You have been focused on ecological and social impact for most of your career, leading companies at a strategic level. What have you learned about communicating these concerns at that level?

Ephi/ Ecological and social impacts must be considered at the forefront versus after the fact. This is easier said than done if there is a lack of understanding about how this impact affects the business. It's important to frame the conversations to start with- how do we impact what and who are around us, including the ecological context and people? In developing the business or product strategy, we have to understand not only what the customers are looking for and the inputs and outputs needed to be to achieve them, at the same time, we have to ensure that the ecological and social impacts and dependencies are embedded there as well.

You've worked in a variety of companies in your career and I imagine most of them weren't led by people who automatically thought that they should be interleaving social and ecological impacts and benefits and strategies with their business. So how do you talk to leaders that don't know how to do this or don't even know that they should do this? What's the conversation like to convince them why it's important and that it is doable?

t takes many forms but what I do first is understand where they (those I have to influence) are and where they're coming from. It's part of a discovery process rather than just convincing them. I have to view them as my customer where I need to uncover what resonates with them and understand what terms they already use. For example, if I'm talking to someone who is in manufacturing, ecological and social impact considerations can manifest in terms of productivity or reduction of waste, which makes it easier to approach a conversation on how to increase profitability while ensuring all these impacts are considered.

The key has always been trying to approach it from their point of view, use language that's already familiar, and not be too caught up with how I would normally talk about it with people who are already like-minded. This helped open-up perspectives and illuminate options.

I have also found that framing ecological impacts, issues and benefits as risk mitigation or efficiency goes a long way with traditionally-minded businesspeople. Have you found other strategies or framing that work besides those two?

Yes. One, in particular. I've not seen this work in every situation, but it has worked in some: knowing that they do care about something, whether that's in their family or community, helps them see this from a personal perspective. For example, in the manufacturing setting, people have kids that will be entering into the workforce. So, I frame it as: ***shouldn't we be thinking about this as an organization that your children would want to work for?*** You can frame this as the workforce in general.

Being able to retain or attract talent is another way of opening that conversation. If you can connect to something near and dear —that has meaning to them that helps in certain situations.

In helping others connect personally, you're also moving past the ecological issues and into the social issues. There are a *lot* of them. How do you help people put their arms around this process in order to have impact?

I often recommend an assessment or inventory, because what could be salient or relevant to one organization doesn't necessarily mean it's the same for another and it also helps with prioritization. That could be a materiality assessment, a human rights impact assessment, or many others. The same inputs and outputs analysis that we would do for an ecological assessment, can work for the social issues. Instead of the environment, the focus is on people and communities. This works for businesspeople who really value rigor. These have been helpful in getting us to something concrete that we create strategy upon.

Existing companies, especially big ones, already have their cultures and policies. You have to work on turning that ship. But, what advice would you give someone starting their own or organization in order to set the right framing from the beginning?

Every new company should have these conversations and considerations from day one. When we were creating our current company, we started with discussions and decisions about social and ecological impacts and started setting up systems so that we were walking the talk. This is an ongoing process. I know it can sound like a luxury, but, I strongly believe no one should be starting any type of business without doing this upfront in the world, today. And, of course, every company should be very clear about their stakeholders. They need some kind of analysis about this, that goes beyond competitors. That's critical to the conversation. It sounds like a really big undertaking, because it can be, but if you start early and just make it part of how you're already building up your business, this can be managed better. I'm living that right now. We are setting up our principles and understanding concerns so we can put guardrails and mitigations in place. It allows us to stay truer to the mission that we're embarking upon, especially as a public benefit corporation.

We decided that even that wasn't enough for us. If we want to participate in regenerating the planet and communities meaningfully and actively, we need to make sure that a part of our company is owned by nature. I know that's maybe more difficult for a lot of organizations to start off with, but setting the intention of how you will be making money, and who will profit from it, is important from day one. We also talked about not just compensation, but the importance of governance and participation in decision making. We don't have all the answers, yet. For example, *we don't know how to put Nature on the board, yet*—especially how this can be recognized legally. *But we're working on this.* We're supporting these efforts and leading discussions to help our clients to make this happen too.

Read the entire interview at www.nathan.com/whole-new-strategy

Even if you don't agree that corporations, specifically, should be agents of social change (or should accept responsibility for social impacts), the world we work in now has preempted this opinion. It's now vital to reduce these risks and it's likely that many of these issues represent significant opportunities to create and capture value. The phrase "doing well by doing good" drives some companies to favor strategies that are both profitable and create positive impact in the world.

Acronym roulette

They are so many different ways impact has been defined so far, reflecting the fact that every system leaves someone wanting. Here are just a few of the most common:

- ESG (Environmental, Social Governance)
- CSR (Corporate Social Responsibility)
- UN SDG (The United Nation's 17 Sustainable Development Goals)
- DEIB (Diversity, Equity, Inclusion, Belonging)
- SROI (Social Return on Investment)
- SIA (Social Impact Analysis)

Each defines different sets of impacts in different contexts. ESG and CSR are most commonly used for corporate goals. The UN's SDGs are often referred to as a kind of standard to check against or validate among non-profits and governments. DEIB is mostly used for human resources goals and metrics in larger organizations. The last two are earlier processes used to evaluate the benefits of initiatives, in quantitative terms.

You can find materials on the above "measurement schemas" and you'll quickly find them inadequate for your purposes. Your industry, partners, or governments may favor (or even require) reporting in one or more of the above. If that's the case, by all means use it as best you can.

You should refer to those that you find helpful or that others in your organization know and respect. The UN SDGs are particularly useful for this, but, its possible that none may suit your needs, too. And the biggest challenge of any of these is to define how you plan to measure performance of any specific issue or impact.

One process that might be helpful is to develop a theory of change: a common thesis format used in the non-profit world. In essence, this is a series of questions designed to clearly define what your change goals are, how you understand them in terms of their impact, who they impact, and what the context for that change might be. Too often, though we may label the kinds of change we hope to make, when we can't be specific about the details, we never reach our goals.

When we get into the specifics of choosing metrics to track, we also have to keep in mind that many kinds of change resist quantitative measurement. You may need to set—and even invent—metrics that can summarize qualitative impacts. Don't fall into the trap of thinking that metrics or data can't be qualitative and can only be expressed in numbers. Some of the most important simply can't be numerical.

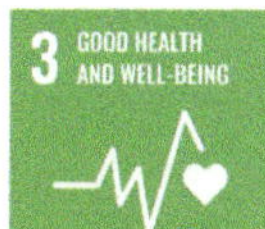

Lastly, beware the drive to compare alternatives and make decisions only on the basis of numbers, especially money. Just because one alternative saves money doesn't make it the "right" one. For example, in the 1970s, Ford Pintos (a compact car) had a regrettable result if they were rear-ended by another vehicle: the car could catch fire or even explode. The Ford Motor Company looked into the issue and found that if they replaced a valve in the fuel system, they could prevent this result. They calculated the cost of recalling every Pinto on the road and replacing the part (including the labor costs). This was quite expensive. They also compared the alternative of not doing so (the costs of litigation and paying off the wrongful death lawsuit judgements). Sadly, this was an extremely narrow, quantitative approach. They decided that it was in the company's best financial interest not to recall and repair the cars as it would cost more to do so than paying legal fees and judgements.

This is the "logical" extreme of the quantitative approach. It's called a ***cost/benefit analysis***. It's relatively easy to perform as everything is reduced to easily measured figures and decisions. Now, today, we might recognize costs they didn't consider at the time: lifetime customer loyalty; decrease in consumer brand recognition; lost partnerships; increased legal, advertising, and PR costs, etc. However, ***even if the resulting, updated costs were still less, the right decision is to fix the cars!***

You may be faced with a similar mindset and argument when trying to measure impact on any of the issues your organization determines should be part of its impact analysis. Some impacts aren't truly measurable, nor numerically, nor fully cover or reflect our values. That's OK.

IMPACT TOOL: THEORY OF CHANGE

Assembling your own scorecard

The reality of all of these systems is that none of them are yet complete, and even if they were, they don't necessarily reflect your values and goals. You'll always need to assemble your own specific scorecard.

Over a decade ago, I created a scorecard for the Design MBA program at California College of the Arts I ran at the time. This came out of my Sustainability Studio class and was a modification of a similar scorecard created by Phil Hamlet for his graduate graphic design program at Academy of Art University. That, in turn, integrated the steps identified in the Sustainability Helix by students at Presidio World College, now a part of the University of Redlands's offerings. Both are described in more detail in the update to my book on sustainable design, ***Design is the Solution.*** You can download this version on my website as well (see the Take it Further notes at the end of this chapter).

Another emerging approach might be more useful: ***Ecological Benefits Framework***. For those who truly want to lessen negative impacts and see real benefits, we need to expand what we consider the benefits. Much of the financial and economic worlds are focused

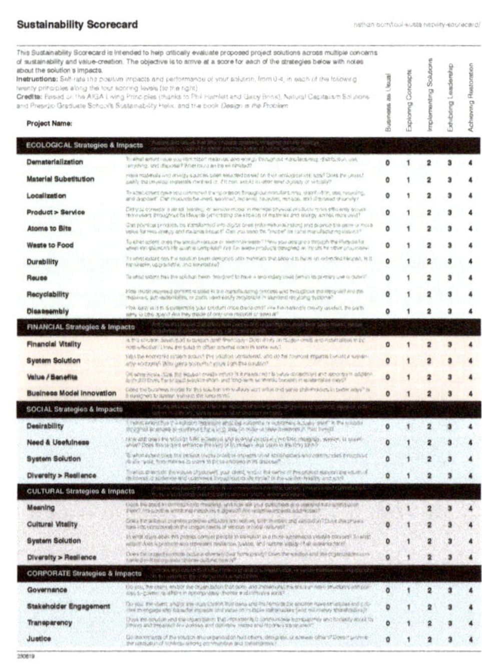

Sustainability Scorecard — nathan.com/tool-sustainability-scorecard/

This Sustainability Scorecard is intended to help critically evaluate proposed project solutions across multiple concerns of sustainability and value-creation. The objective is to arrive at a score for each of the strategies below with notes about the solution's impacts.
Instructions: Self-rate the positive impacts and performance of your solution, from 0–4, in each of the following twenty principles along the four scoring levels (to the right).
Credits: Based on the AIGA Living Principles (thanks to Phil Hamlet and Gaby Brink), Natural Capitalism Solutions, and Presidio Graduate School's Sustainability Helix, and the book *Design is the Problem*.

Project Name:

Strategy	Business as Usual	Exploring Concepts	Implementing Solutions	Exhibiting Leadership	Achieving Restoration
ECOLOGICAL Strategies & Impacts					
Dematerialization	0	1	2	3	4
Material Substitution	0	1	2	3	4
Localization	0	1	2	3	4
Product > Service	0	1	2	3	4
Atoms to Bits	0	1	2	3	4
Waste to Food	0	1	2	3	4
Durability	0	1	2	3	4
Reuse	0	1	2	3	4
Recyclability	0	1	2	3	4
Disassembly	0	1	2	3	4
FINANCIAL Strategies & Impacts					
Financial Vitality	0	1	2	3	4
System Solution	0	1	2	3	4
Value / Benefits	0	1	2	3	4
Business Model Innovation	0	1	2	3	4
SOCIAL Strategies & Impacts					
Desirability	0	1	2	3	4
Need & Usefulness	0	1	2	3	4
System Solution	0	1	2	3	4
Diversity > Resilience	0	1	2	3	4
CULTURAL Strategies & Impacts					
Meaning	0	1	2	3	4
Cultural Vitality	0	1	2	3	4
System Solution	0	1	2	3	4
Diversity > Resilience	0	1	2	3	4
CORPORATE Strategies & Impacts					
Governance	0	1	2	3	4
Stakeholder Engagement	0	1	2	3	4
Transparency	0	1	2	3	4
Justice	0	1	2	3	4

/The Sustainability Helix

Aside from being a corporate-level tool for describing the various aspects of sustainability strategy inside organizations (as opposed to one focused on the product or service level), the Helix is a unique aspect not found in nearly any other sustainability tool. This one is critical to many strategies.

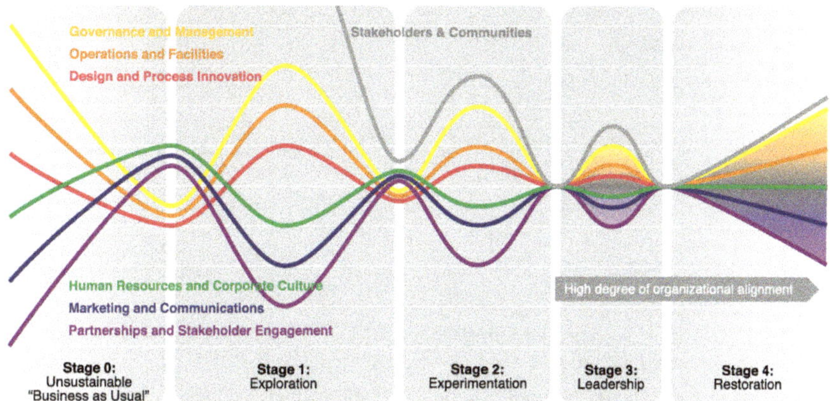

I'll illustrate this with a story: one upon a time in the early 2000s, a large US manufacturer of building products wanted to investigate what it could be doing to improve its impacts on the environment. It was earnest in this goal and did all of the right things: it planned a two-day workshop with representatives from all over the organization (manufacturing, various product lines, operations, finance, marketing, legal, human resources, research & development, etc.). To kick off this focused workshop, they invited one of the most prominent "visionaries" in the sustainability world to give a motivating talk. The morning came, everyone was assembled in a large board room, the luminary was introduced, and the first words out of his mouth were, essentially, "your company's products are hurting people and if you don't do something about it, I'll make it public." This was well-meaning but tragically naïve.

The next words spoken in the room were from a man who stood up, immediately: "This meeting is over. Please leave now." Any guesses as to who this was?

It was one of the company's lawyers. In the US, there is an impossibly tenuous legal situation where organizations have to accept the results of their impacts when they're made known to the organization. Here was someone beginning to make these clear to the leadership throughout the company. After that point, anyone could sue the company for any of these negative impacts and it would be easy to establish that the company knew what they were doing and the impacts. The company tabled any discussion or progress in this aspect from that point on. While the visionary speaker had noble motivation, his approach was, strategically, a disaster as the company never again entertained ecological progress.

The Sustainability Helix measures programs in only positive terms. The baseline is "business as usual" and assumed to better than any of their competitors. With the Helix, there is only one direction to move, towards better and better performance. There is no going backward and never a negative assessment precisely because of this legal condition. When you identify and plan your organization's impact metrics, you might keep this in mind, if only to make your legal counsel more comfortable—and mitigate these risks they will surely identify.

only on carbon dioxide measurement. While CO2 is important, it is hardly the only critical impact and may not be even the most expedient. Here are six that truly define the health of our ecology: ***air, water, soil, biodiversity,*** and ***carbon,*** as well as our society: ***equity***. Think of the last as a catch-all for all social impacts and issues. We are only now developing usable metrics for all of them (carbon has had a lot of support so it's the furthest along).

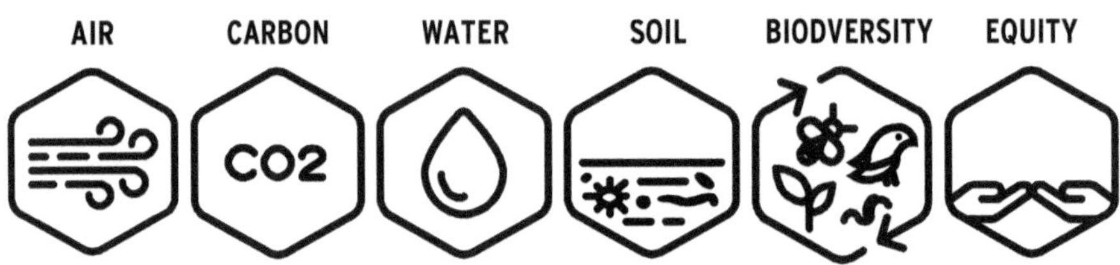

Here, Equity is a big category that contains all of the social impacts. In addition to literal equity, it would include all of the social issues in the Risk Mitigation discussion in the previous chapter. Specifically, it includes governance and democracy, as well.

Hurt and hate

One of the responsibilities you have is to proactively limit the harms your organization and it's offerings can have. This has never been a part of traditional strategy but can no longer be ignored—by any kind of organization. No one goes into business looking to hurt people. Yet, too many organizations do just that, often out of ignorance or accident. It's impossible for organizations to predict every potential harm. Yet, you need to take a moment to explore potential harms, regardless. Can you start or run a successful business without care to these issues? Probably yes, though that's becoming increasingly difficult in our hyper-connected, socialized, technological world. But, do you want to be the kind of person that harms others and doesn't care about your impact on the world, physically or socially? Only you can decide this for yourself. I'll just say that it's becoming increasingly strategic and competitive to be a positive actor in the world.

The first step on this part of the strategic journey is to simply arrange a diverse cadre of people with different perspectives and experiences and simply ask them how they would react to your offerings. This group might include ***gender, age, race, equity***, and other social differences but can also include ***neighbors, partners,*** or people in ***different fields and industries***. You can do this with a focus group, in one-on-one interviews, by setting-up a review board or council, or during user or other testing. The only wrong way to do this is to not do it at all.

You may need to engage non-profits, charities, or government agencies to find and enlist help from some of the most important constituents, but they may be disadvantaged people in many ways. To properly engage with them, you may need to pay them for their time—and it's well worth it. You should approach them carefully, with an abundance of respect, and with trauma-informed engagement techniques.

The second step is to present your offerings, describe their capabilities, and ask people how they would respond or react using them (or having these offerings used on them). What are their concerns? This can be an excellent way to learn about secondary uses and opportunities as well, since people will invent uses that you may have never intended or foresaw (positive ones).

Many of the harms caused by social media, however, could have been predicted and then alleviated long before they became problems. Likewise, ***bias in algorithmic technologies,*** like facial recognition systems, loan approval systems, sentencing and parole systems, and predictive policing would have surfaced during development if the companies behind these technologies simply had a wider, more diverse pool of people involved with their development and testing.

Lastly, don't forget to engage with the haters. Shiny, happy, wonderful people may divulge a set of concerns or uses but hate groups or those opposed to others for any reason will quickly show you how the fruits of your hard work may be used to hurt others. Of course, you should perform these steps at different times. Never mix hateful people with those whom they hate. Unfortunately, hate is a reality in the world and ignoring it can set an organization up to become a conduit for it. Consider Twitter's recent existential troubles wrongly assuming free speech, even hate speech and disinformation, was an infallible ideal. Hate speech and harassment has spiked within the service, driving users and advertisers away in droves.

Even if you don't want to engage haters, you might still use a separate team, entirely, within your organization to work on identify negative impacts. It's often too difficult for a team that has been focused on building something new to imagine how it might break things. In my own classes, I sometimes make teams switch projects for a week to break the things being built because their fresh eyes see new opportunities and threats than those who know the project intimately. They also have different incentives.

There may be no watchdog groups for the offerings you plan to provide but there are almost certainly ***adjacent groups*** that focus on relevant issues. Traditionally, many companies see these groups as problematic and adversarial players. Indeed, some may be stuck in a frame of reference that doesn't allow for the possibility of good actors—especially from the private sector. However, if you're serious about not creating offerings that harm others, you're responsible for seeking the partners that can help you determine if that's a possibility. By reading this paragraph, you are no longer unaware of either the fact that this is possible, your responsibility to act, nor how to start the process. Sorry about that.

It's not unusual that issues other than financials are routinely ignored in business decisions. It's been "business as usual" for many decades. And, business schools have reinforced this thinking for even longer (this is only, now, being addressed by too few schools). However, there are often ways around these common refusals to consider any issues but money. Sustainability professionals learned a long time ago that Nature and the Planet aren't top-of-mind for most people and there are only a few people, even today, that take these into account when making buying decisions—yes, even when it effects their own futures on the Earth.

You may get further making ecological and social gains by not mentioning them at all (bake them into your work regardless of others' criteria) or simply reframe them into real concerns that your peers and leaders do care about. For example, sustainability is often achieved not by using that term explicitly, but by framing it as ***efficiency*** or ***risk mitigation***. Both are still true and both get much more attention and appreciation from traditional businesspeople. Often, if social concerns are framed as ***customer loyalty*** or ***brand value***, they are given more consideration as these two are also triggers for businesspeople who understand them as directly connecting to revenue.

The never-ending story

Perhaps the most important planning you can do is to plan methods of feedback and assessment that you can use over time to measure or understand the impact you're having and whether you need to change strategies. In addition, you should calibrate what level of transparency is important at which levels, inside and outside the organization and among your various stakeholders. If you operate in different countries, they may require this anyway so even if you can get away without worrying about it in the USA, China, or elsewhere, if you're doing business in the EU or other places, you are already required to meet these standards. So you might as well avoid corporate multiple personality syndrome and do this across your entire organization. Refer back to your stakeholder analysis from Chapter 10. If you haven't already identified the partners that may aid (or oppose) your efforts in these regards, now is a good time to do so.

You need a strategy to mitigate harm that's every bit as supported and communicated as your strategies to do everything else in your organization. It needs to be baked-into your organization's structure, reporting, reward system, responsibilities, reports, etc.—in effect, your culture. If not, it can and will be ignored—especially when times get tough.

One of the simplest ways to assess your impact is simply to ask those around you what they think it is. Ask your managers, your employees, your customers, etc. what their concerns are. Ask them about their understanding of your business and how it effects them. If you're interviewing at an organization, ask them what their sustainability strategy is. Ask them about their social or equity strategy. Ask them about where they stand

/Integrated Bottom Line

Since at least the 1990s, the sustainability world has called for a "triple bottom line" approach to business. The first bottom line is, of course, the financial one that common accounting tools already track and leaders use to gauge success. The second is a new kind of accounting for the ecological costs, benefits, impacts, and issues tied to the organization's operations. The third is the same for social context: the benefits and costs in social terms to all of its stakeholders.

While many leaders agreed with this approach, and even made attempts at calculating, reporting and managing their organizations with these three summaries in mind, more often than not, when the economy got difficult or money became critical, these leaders immediately ignored the other two bottom lines in favor of only the first: the money. Yes, it's critical for a company to survive if it's ever going to do any good at all but, often, these two other accountings aren't at odds with the financial accounting and, in some cases, they actually help it.

Traditional accounting and management ignored the interconnected value created by operations, decisions, and culture. Most sustainability initiatives result in money saved and risk mitigated. Many policies and activities seen as frivolous benefits for employees are often responsible for attracting and retaining the best talent (saving money in hiring and training costs). These three bottom lines aren't disconnected and should reflect their interdependencies and intervaluations.

In 2004, students in the first class in the MBA in Sustainable Management program at Presidio Graduate School in San Francisco, recognized this and called for an ***Integrated Bottom Line***. This would be a single bottom line for organizations to manage themselves; all issues, impacts, values, costs, and benefits, would be calculated together with their connections intact. This would help better decisions to be made and supported within the organization as well as externally. While absolutely correct, no one (to date) has created the accounting tools for this. Nor has anyone done the same with the triple bottom line.* Sadly, if you decided tomorrow to manage your organization from these perspectives, there are no tools available for you to use in place of the traditional ones. But while we await their development, we have no excuse to take them into account. In fact, perhaps, this is an opportunity you've been waiting for to build a meaningful, impactful business helping make the world better in a material way: helping others do better business.

---

* The Sustainable Accounting Standards Board has been making slow progress to develop these tools but they have yet to issue tools ready-for-use.

on any issue important to you and what they're doing about it. More likely than not, at least for now, they won't have good answers. Their inability to answer or discuss your concerns is an important indicator and something you should take into account. Can you accomplish your personal impact goals at this institution? Are they open to change? Can you be the change they need and support?

/Highlights

- There are no commonly accepted ways to measure social and ecological impacts, only many diverse measures across many categories of issues and impacts. This lack of standards shouldn't deter you, however, from analyzing and planning positive impacts and mitigating negative ones.
- There is a history of social impact measures, from SROI (Social Return On Investment) to SIA (Social Impact Analysis) to, currently, ESG (Environmental, Social, Governance) regarding external impacts and DEIB (Diversity, Equity, Inclusion, and Belonging) regarding internal ones.
- Any impact analysis should include a *Theory of Change* that acknowledges the systemic aspects of impacts (and their responses).
- You'll likely need to invent or assemble a scorecard for your organization that fits its social and ecological goals. You may be able to modify existing scorecards but you may also need to develop your own from scratch. Hopefully, in the near future, there will be more solutions readily available.

/Explore More

- *Design is the Solution* by Nathan Shedroff
- *Leading Change Through Sustainability* by Bob Doppelt
- *Humanetech's Ledger of Harms* ledger.humanetech.com
- *Climate Capitalism* by Hunter L. Lovins & Boyd Cohen
- *Strategy for Sustainability* by Adam Werbach
- *United Nations Sustainable Development Goals for 2030* sdgs.un.org/2030agenda

Your Future

The future is always heading toward you, in small or large timelines. There is no escaping it. However, we can approach the future in very different ways: we can fear it, we can be overly optimistic about it, we can look at it deterministically, or even be indifferent. However, we can also be strategic.

Foresight is a set of strategic processes to examine the richness of the future in front of us. It is always done best when approached *systemically* and *collaboratively*. No one can see all of the potential future so we all see a fractical piece that helps illuminate the whole.

Think about the future as a set of modifications on the present that you know. If you've done the research to understand trends, stakeholders, and competitors, as well as the decision-drivers of your customers, then the fundamental data your've built your strategy upon is already sound. Looking into the future, any specific potential scenarios, is merely a different set of decision-drivers, trends, and responses by various stakeholders that shuffles into that strategy. With new conditions, you need to evaluate if your decisions, insights, and opportunities from the Market sequence are still valid. If not, you need to modify these and then address them in the Operations sequence.

By simply duplicating your work and modifying the changes under a specific scenario, you can endlessly consider new cases and alternative conclusions, each one a new perspective on the future and each one, a different strategy to take as the world evolves.

Chapter 15

Your Vision

Vision and Mission are often confused. In many organizations, the Mission and Vision are so similar, there's no point in having one or the other. Consider these:

- Our *Mission* is to deliver the best online customer banking experience!
- Our *Vision* is a vibrant bank that helps customers realize their goals and changes their lives!

Really, there's no difference between these. Your vision can't merely the completion of all or part of your Mission. It's not a vision of your own success.

or, consider these:

- Our *Mission* is to provide exceptional online financial services and solutions to our customers, ensuring their financial well-being and prosperity. We strive to uphold the highest standards of integrity and professionalism.
- Our *Vision* is to be the leading provider of online financial services, renowned for our commitment to customer satisfaction, financial stability, and growth. We aim to be recognized as a trusted partner, offering comprehensive solutions and contributing to the success of individuals and businesses in the communities we serve.

There's nothing wrong with either of these statements but they speak to exactly the same thing. There's no functional difference between them. One is simply the achievement of the other.

Certainly, you should have a strong, concise, clear *mission statement* as was discussed in Chapter 11. Then, what purpose does a *vision statement* serve? That's the billion-dollar question. If these two are so often confused, what is the intent? According to Wikipedia:

> A vision statement is an inspirational statement of an idealistic emotional future of a company or group.

The definition from the Corporate Finance Institute (CFI) might be better:

> A vision statement describes what a company desires to achieve in the long-run, generally in a time frame of five to ten years, or sometimes even longer. It depicts a vision of what the company will look like in the future and sets a defined direction for the planning and execution of corporate-level strategies.

In the first case, Wikipedia's editors describe the difference as emotional. But, if your Mission statement doesn't either reflect emotional value or account for it, there's little likelihood that your company is set to generate any for customers, partners, etc.

In the second definition, CFI defines a vision as being longer-term but 3-5 years is also what a mission statement should cover (it shouldn't be something a company changes every year). I agree with the idea of longer-term horizons but disagree with the time frame and, also, with the definition being limited to the company's future. As I described in chapter 10, the world around the company is critical to understand.

Added to this confusion is the fact that vision is used elsewhere in business for other purposes. In particular, vision is a component of foresight and the long-term strategic processes companies use to peer into the future in order to project their needs and opportunities.

All of these issues flow into the same solution: the Vision statement should be a description of the future an organization is expecting and planning for. This can be at any time frame, from 3 years to 20 years or more. It can change with conditions or it may be appropriate to have more than one, preparing for different future conditions. Instead, consider these:

- Our **Mission** is to provide exceptional online financial services and solutions to our customers, ensuring their financial well-being and prosperity. We strive to uphold the highest standards of integrity and professionalism.
- Our **Vision** is for people to more easily manage their money so that they have a more successful, stable, and thriving financial future without anxiety, fear, or depression about that future.

This vision statement speaks to the benefits to customers lives (and, potentially, the world). An even stronger, more aspirational version might be:

- Our **Vision** is for business and technology to make the complicated world or personal finance more human, fair, and clear. We envision leading in an industry that doesn't prey on its customers with features and policies that hurt their financial success but helps them effortlessly manage their money, grow the value of their portfolios, thrive financially, and live more confidently and peacefully regardless of the changes the future may bring.

This one is more exciting for people to join, making it easier to manage people who do. It inspires not only offerings but clear alignment for employees and partners to act. It is a statement about a better world, not merely a successful company.

What Vision—and Who's?

This brings us straight into Strategic Foresight, a set of tools and processes for imagining possible futures, positioning both their probabilities and preferabilities, and generating plans that allow organizations to act on them.

There are several, common foresight tools and processes. Generally, they are all a variation of Scenario Planning, a technique originally developed by the US military in the 1950s and further developed in think tanks: by Herman Kahn at RAND and Gaston Berger at the Centre d'Etudes Prospectives. It was famously used in business by the 1970s by Pierre Wack at Royal Dutch Shell, helping them to quickly react and recover from the Oil Shock of 1973. By preparing a realistic number of potential scenarios and responses well in advance of a major event, the leaders of Royal Dutch Shell were able to pull these plans off the shelf, reconsider the context, and start implementing immediately. This story also solidified the value of scenario planning to strategy.

Most industries have a variety of tools that function as a type of scenario planning or disaster preparation. Major airlines create "dark sites" in advance of crashes or other issues to respond more quickly in real time when something bad happens. Even newspapers and magazines pre-write obituaries for famous people, often decades in advance, revising them periodically, so they can publish immediately if a celebrity dies.

Using scenarios to inform strategy isn't an easy process but the steps are more or less straightforward. The difference between successful scenarios and unsuccessful ones is in how the process is managed and who is involved. In particular, this is an iterative, collaborative, and generative process so trying to manage it as if it were a quality assurance issue, like with Six Sigma tools, is the wrong way to get results.

Scenario Planning requires a broad, diverse cohort of experts from many fields. They can't all be in the industry of the company. Some should come from government, science, the public sector, related industries, etc. and the participants should have different skills and experiences. Some might be designers or artists, others scientists of varying types, even philosophers. The point is to build scenarios with the help of multiple perspectives so that the vision of the possible world is as well-rounded and profoundly "real" as possible. These visions can push boundaries of what is possible and don't all need to relate to what is preferrable. For example, no one at Royal Dutch Shell was hoping for an oil-based economic downturn yet the fact that they prepared for it was invaluable! As is often said, "Hope for the best, but plan for the worst."

Context changes vision

Chapter 10 was all about the current context and how it impacts strategy. Foresight is all about envisioning future contexts for the same purpose. As such, most of its impacts simply change the forces, issues, and concerns of stakeholders and trends. Also, your customers' decision-drivers will likely change under that scenario, as well. Think of a scenario as an instance of a new set of trends and stakeholder motivations—sometimes a radically different one. As you can imagine, these will change your decisions throughout the strategic process but it doesn't change the process, itself. Everything else is still relevant.

As conditions change (or as you imagine them changing), your decisions will need to evolve, as well. You might even, eventually reconsider the highest-level priorities for your organization—such as your Mission and Goals. This is why Mission and Vision are so often tied together.

What time is it?

One of the first considerations in foresight is the time horizon you consider appropriate. A one-to-three year timeframe is really focused on Operations. This is a level appropriate to operational strategies (technical strategy, design strategy, supply chain strategy, etc.). This isn't really the domain of foresight tools but more for standard planning tools.

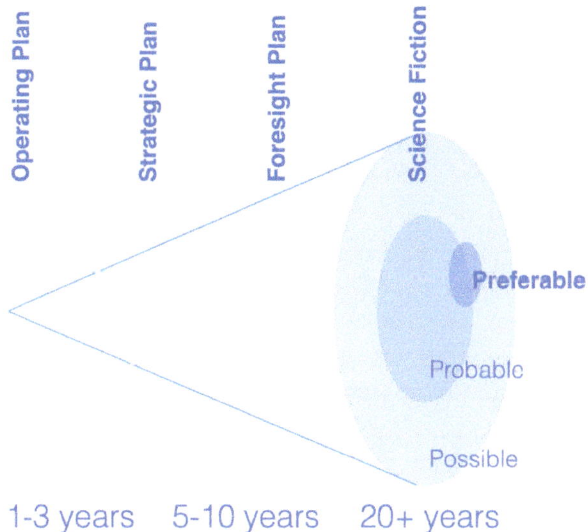

It's important to differentiate, here, between trends and fads. The latter are fun, often frivolous, and don't last long. They engage our pleasure centers (or our insecurities) but they don't have lasting change, either for ourselves or society. The Pet Rock™ is a perfect example. It was simply a rock set in a "nest" of shredded paper and put in a box that looked like a miniature animal carrier. It didn't even have googly eyes pasted on it. It didn't do anything. It was a humorous gift promising fun and no responsibilities—and it sold millions of units in 1975 on just this basis. Just like the Beanie Baby™ craze, the spinner craze, micro mini skirts, and that

Nathan/ How do you describe the value of strategic foresight to leaders and when they should and shouldn't employ it?

Radha/ Imagine having a set of tools, frameworks, and methodologies that can put you in a place where you have some ***agency and ownership over the future.*** And, you don't have to resign to the future happening to you. You're not chasing the market, you're not just guessing what's happening. We can scan for ***signals of change***. We can build our own point of view. We can build visions of futures that are preferable for us and work towards them. And we can do that along the way while diminishing blind spots and gaps. When you bring that to a CEO, they're usually pretty open to having a conversation. So, that is often where I start: "How do you ensure that you don't have to resign to the future happening to you, with agency ownership and understand where you have accountability, over a particular future?"

That's probably the most concise definition I've ever heard.

It's taken years to come to, but once you land on that, you don't let it go. Oftentimes, the language we use to talk about the future can be alienating to folks who don't operate in the foresight space. And, we see that across critical design, speculative design, anything under the umbrella of "future studies." For people who have an MBA or marketing degree or any business degree, for that matter, Foresight doesn't always make sense. But, when we talk about foresight, this is what we actually mean: ***"How can you understand the uncertainty that's taking place in your immediate environment—your business, your industry, your customers, your employees, and the external environment, and the global drivers of change?"*** Then, ***"How do you capitalize on that change in a meaningful way?"***

A lot of foresight and future studies work can feel like science fiction to folks and, oftentimes, the outcomes of foresight work tends to end up in marketing and communication strategies, which isn't terrible but doesn't realize it's true, potential impact. Often, this comes down to the positioning of a foresight team within an organization. At Autodesk, it was critical that we didn't sit in the Mar/Comms group, but that we sat instead in the research group and that we reported directly to the CTO. Even at Arup, foresight is positioned directly with leadership, working in the most strategic parts of the company to drive forward long-term strategy.

When you can link foresight and strategy, that's where it has the most value. If you go in asking to build visions of the future, that's not where the value lies, honestly. To me, scenarios and visions of the future are prototypes. It's like how we build architectural models. It's a tool for you to see what a possible future might look like for you to pull it apart and repack it in some way. It's not the final outcome. Unfortunately, what often happens is that the scenarios end-up being the final outcome. And that's what people think foresight is. So, I always talk about scenarios as prototypes.

It sounds like you're basically suggesting that the journey is at least as much of the value as the thing that comes out of the journey. Putting people in that space—especially leaders—to consider things they haven't seen or don't usually consider is half the value, if not more.

Exactly. I place strategic foresight on a continuum between provocation and planning or science fiction and strategy. Foresight will pull from or be inspired by or build visions that feel science fiction. They're provocations. But, the real work and the real value of foresight is being the mechanism that delivers you back into implementation, planning, and strategy. If you only focus on the cool part and you don't focus on what do you do about it, you've ignored your agency. That's where you lose a lot of folks.

What are those pieces that aren't just about the vision—the more pragmatic pieces that have immediate value to a company?

At Autodesk, it was like taking a scenario, going to the industry strategy groups, saying, "What do you now do about this? If this is what executive leadership is saying is our vision, how do we actually help you backcast and build a roadmap toward realizing these things? How does it impact your strategic realization and strategic intent?" Then, we take that to product development and ask, "How does this impact the tools in the tech?" We do this with clients of Arup, too, which is to say, "If this is your 10 year vision on climate action, what does that actually mean for your business?" Let's run this through a futures wheel. Let's run this through a visioning and road-mapping exercise.

We work toward getting them to a place where they can translate the change that we're seeing in the environment and determining what they need to do to have control over that change. And, for the things they don't have control over, is it a matter of upskilling our people in some way? Is it a matter of partnering with folks who do it better or acquiring someone who does it better? Is it a matter of building something internally to address the change?

I imagine that you can tell those different kinds of companies in the first conversation. What are the "tells" that help you understand where companies are going to end up?

There are two models of foresight. One is coming from the outside, as a consultant. And, the other approach is to embed yourself inside of an organization. I almost prefer the second because, then, you can really ensure that there are resources, time, and effort being invested in bringing these things to fruition. When you come into a company as a consultant, you can only go as far as the scope allows you to. You don't usually have the opportunity to come back to a client and ask "Hey, how did that thing go? Did you actually do it?" We do have some clients that we have trusted relationships with that span years.

Foresight is not helpful for quick a solutions. It's robust and it's not great when you operate in silos. It requires diversity of thought, networked thinking, and divergent thinking. When something's a trend, it's already too late for foresight work.

Read the entire interview at www.nathan.com/whole-new-strategy

terrible thong in the movie Borat, these fads come quickly, shine brightly (if they're lucky) and die just as quickly.

Trends have long-term impact. Crocs, the funny-looking, plastic, casual shoes seemed like a fad when they were first introduced in 2002. But, they're still here two decades later and have inspired many imitators and variations. They are beloved by their owners (often despite embarrassment) and have become a category of their own.

Your mission is to identify trends that have big and lastly impact. It would be a waste of your time to focus on fads for foresight work because they don't last long enough. However, fads can sometimes point to actual trends if you bother to investigate.

For most of the last century, the future was exaggerated. We don't have floating cities, personal robotic maids, flying cars, or antigravity boots. Technology often takes much longer to develop and deploy—particularly affordably—than even technologist predict. However, in the last decade, many technologies have advanced so quickly (like personal devices, apps, and machine learning) that it can sometimes be difficult to imagine the future. Everyday, it can seem that we already live in the only future we might need. This makes it more challenging to envision scenarios that are meaningful, impactful, and still realistic.

Once we can imagine a plausible, important future, we need to expand that vision with enough details to make it seem real and then consider how it changes the context for our organization (and our customers, ourselves, and any of our other stakeholders). What happens to us in that future? What are the new opportunities and threats? What must happen to make that future occur (and what might prevent it)? And, finally, what can we do to create, respond, influence, or thrive in that future?

To really expand that scenario, we might look at more reverberating effects of it. For example, once you create a future, what comes next? You might have another team build on that future to uncover secondary, tertiary, or even deeper effects. For sure, you're expanding the timeline but your also enriching your understanding of the impacts and influences that future might have.

The three-to-five year time frame is more appropriate for strategic planning. It's the most common timeframe for strategic plans, as it allows for thoughtful consideration of the future while not questioning every possible thing that might occur.

Foresight really shines in the five-to-twenty year time frame, as it's possible to read the current state of science, technology, society, etc. with a critical eye and still set reasonable expectations about the changes those developments might bring.

Lastly, any timeframe beyond 20 years is really the domain of science fiction, which can be a useful investigation into current attitudes, understandings, and conditions, as well, but it's not the same as engaging organizational strategy. Science fiction can be a potent force in imagining new opportunities, particularly when paired with the design process. Science fiction prototyping, for example, has been used in many companies, big and small as a prompt for legitimate reimagining of an organization's business (or their customer's lives). I've run these workshops at Intel and global conferences and they help engineers, designers, researchers, and managers quickly break old assumptions and see new possibilities, but while the ideas that emerge are great prompts for strategy, they aren't the same as strategy.

Qualitative Scenarios

An easy way to approach scenarios is to assume one major change, such as the economy goes bad (recession or depression) or becomes utopian. Or, perhaps, what happens if the West Antarctic ice sheet breaks off and begins to melt? That could raise sea level, quickly, by 16 feet! That's a scenario that would affect nearly everything and nearly everyone.

Scenarios based on quantitative changes or extreme events are easy to define and ponder. But, consider other kinds of scenarios, based on more qualitative changes. When I ran brand scenario workshops for AIGA with my colleague, Davis Masten, we explored scenarios like: extreme individuality (represented by mass-customization technology), extreme belonging (a desire to connect with others—basically the opposite of individuality), rare privacy, or the rise of Latin America. Each scenario posited a single, major qualitative change in the world and the results flowed from that assumption. As with every other point in strategy, focusing only on the quantitative will often preempt the qualitative and the later often yields more interesting questions and results.

Note, that utopian scenarios aren't usually interesting. If the world is wonderful, money is plentiful, the impact, necessarily, eliminates many sources of conflict or difficulty. This is great for society but doesn't always create meaningful, actionable plans for many organizations. Instead, specific advances that make change—even better change—are more helpful. For example, consider what might happen if fusion energy becomes commercially viable. As many experts attest, the price of energy will plummet, making electrical power exceedingly inexpensive—potentially negligible. That's certainly great for society but will create many changes to organizations and governments worldwide who thrive off the opposite. For anyone in business, even if not in the energy sector, this is a worthwhile scenario to consider. But, "everything for everyone is awesome" isn't either specific enough or constrained enough to be helpful.

Some common scenarios you might consider include:

Economic depression
Mass customization/personalization
Rise of fascism
Environmental collapse
Massive immigration or refugees
Demographic shifts
Ecological collapse

Inexpensive fusion power
Death of a celebrity or key person in your organization
Apple entering your market (Competitor X)

In addition, you might go back to the opportunities and threats you identified in the Market or Operations sequences and create a scenario based on an extreme example of those. The only "right" scenario is one that causes you and your organization to consider a plausible, alternate future. The only "wrong" ones are the ones that don't push far enough to stimulate change or make things too easy (like utopia).

Foresight Variations

Once you understand the process for scenarios, there are many ways to riff on these. ***Backcasting***, for example, specifically looks at the plausible lead-up to a preferable scenario. So, if you've carefully created a scenario outcome you like, backcasting is the process of considering what steps between today and that scenario might lead to it becoming a reality. It acknowledges that one change can lead to another and asks the question: "what steps, specifically, could this future develop upon." Then, you can imagine how to make each of those steps real.

Another variation was created by Brian David Johnson, a notable expert in foresight, to specifically look at potential threats. He runs ***threatcasting*** workshops twice a year for the US Department of Defense to identify potential threats no one else has identified. He brings together experts from all over the Department of Homeland Security (including the DoD, FBI, CIA, and Secret Service), as well as all of the military branches) and mixes in scientists of all types (including political and social sciences), businesspeople, and others to form a diverse set of teams working together on specific prompts. The results of this work at Arizona State University's Threatcasting Lab are published on their website.

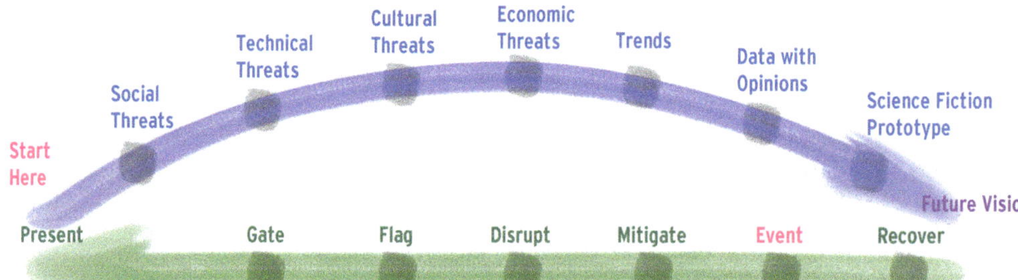

The threatcasting process identifies not just the threat but the "gates" that must be crossed for it to become a reality. In examining the threat timeline, participants can imagine how it happened, how it could have been disrupted in progress, how the effects could be mitigated or even how to recover from the threat events. Reading any of their publications is both mind-blowing and eye-opening. There is no reason why this same process couldn't be employed by any organization to identify, disrupt, and mitigate potential threats to their own goals.

Developing Your Organization's Vision

Where does this all apply to Vision for an organization? Any of these techniques can be used to change the context considered for strategy. In doing so, the organization can plan a response to that new context. In reality, any new context is only a prediction—one that is unlikely to come to pass exactly as envisioned. Even the Oil Shock of 1973 didn't unfold example as in Royal Dutch Shell's scenario. But, perfect prediction isn't the goal. Imagine having a suite of scenarios that describe different responses to circumstances. Responses from more than one scenario may be relevant to consider, not merely from a single one.

In the Brand Futures scenarios work I did with AIGA, it was often the case that many of the scenarios related (either through similar technologies or mechanisms of change in people's attitudes). Having a suite of scenarios helps understand the others, and their interconnections. One scenario is only useful to explore if that very thing happens, exactly as imagines. Therefore, scenarios are almost done plurally. There is need for several, not merely to have multiple possible solutions but because the plurality informs each individual investigation, strengthening and deepening it.

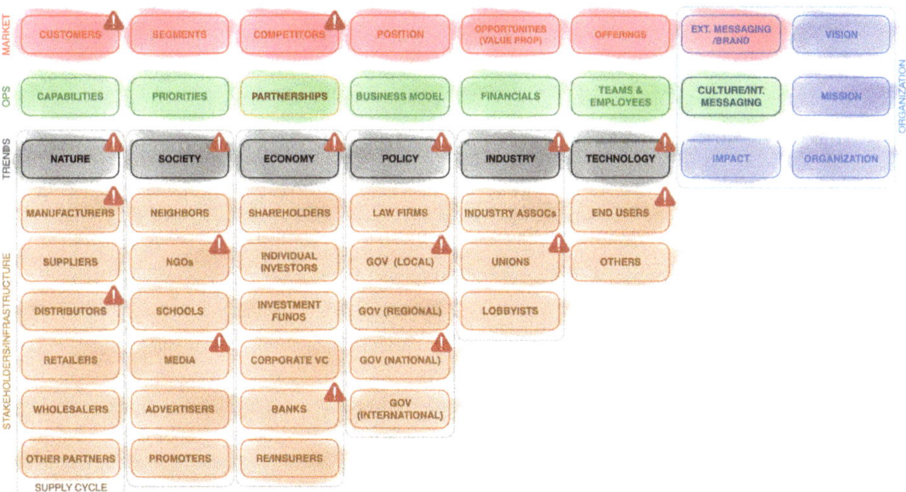

Think of a scenario as a set of changes to your stakeholders and trends. In a different context, what changes most are the decision-drivers of customers, competitors, and specific stakeholders. You may need to consider stakeholders that you didn't before because, under this scenario, their reactions, concerns, and impacts may suddenly be of consequence to your business. Your ecosystem can't help but shift under any new scenario. In addition, trends will change, too. It's not only that there may be new trends. The rankings of importance of trends you previously identified may have changed as well. The same goes for the decision-drivers of your stakeholders. You may or may not have new customers or segments due to the scenario but it's reasonable to consider that the drivers of all of your stakeholders' decisions have been reset. There may be now concerns that driver their decision but, for sure, the ranking of importance for past decision-drivers will have likely changed, as well.

Nathan/ Should every organization be thinking about —and acting on—strategic foresight?

David/ Companies need to reach a certain level of maturity to take advantage of foresight. Not every organization is ready to do it or use it. And, there's a spectrum. All organizations look into the future, at least a little bit. Anytime they make a plan, they're operating in the future. But, they don't always imagine how the future might be different before they make that plan. Most assume that conditions will be, more or less, the same as they've been. Of course, that can work well—for a while—depending on your business or industry. But, as we all saw with the pandemic, the future has a way of disrupting the "normal." You can't be ready for everything but every business environment and market is changing all of the time, and there are certainly things that more businesses should take into account that they usually don't.

Some plans look out a quarter or a year. Others, 2-3 years, Still others, 5-10 years. And, some look out even further: 20 years or more. Those are all different animals and require different techniques. This isn't about predicting the future but looking at possibilities, focusing on the most interesting or advantageous, and then planning how to react if they happen.

Who should be in charge of foresight?

it really depends on the leaders and the overall culture of the leadership team. Because it's an emergent discipline, leaders value different (and at times inconsistent) sets of inputs and they each have different expectations of change in the markets based on their personal frame of reference. Some leaders absolutely don't think foresight is important or even a thing. That's fine. Hopefully, they can react well in realtime, as their industry or the world changes. Whoever should be in charge of foresight should strive to influence their leadership while acknowledging some leaders are completely focused on the "now." Foresight deals with understanding how leadership cultures make decisions. If they find that things need to change, they'll do that in the next revision or cycle. Some leaders are reluctant to pivot, based on what they find, which is understandable. They think in quarters or six month cycles.

Others are comfortable with some type of foresight tools and processes but not others. That's fine, too. I look for what works for different leaders and company cultures. Some won't stick with the process very long before they give up. It really takes at least a six month commitment to get to usable insights on the efficacy of foresight and innovation. When you talk to fitness instructors, most will tell you that you need to sustain a commitment to new activities—to change—for at least 28 days. Otherwise, you haven't made new habits. That principle also applies in foresight work. I don't think you can find meaningful insights within your market in a month. Teams should be looking at conditions for longer, to find the best value. It takes discipline, not unlike working out. It also takes discipline to apply the insights you find to new activities and behaviors.

Foresight is relatively new to most professionals; it certainly was for me before I joined the DMBA program. On the other hand, strategy is more widely recognized among a broader audience. However, strategy can be somewhat abstract for many people, and adding another layer of abstraction with foresight on top of it can be especially challenging for those who tend to think in more concrete terms. So, I make an effort to identify practical use cases that illustrate foresight's distinctiveness from strategy. Frameworks play a pivotal role as well as having dedicated workshops with enough time to think through them.

Furthermore, I've observed a growing trend in organizations valuing insights almost as much as they do analysis. My firsthand experience in consulting involved gathering insights while collaborating with coworkers focused on data analysis and strategy. The most successful projects were those that effectively combined both approaches. Foresight enters the picture as customer insights help shape strategic decisions. One valuable framework I learned in my foresight class draws inspiration from Pierre Wack's scenario planning methodology. This framework introduces nuance to insights by considering the differences between predetermined elements and critical uncertainties. By incorporating time as a dimension into the insights, this framework helps categorize insights - trends that will be around for 20, 30 years or variables that are more malleable to macro change.

Predetermined elements have a certain level of predictability in their evolution whereas critical uncertainties carry an element of unpredictability regarding their trajectory. In a given business environment, both elements are present. For instance, let's say we're building a new B2B product and we want to really understand the value proposition in a particular market, and we need to really solve someone's pain. During research, we want to understand the nature of the challenge so we can use this framework as one lens to organize our findings. When working on discovery-oriented research, we might ask: "How long has this problem been going on? Is this something that you think is endemic to the industry? Or, do you think this is more nuanced? Talk about what triggers the pain points." The answers we hear, how they describe the situation, all will help to make sense of the magnitude of the problem and how long it has been around.

For example, in the facilities operations industry, a ***predetermined element*** would be the belief that this business function will always be a cost center. Therefore, we can expect workers to continue having the mindset that 'less is more' thus influencing the way they construct value. An example of a ***critical uncertainty*** is that brick-and-mortar stores will remain important in retail going forward. The pandemic exposed its fragility but it remains one that requires the industry to plan mitigation strategies. This begs the question: "What degree of uncertainty does this element have?"

Read the entire interview at www.nathan.com/whole-new-strategy

You can think of a scenario or a vision for the future as a distinct set of these conditions (trends and decision-drivers). That's a convenient way to frame a scenario because all of the other parts of your strategy remain the same. By entering or overlaying these new conditions, into the same framework, they impact your strategy in exactly the same way that your previous context did. Of course, you need to start back at the beginning of the Market sequence, customers, to see what's changed, and then pull through all of your new rankings and decisions until you get to the end and restart your Operations sequence to reflect these new options and priorities. While it sounds like a lot of work, it's the same process and sequence as before—and, many of your prior decisions and data may still be valid. So, really, it's a big time-saver to have your information and data in this format. It makes considering alternative futures much easier.

Once you have scenarios imagined and explored, it's time to choose either a preferred scenario you want to focus on bringing to reality, or the one you believe is most probable (and, therefore, need to content with in your organization's strategy). The former runs the risk of choosing a scenario that is desired but not likely. This would be a mistake, obviously. The latter is usually the safer way to go.

This chosen scenario is your vision. This should form the basis for your vision statement, that description of the world your either expect or are prepared to work within. If you think that the world is becoming a more open place, your vision should reflect that. This is a grounding for your strategic work—and certainly your mission statement. ***There should never be a conflict between your mission and vision statements.*** The first should comfortably exist in the context of the second. If it doesn't, your strategy can't be coherent.

Operationally, your vision statement is more of a description than a plan. In the context of your strategic plan, it may take up no more than a paragraph. Yet, it sets context for everything else.

Behind your vision statement may be an entirely different strategy that outlines how that vision may come to be, what the other potential visions might be, how to respond to these scenarios, and what steps might be taken in further strategic plans to keep working toward that scenario. This is where your scenarios will "live" within your strategy, even if they aren't consulted day-to-day.

Ultimately, it's the investigation that is the most valuable part of the foresight process, not the end results. Like much regarding strategy, merely asking questions and considering new contexts often gives us the important insights we need to make decisions. The process is the most valuable part, not the deliverable (though that deliverable may be critical to communicate to others). The best way to do this poorly is to not do it at all.

Science Fiction Prototyping

Because it's so difficult for people—especially managers and leaders—to consider a context that isn't their day-to-day context, it's sometimes helpful to provide an opportunity to really push the boundaries of what they imagine is possible. Futurist Brian David Johnson often uses science fiction prototyping to do just that. I, too, have run workshops for companies to help their teams identify new opportunities.

The process starts with an overview of some of the impacts that science fiction has had on business and other parts of society. It helps to have some fun and thoughtful scifi video clips from popular and uncommon scifi films and televisions. Then, the workshop leader can step people through a process of choosing a scifi context, a character, and imagine how they would solve a challenge in their world. The leader might overlay edgy technologies to push teams even further.

When the teams have built an interesting story, the leader helps them "pull it back" to present day, shedding some of the more unrealistic or impossible aspects but keeping the central story and solution intact as much as possible. While this seems frivolous, I have seen teams identify new, realistic opportunities they would have never identified before.

For example, in one of my workshop attendees chose his favorite film, Aliens, and the character of the Alien Queen to explore. I suggested Ripley might be a more helpful character as I had remembered that he introduced himself as someone who worked on the back-end software for an international transportation company (Ripley, the central character of Aliens, manages cargo as her job). It wasn't a big surprise to anyone but him that, when he finished, he had designed a new kind of interface for package handlers to better do their jobs—today.

The context of science fiction often gives people permission to explore possibilities they otherwise wouldn't. When imagining the possible futures for your organization, you may have to employ techniques like this to explore more widely and deeply those futures.

/Highlights

- Your vision should be just that, a statement about the world you expect to inhabit. Your mission should be your goals and actions within that world.
- Your vision is a statement about foresight that can range from the very near term (next quarter or next year) to the somewhat far (10-20 years away). Past 20 years, is likely too far to make effective strategic plans, though some organizations and leaders try.
- Foresight tools don't predict the future but help us imagine possible futures that we prefer and want to help occur.
- Effective visions require perspectives and experiences from a diverse set of people and research: science, medicine, government, technology, various industries, academia, communities, etc. A wide, diverse, informed context is just as important to foresight as it is to the Market sequence described in this book (and uses the same categories).
- Think of foresight as a set of new trends, customer decision-drivers, competitors, and stakeholder decision-drivers that impact your strategy in ways that current ones don't. The same process you've used to develop near-term strategy can be used for far-term strategy.
- Most foresight work is a variation of scenario planning.
- Great foresight planning requires both qualitative and quantitative indicators. In fact, qualitative projections will likely be more useful than quantitative ones.
- Backcasting is a process to fill-in the timeline for a scenario developed to describe a possible future. By assuming this future, backcasting asks us to imagine the necessary steps required for that future to become reality.
- Threatcasting is used to focus on imagined or emerging threats and, then, developing mitigating strategies and tactics. It is commonly used by governments and military organizations but can also be used to great benefit by corporations of all types.
- Science Fiction Prototyping is a process to break people out of rigid assumptions that may hinder their ability to imagine more "radical" innovations. This is useful inside large corporations and teams with both long-standing team members and rigid operational processes.
- Your vision statement is an understanding of a near-term future. As such, it is a foresight tool (though most don't recognize it as such). It represents the nearest point on a timeline (or time horizon). The furthest points can be 50-100 years in the future.

/Explore More

- *Science Fiction Prototyping* by Brian David Johnson
- *ASU Threatcasting Lab:* threatcasting.asu.edu
- *Thing from the Future* by Stuart Candy situationlab.org/project/the-thing-from-the-future/
- *AI Meets Design Toolkit* aixdesign.com/toolkit
- *The Future of You* by Brian David Johnson

CONCLUSION/
YOUR PROFESSIONAL STRATEGY

Photo: Denise Jans

The model presented in this book was designed to be generalizable so that it not only applies to organizations of all kinds but building strategies for individuals, as well. Hopefully, at this point, you have a good feel for the elements that make up great strategy. You understand the importance of understanding the context for strategy and action as well as the need to deeply understand the organization and its customers and constituents. At the end of the day, the most important organization to strategize for is **you!**

Because so many parts of this model are really context-dependent and look at the world around an organization, most of them already address the same things you should consider when making your own professional strategy. And yes, you can probably use this model for your personal goals, as well.

If you've taken away anything from this book, it should be that strategy is all about context (understanding the various contexts around you) and prioritizing the paths through that context that best create success for you.

Your professional context must respond to important trends; the needs, desires, and drivers of decisions for your employers (or clients) and other partners; and your operational needs. How you message about yourself should mirror what you come to understand about your employers' and clients' biggest needs, crossed with those that that make you stand out (your position). You should look for partnerships among your stakeholder ecosystem the same way an organization would and the things you need to do to successfully prepare and manage yourself (your operations) are nearly identical to those of an organization. They aren't exactly the same, but they're close enough that with a few tweaks, the elements of professional strategy look something like this:

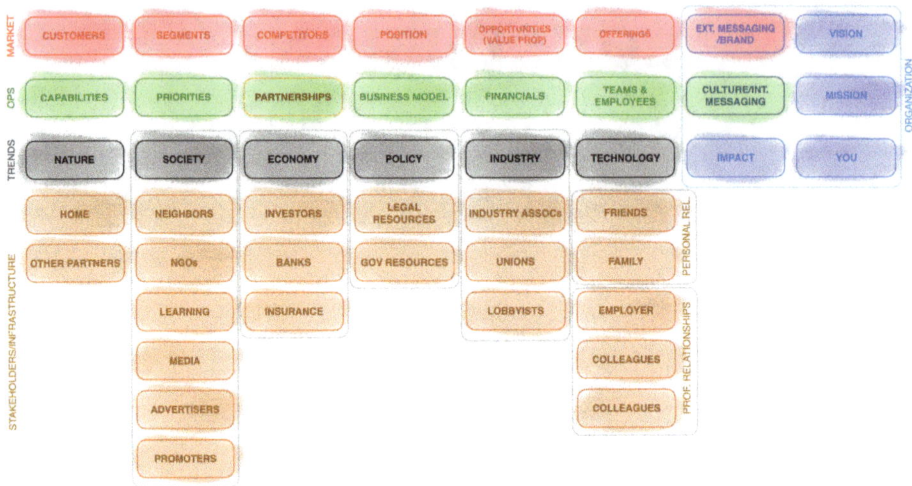

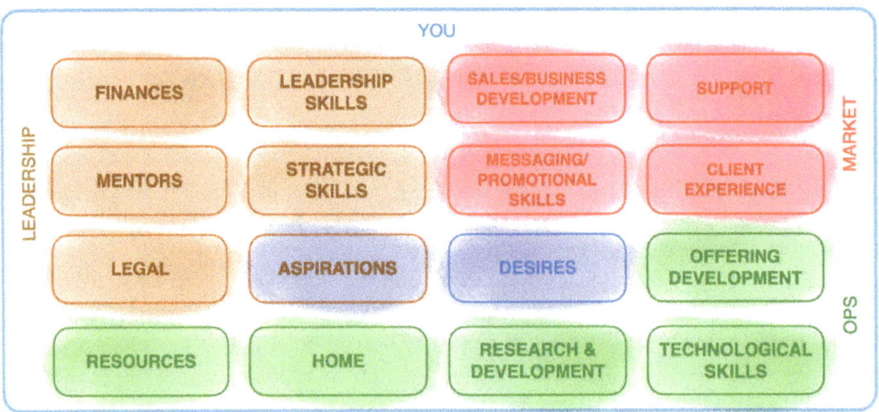

The most notable differences are the severely shortened lists in your professional "supply chain" and Policy columns, as well as the greatly-expanded one in your personal network (the first and last columns in the stakeholder section). Likewise, your internal organizational matrix mirrors that of an organization's and each should be addressed in a similar way.

What you can do to increase your value

There are many things you can do to make yourself more professionally successful. Most revolve around differentiating yourself from those in similar roles, with similar skills, or that deliver similar value. This is no different than organizations. And just like organizations, you may find that the most strategic moves you can perform are building new skills to deliver the same or new kinds of value. Therefore, learning is your primary catalyst for change. It doesn't need to be a new degree or even a certification but, once you focus on the priorities you've determined are the best position for yourself, these should naturally identify capabilities that you need to build or obtain through partnerships.

Simply learning more about strategy—like you've done by reading this book—and demonstrating that you can perform strategic processes can often "up your game" to employers. Certainly, being able to have a conversation in the language of your peers (I'm talking about business-speak here), changes the conversations you have and helps you access those you've been unable to participate in before. Sometimes, this is simply a matter of vocabulary, but as in engineering, it's not just new terms but new concepts, processes, and perspectives that learning unlocks for you. This allows you to better understand what your peers care most about, how they approach challenges, and what goals they work toward, which is not unlike learning these things about your customers or constituents.

By learning these new tools, like stakeholder maps, impact assessments, and this very model of strategy, you don't just increase the value you can provide to your organization, you can even be the person who introduces them to the rest of your colleagues. You may even cement in your peers' and managers' minds that you're the expert in their use. You can ask questions that others don't and provide answers that elude them. You see stakeholders, trends, and decision-drivers where they may be focused only on features. You will identify opportunities, theats, and new competition that are otherwise invisible to others. You can see where data and communications flow (or not) simply because it never occurred to others to look.

Along the way, you will learn a lot about your organization's culture and ability to deal with new information (and its source). You may find you are in an organization that cannot support, understand, or value the kinds of customer insights you uncover and sharing. That's not unusual, but it's a signal that it may be time to move to a place that values and can use your research and perspective. You may find that the information you share is a threat to others, particularly of authority. That, too, is valuable information.

It takes time to understand the innovation culture within your organization. But, the description of different innovation cultures in Chapter 8 should help you identify what kind of organization you're in.

You can also develop your ***leadership skills:*** You don't have to become ***the*** leader of the organization but you can certainly become ***a*** leader of the insights you're able to share. It's not as difficult as it might feel. Introverts might feel reticent but if you can clearly communicate insights from your research and those can improve the organization, you are automatically becoming a leader. People regularly lead from all over an organization. From the top, from the bottom, from the middle, and even from the outside. ***Leadership is simply the ablity to communicate a new future that others want to follow*** and your insights may make that possible. The books, ***Rise of the DEO*** and ***Changemakers,*** both by Christopher Ireland and Maria Giudice, describe the traits that make leaders and changemakers.

Most people fear change, even when they hate the current state of things, processes, and outlooks. They fear new metrics even more. For example, it took a long time for traditional businesspeople to accept Net Promoter Scores (NPS) and it will take a long time for them to give that up. Past processes and success are the biggest impediments to change. Your research will likely warp their worldviews so you will need to help them find comfort in understandings, perspectives, tools, metrics, and processes.

You may need to help people get over their fear of losing influence. Understand that they likely have a limited understanding of strategy, value, and context. They may not have any experience working with your insights or processes. It may even confront their own cultures and beliefs. Most organizations, and the business world itself, suffers from analytical reductionism. Templates replace mindfulness, systems are oversimplified to the most immediate context. Qualitative concerns are often reserved for personal, not professional realms.

At every point, you will need to contextualize your insights in terms of how it impacts the organization's mission, goals, and performance. You will likely need to frame your insights in familiar language and concerns of your peers and leaders. You may not even be able to get "into the room" where strategy is discussed, so you may need to prepare materials, reports, or other artifacts that you can send into that room without you. Over time, these materials may be the very thing that gets you invited into the strategic development process within your organization.

In addition to expanding your ability to interact with others on their terms, actively building relationships and then partnerships across your stakeholder ecosystem is probably the second most powerful strategy for changing your current situation. Building your network, particularly outside your industry or profession, opens up opportunities and build respect with others that can introduce you to new opportunities.

Your professional strategic plan (or your personal one, for that matter) may not need to be shared with investors or others but it will help you not only organize your priorities but also clarify your story of the future (even if that story isn't shared with others). Your future success pivots on your ability to clearly envision a new future for yourself and that is perhaps the most important story you can ever tell (even if it's just to yourself).

However, *you will need a brief story to share with others.* Whenever someone asks you "what do you do?" in a professional context they're really asking you *"what value do you provide others?"* You should have a good sentence that describes that in a way that amplifies your professional strategy.

Every conversation you have may become an important new relationship. Starting it out clearly, aligned with your strategy, will help quickly either build that relationship or determine if it's one you should prioritize or not. Regular contact with those most strategic can build the most impactful relationships. However, don't make commitments that you won't easily be able to continue. Keep things vague unless you know you can deliver. For example, circulating regular research reports, items of interest, or self-written thought-pieces is a great way to provide value and remind people of your work—until you can't keep up. Better to make these periodic than set a schedule you can't maintain.

The more you can connect the dots for your peers and partners, the more you can differentiate yourself as someone they can rely upon to provide a much-needed, valuable perspective. Putting things into their context shows that you can speak their language, keep their needs in your mind, and work for goals greater than just your own. Share your insights, not your processes (unless asked). Too often, we launch into detailed descriptions of how we work, thinking that this will differentiate ourselves or impress others. Until it's appropriate, your partners will be more interested in your insights on their business than how you will work for them. You can get to that later, as they ask, when you've already impressed them with your perspectives.

You should also build a professional feedback mechanism. I'm not suggesting that you send a survey to all of your employers, partners, and clients but you should make a point to periodically check-in with current or past ones.

Of course, you can always suggest that professional contacts write a recommendation for you on LinkedIn or give you a testimonial when you've completed a project for them. This can be as easy as asking "how well am I serving you and how could I be of more value?" If you leave an employer on good terms, you're always allowed to ask if they would write a letter of recommendation for you.

When you have your professional strategic plan, your story, your goals, or your vision, externalize it by physically realizing—even print it out. Create a poster or a physical reminder of what you what to accomplish. Make a ***physical mnemonic*** of who you want to be next and what you want to become. Or, at least, what you value. When Tom Arnold bought a multi-million-dollar ring for his wife, comedienne Roseanne Barr, it wasn't meant as an outlandish expense or even merely a show of the amount of his love for her. In an interview in 1993, he explained that he bought a ring that equaled her property in Iowa because he wanted her to have a physical reminder that she could always say "no" to a deal or project she didn't like. He wanted her to have a physical symbol of her ability to turn down something she didn't feel was right for her and return to her happy life. She didn't have to compromise her values or work on anything she didn't want to. That ring was a reminder of her independence.

Lastly, you should revisit your professional strategy periodically—sooner than every three-to-five years!

/Highlights
- The same strategic model and process for organizations can be used for you to plan your personal or professional strategies.
- The strategic model for You has the same groupings but several of the categories change. However, these modules and processes contribute to the same, improved outcome.

/Explore More
- ***The Future of You*** by Brian David Johnson
- ***Rise of the DEO*** Maria Giudice & Christopher Ireland
- ***Changemakers*** Maria Giudice & Christopher Ireland

TOOLS & RESOURCES

Traditional Strategy
* *War Fighting* by US Marine Corps:
  www.marines.mil/Portals/1/Publications/MCDP%201%20Warfighting.pdf
* *What is Strategy?* by Michael E. Porter: hbr.org/1996/11/what-is-strategy

Customer Research
Blind Spot by Steve Diller, Nathan Shedroff, & Sean Sauber
Just Enough Research by Erika Hall
Interviewing Users by Steve Portigal
Doorbells, Danger, and Dead Batteries by Steve Portigal
* *How Many Interviews Are Enough?: An Experiment with Data Saturation and Variability:* Greg Guest, Arwen Bunce, and Laura Johnson
  doi.org/10.1177/1525822X05279903
* *Selling the Invisible* by Harry Beckwith
* *Why We Buy* by Paco Underhill
* *Design Research* edited by Brenda Laurel

Economics & Finance
* *Financial Intelligence* by Karen Berman, Joe Knight, & John Case
* *Fixing the Game* by Roger Martin
* *Interest and Inflation Free Money* by Margrit Kennedy

Business Models
* *Business Model Generation* by Alexander Osterwalder & Yves Pigneur
* *Designing for Growth* by Jeanne Liedtka & Tim Ogilvie
* *Utopian Entrepreneur* by Brenda Laurel
* *Guide to Organisation Design* by Naomi Stanford

Culture & Communications
* *Great Mondays* by Josh Levine
* *Moments of Truth* by Jan Carlzon
* *The Catalyst* Jeanne Liedtka, Robert H. Rosen, and Robert Wiltbank
* *Rise of the DEO* Maria Giudice & Christopher Ireland
* *Changemakers* Maria Giudice & Christopher Ireland
* *The Team That Managed Itself* by Christina Wodtke
* *Innovation Culture video:* www.youtube.com/watch?v=HqTUThYBm7U
* *Innovation Culture article:* www.nathan.com/tool-innovation-cultures/
* *Generative Communication workshops* by Bob Dunham generateleadership.com
* *Conversations for Action and Collected Essays* Fernando Flores & Maria Flores Letelier
* *Powers to Lead* by Joseph S. Nye
* *Difficult Conversations* by Douglas Stone, Bruce Patton, Sheila Heen, & Roger Fisher
* *A General Theory of Love* by Dr. Thomas Lewis
* *The Power of a Positive No* by William Ury
* *Moments of Impact* by Lisa Kay Solomon & Chris Ertel
* *Concise Communications* by Nathan Shedroff (2024)

Systems Thinking
- *Thinking in Systems* by Donella Meadows

Impact
- *Design is the Solution* by Nathan Shedroff
- *Leading Change Through Sustainability* by Bob Doppelt
- *Humanetech's Ledger of Harms* ledger.humanetech.com
- *Climate Capitalism* by Hunter L. Lovins & Boyd Cohen
- *Strategy for Sustainability* by Adam Werbach
- *United Nations Sustainable Development Goals for 2030* sdgs.un.org/2030agenda

Foresight
- *Science Fiction Prototyping* by Brian David Johnson
- *ASU Threatcasting Lab:* threatcasting.asu.edu
- *Thing from the Future* by Stuart Candy situationlab.org/project/the-thing-from-the-future/
- *AI Meets Design Toolkit* aixdesign.com/toolkit
- *The Future of You* by Brian David Johnson

INDEX

INDEX

INDEX

ABOUT NATHAN

Nathan Shedroff is a serial entrepreneur in various technology and strategic sectors, including blockchain, conversational interfaces, software services, media, and new tools. He led the *Foodicons.org* project to develop an extensive visual language to unite the food systems around the world. He is a design pioneer turned entrepreneur and an international educator, speaker, and consultant.

His new company, *ASTRA*, plans to disrupt the strategic consulting industry with a new strategic model, tool, and services: *astra.tools*

Nathan was the founder and chair of the ground-breaking *Design MBA programs* at California College of the Arts (CCA) in San Francisco, CA. These programs prepared the next-generation of innovation leaders for a world that is profitable, sustainable, ethical, and truly meaningful by uniting the perspectives of *systems thinking, design thinking, sustainability, and generative leadership* with *strategic tools* that lead people through ambiguity.

He is a pioneer in *Experience Design, Interaction Design,* and *Information Design*, is a serial entrepreneur, and researches, speaks and teaches internationally about meaning, strategic innovation, business value, and science fiction interfaces. He's authored more than 10 books, including: *Experience Design 1.1, Making Meaning, Design is the Problem, Design Strategy in Action, Make It So*, and *Blind Spot.*

He holds an *MBA in Sustainable Management* from *Presidio Graduate School* and a *BS in Industrial Design* from *Art Center College of Design*. He worked with Richard Saul Wurman at The*Understanding*Business and, later, co-founded *vivid studios*, a decade-old pioneering company in interactive media and one of the first Web services firms on the planet. vivid's hallmark was helping to establish and validate the field of information architecture, by training an entire generation of designers in the newly emerging Web industry.

www.nathan.com
www.experiencedesignbooks.com